Rhetorical Philosophy and Theory
Series Editor, David Blakesley

Other Books in the Rhetorical Philosophy and Theory Series

Writing Genres

Writing Genres

Amy J. Devitt

Southern Illinois University Press
Carbondale

Library of Congress Cataloging-in-Publication Data
Devitt, Amy J.
   Writing genres / Amy J. Devitt.
      p. cm. — (Rhetorical philosophy and theory)
   Includes bibliographical references and index.
   1. English language—Rhetoric—Study and teaching. 2. Creative writ-
ing—Study and teaching. 3. Report writing—Study and teaching. 4. Literary
form—Study and teaching. I. Title II. Series.
   PE1404 .D416 2004
   808'042'071—dc21
   ISBN-13: 978-0-8093-2553-5 (cloth : alk. paper)   2003006161
   ISBN-10: 0-8093-2553-5 (cloth : alk. paper)
   ISBN-13: 978-0-8093-2869-7 (pbk. : alk. paper)
   ISBN-10: 0-8093-2869-0 (pbk. : alk. paper)

Dedicated to my colleagues in genre theory,
for their generosity of time and depth of scholarship

Contents

Acknowledgments

This book has developed over many years, and I owe thanks to far too many people to be able to list them all, or even a respectable portion of them. In keeping with the genre of acknowledgment, though, I will make an effort to name a few. My interest in genre began far back before 1982, when I discovered in my dissertation research that language change varied significantly in different genres. Genre had been a variable I was controlling for, along with audience and medium, just to ensure that my results were not skewed by some odd rhetorical difference. I cannot remember if anyone suggested that I control for genre or that genre might be significant, so where I got the idea is a mystery to me. It surely had something to do with the education I was receiving at the University of Michigan from my dissertation director, Richard Bailey, and my other teachers there, Jay Robinson, Thomas Toon, and James Downer. Perhaps it also came from my fellow graduate students, with whom I discussed language, writing, and teaching for many hours, or from my students there, who challenged me to figure out what I was teaching them.

I began trying to figure out more deeply why genre would be so significant as I worked on my book for Cambridge University Press, *Standardizing Written English: Diffusion in the Case of Scotland, 1520–1659.* Conversations with my colleagues at the University of Tulsa, including Winston Weathers, Otis Winchester, Anita Handleman, and George Otte, surely influenced my thinking, though I cannot now point to specific discussions or insights we had. My colleagues at the University of Kansas similarly have influenced my thinking in ways not always specifiable but no less important. My perspectives benefit when Richard Hardin comments that genre seems connected to notions of decorum, when Maureen Godman asks me whether literary genres are different from rhetorical genres, when Janet Sharistanian asks me to explain my work to her, when Kirk Branch asks me to explore how our research areas might be related, or when Frank Farmer explores a Bakhtinian concept with me. The daily interactions I have had with my colleagues for twenty years have enriched my thinking in ways that often go unnoticed.

My students, too, deserve my thanks. All of my students over the years have helped me learn how to explain things more clearly, to consider multiple perspectives on any issue, and not to be satisfied with an easy resolution of a problem. My writing students in particular have forced me to attend to my own prose and to insist on revision, as well as to consider what they might benefit from understanding about genre. Two groups of seminar students actively explored the research on and my thinking about genre intensively and insightfully. Some of them read early drafts of several chapters; others asked questions at pivotal moments or suggested new views of established scholarship. I thank them all: Anis Bawarshi, Donna Binns, Lara Corkrey, Angela Crow, Wendy Doman, Emily Donnelli, Scott Hendrix, Lee Hornbrook, Daniel Kulmala, Susan Malmo, Amanda McGinnis, Andrew Moody, Mary Jo Reiff, Jean Reitz, Aaron Rosenberg, Elizabeth Rowse, Amy Southerland, Lisa St. Ledger, and Thomas Veale. Two former students and now colleagues, Anis Bawarshi and Mary Jo Reiff, deserve special comment, since we have collaborated on other genre projects over the years, including conference panels, coauthored articles, and most recently a coauthored textbook, and they have gone on to produce their own scholarship in the field. Having such agile minds to explore ideas with and such energetic colleagues to try ideas on has proven invaluable. My work with them on the textbook has affected the final revisions of this volume in some unexpected ways, as I discovered that I had developed new insights from applying genre theory to first-year writing courses.

Some who have contributed to my understanding of genre remain nameless to me, for anonymous reviewers of several articles and of this volume have made comments that provoked new explanations and discoveries. Although only one chapter in this volume, chapter 6, remains closely similar to a work I published previously, several chapters began in early drafts with the use of my previous work. Chapter 6 is a revised version of my article "Integrating Rhetorical and Literary Theories of Genre," originally appearing in the July 2000 issue of *College English* (copyright 2000 by the National Council of Teachers of English; reprinted with permission). Parts of chapter 1 and a bit of chapter 7 draw from an earlier article that was supported in part by the University of Kansas general research allocation no. 3629-0038 and that was published in *College Composition and Communication* (December 1993) as "Generalizing about Genre: New Conceptions of an Old Concept" (copyright 1993 by the National Council of Teachers of English; reprinted with permission). I originally developed the comparison between language standards and genre in chapter 5 for an article "Genre as Language Standard" that appeared in *Genre and Writing: Issues, Arguments, Alternatives,* edited by Wendy Bishop and Hans Ostrom and published by Boynton Cook/Heinemann in 1997. The tables showing my data from the Scots-English and early American English study in chapter 4 I created originally for my article "Genre as Textual Variable," published in *American Speech* in 1989. The epigraph that begins chapter 6 is copyright © by Sidney Harris.

This volume developed over many years and many versions. I am grateful for the support of the University of Kansas in the form of a sabbatical and research semester, necessary time to write both before and after the arduous work of directing KU's writing program. And I am grateful to David Blakesley, the editor of this series, for his interest, enthusiasm, and advice. The volume is better for his input. He also elicited the comments of an exceptional anonymous reviewer for this work; the reviewer's comments prompted my rethinking of several issues, including that of how better to situate my work among that of other scholars. Karl Kageff has been a pleasure to work with at Southern Illinois University Press, always prompt, gracious, and encouraging, and Wayne Larsen offered copyediting suggestions that were consistently reasonable and helpful.

I am also indebted to my colleagues in genre theory, to whom this volume is dedicated. Since I discovered the first international colloquium on genre at Carleton University in 1992, I have benefited from the hard work and research, thoughtful arguments, astute examples, and collaborative exploration of other scholars in the study of genre. Those with whom I have been able to talk in person have contributed their time, ideas, sources, and feedback with generosity and intellectual enthusiasm. Although I can not possibly name everyone whose conversations at every conference have helped me to think better, I wish to thank the several whose continuing discussions have encouraged my work: Charles Bazerman, Carol Berkenkotter, Irene Clark, Aviva Freedman, Janet Giltrow, Tom Huckin, Carolyn Miller, Randall Popken, David Russell, and Tatyana Yakhontova. Their published works add to those of scholars whom I have known mostly through their writings, and I hope I have adequately acknowledged them all in my citations and references. After twenty years of reading and thinking about a subject, I doubt that I have been able to retrace the origin of every thought or idea, though I have tried earnestly to credit those whose ideas have prompted my own. The study of genre has been a rich endeavor for its community of scholars as well as its wealth of ideas.

Finally, I thank my family and friends, whose support always makes my work go more smoothly even as it makes me wish I could spend more time with them. In particular, I thank my husband, James Hartman, an exceptional scholar in his own right. He has always been my best reader, and his questions on the near final draft helped me see my way through to one more round of revision, for which the readers of this volume should also thank him. He contributed to my completing this project as well, through his willingness to take on even more Saturday chores so that I could finish one more section. As always, I have achieved more because of his support and encouragement.

In the end, I have been alone with my thoughts and am solely responsible for what I have written in this book. My most ambitious hope is that some idea in this volume sparks someone else's thinking so that, twenty years from now, another book appears in which this volume has played a small, though even unacknowledged, part.

Writing Genres

1
A Theory of Genre

You've got to fit somewhere, and for the sake of fitting, I'm country.

—Shania Twain, *Lawrence Journal-World*,
4 September 1998

The significance of generic categories thus resides in their cognitive and cultural value, and the purpose of genre theory is to lay out the implicit knowledge of the users of genres.

—Marie-Laure Ryan, "Introduction:
On the Why, What and How of Generic Taxonomy"

Genre pervades human lives. As people go about their business, interacting with others and trying to get along in the world, they use genres to ease their way, to meet expectations, to save time. People recognize genres, though not usually the power of genres. People say, "I heard the best *joke* today," "I have to give a *lecture* at nine thirty," "I've gotten into *mysteries*," and "Do you have a *travel brochure* for the Apostle Islands?" Genres have the power to help or hurt human interaction, to ease communication or to deceive, to enable someone to speak or to discourage someone from saying something different. People learn how to do *small talk* to ease the social discomfort of large group gatherings and meeting new people, but advertisers learn how to disguise *sales letters* as *winning sweepstakes entries*. Outraged citizens can express themselves in *letters to the editor*, but first-year college students may struggle to dissociate their personal experience from their *research papers*. Genre has significance for people's lives.

Scholars have studied genres for centuries; neither is it a new topic in English studies. In recent years, however, views of genre have changed, shifting from a formalistic study of critics' classifications to a rhetorical study of the generic actions of everyday readers and writers. This shift is possible in part, of course, because of the work done by previous genre critics and theorists, but it represents a substantial change in what is considered interesting and significant about genre. The theorists most directly contributing to this new conception of genre come from the whole range of English studies: from literature (M. M. Bakhtin, Tzvetan Todorov, Thomas Beebee, and David Fishelov), linguistics (M. A. K. Halliday, John Swales, Aviva Freedman, and Vijay K. Bhatia), and composition and rhetoric (Kenneth Burke, Lloyd Bitzer, Karlyn Kohrs Campbell and Kathleen Hall Jamieson, Carolyn Miller, Charles Bazerman, Carol Berkenkotter and Thomas Huckin, and David Russell), to name just a few. Because genre so significantly impacts how people use language, read literature, and write and read nonliterary texts, theories of genre can contribute new perspectives and approaches to many endeavors within English studies as well as a better understanding more generally of how people operate and have operated within their societies and cultures.

This volume examines, interprets, illustrates, elaborates, critiques, refines, and extends a rhetorical theory of genre, a theory that sees genres as types of rhetorical actions that people perform in their everyday interactions with their worlds. A rather complex theory of genre has developed over the last twenty years in the field of composition and rhetoric in particular, building in North America especially on the theoretical synthesis and argument proffered by Carolyn Miller in a 1984 article, "Genre as Social Action." Miller drew from a wide range of rhetorical scholars and theorists to synthesize and then extend a semiotic theory of genre. To explain and develop different issues in this rhetorical and semiotic theory of genre, other scholars have incorporated bits from Mikhail Bakhtin's theory of speech genres, from M. A. K. Halliday's functional theory of language as a social semiotic, from Anthony Giddens's structuration theory, most recently from Soviet activity theory, and from other theories and perspectives that have proven useful and enlightening. The results today are enhanced rhetorical theories of genre, much indebted to Miller's original examination and extension of then current genre scholarship.

What I attempt in this volume is not a history of that scholarship nor a detailed, blow-by-blow account of each addition to our understanding of genre. What I hope to do is to synthesize much of the existing scholarship in order to clarify where genre theory stands today; to elaborate and illustrate what I consider to be the essential ideas of contemporary genre theory so that readers may better understand our claims; to critique current theories where I see disagreements or opportunities; and to extend genre theory in order to add new directions or argue for particular perspectives. Although many scholars have advanced theories of genre upon which this book will draw, some essential assumptions have not been fully examined and some implications have not been considered. Nor has anyone attempted the perhaps foolhardy task of elaborating a comprehensive theory of genre, one that encompasses synchronic as well as diachronic perspectives, literary as well as rhetorical genres, and individual as well as social views. In making this attempt, I hope to provoke new questions, not supply all the answers.

Following current genre scholarship and therefore drawing heavily from Miller, this first chapter establishes the basic definitions and tenets I find most significant and productive in current rhetorical genre theory. Readers interested in the scholarly history of these ideas might wish to review Miller's 1984 article, in which she establishes the sources of many of the ideas that current composition theory in North America most often draws from her work. One of the ideas current in genre theory and explained in this chapter is that genre should be redefined rhetorically according to the people who participate in genres and make the forms meaningful, a shift from genre as defined by literary critics or rhetoricians to genre as defined by its users. Breaking with older, traditional notions of genre and moving toward contemporary views, this chapter explains why genre cannot be equated with classification, though genres do classify, and why genre cannot be equated with forms, though genres are often associated with formal features. More current and rhetorical theories of genre tend to follow Miller's definition of genre as typified social action associated with a recurrent situation. Agreeing with this essentially rhetorical nature of genre, this chapter draws out and extends threads introduced by Miller and other scholars to weave a detailed tapestry of genre. It amplifies Miller's challenge to the existence of recurrence as anything other than a construction, and it defines the relationship between genre and its situation as interactive and reciprocal. In fact, as David Russell does using activity theory, this chapter rejects situation as singularly defining of genre. Instead, I expand from situation to include an interaction of contexts at different levels, encompassing the impact of preexisting genres as well as situational and cultural context.

After this initial weaving of a definition and theory of genre, the remaining chapters examine some of the most significant and sometimes unexplored implications of such a theory. Each chapter examines genre from a different angle: the social, historical, individual, literary, and pedagogical. Chapter 2 elaborates the social nature of genre, its functioning within social groups and social spheres and its embroilment with issues of power. These basic social principles will be illustrated and complicated in chapter 3 through reconsideration of a study of the particular genres written by tax accountants. Chapter 4 focuses on how genres change and their dynamic and historical nature, using examples from others' studies of business genres, genres used by presidents, and freshman themes, and drawing from my own study of change within sixteenth- and seventeenth-century genres. Chapter 5 examines the role of genre as norm, as standard to enforce similarity among different readers and writers. The chapter examines the issue from a linguistic perspective, considering how genre compares with other language standards and demonstrating how genre affects the process of linguistic standardization in even small textual features. Drawing on linguistics and creativity theory, I also argue that genre both encourages standardization and enables variation and that, similarly, genre both constrains and enables individual creativity. Chapter 6 examines whether such a social and rhetorical theory of genre can apply to literary genres as well. It finds that the different fields within English studies ask questions and raise issues that challenge each other's assumptions and advance our understanding of genre for both. Chapter 7 considers the question of whether to teach genres explicitly, especially in light of arguments about language acquisition critiques of genre pedagogies. It proposes that we teach genre awareness, not specific genres, and that we consider carefully the genres we have students write with a view to the antecedents those genres may provide for future writing tasks. Finally, chapter 8 considers implications for the study of reading and writing and suggests questions for future research.

Before addressing these implications and extensions, however, I need to establish the views of genre current in composition and rhetorical theory. I will begin, as others often have, with an explanation of why traditional views of genre are inadequate to capture the complexity of genre as it operates in people's lives.

Genre as Classification and Form

At its worst, genre is a trivial and dangerous concept. It merely names what writers have created (the sonnet) and specifies formal features (fourteen lines), yet it artificially compares unique authors and works of art (Shakespeare and Donne) and stifles true creativity (forcing modern poets to break out into free verse). That negative perception leads to labeling as "genre writing" what are considered by many the least interesting literary works—formulaic mysteries, romances, westerns, and science fiction. Even at its most positive, genre is traditionally known as artificial and arhetorical, a classification system deriving from literary and rhetorical criticism that names types of texts according to their forms. No wonder that genre has become a topic of little interest to postromantic scholars, who do not care to consider such traditional topics as whether a text belongs to one genre or another, whether one type of text is its own genre or a subgenre of another, whether a new genre derives from this genre or that genre, and what comprises the essential features of a particular genre.

Such a view of genre holds little interest for contemporary language, composition, and rhetoric scholars as well, for, in the past, genre has not only been equated with literary texts exclusively but has also been divorced from contemporary understandings of how language works. Simplified views of genre encourage the very dichotomies in the study of writing that contemporary composition and rhetoric scholars have been undercutting: splits between form and content (and the related form and function, text and context), product and process, and individual and society. Treating genre as form requires dividing form from content, with genre as the form into which content is put. This container model of meaning has been superseded by a more integrated notion of how meaning is made, of the inseparability of form from content, as argued by such theorists as Kenneth Burke in "The Philosophy of Literary Form," and M. M. Bakhtin: "Form and content in discourse are one" ("Discourse" 259). Similarly, treating genre as form and text type requires binding genre to an emphasis on writing as a product, without effect on the processes of writing or, worse yet, inhibiting those processes. As a product-based concept, in fact, this view of genre seems to have more to do with reading than with writing. Genre interpretations have been popular among literary critics, those who have traditionally been more concerned with the reading of texts than with the writing of texts. Even in literature, though, the emphasis with genre has been on the product one reads rather than on the process of reading. Finally, a formal view of genre exaggerates one of the most troubling current dichotomies, that between the individual and the group or society. It makes genre a normalizing and static concept, a set of dictated forms that constrain the individual; genuine writers can distinguish themselves only by breaking out of those generic constraints, by substituting an individual genius for society's bonds. The individual and society are at odds rather than integrated. Although such

simplified versions of traditional views of genre are being replaced by
new versions—genre as rhetorical and dynamic, integrating form and
content, product and process, individual and society—the conceptions
of genre as classification system and formula have such a long history
and are so well established that they are not easily dethroned. They also,
of course, have some truth to them. An explanation of new theories of
genre thus begins with the old.

Genre as Classification System

The conventional conception considers genre a classification system of
texts based on shared formal characteristics. Since formalisms in general have sustained much of the work in linguistics, rhetoric, and literature in the past—the fields out of which genre theories have developed—
it is not surprising that most genre theories in the past have been concerned
with classification and form, with describing the formal features of a
particular genre, describing the embodiment of a genre in a particular
work, or delineating a genre system, a set of classifications of (primarily literary) texts. The emphasis on classification can be traced back to
the followers of Aristotle, who turned his initial treatment in the *Poetics* of the epic, tragedy, and comedy into an infinitely modifiable classification scheme. The rhetorical division of discourse into epideictic, ju
dicial, and deliberative can be seen as a similar classification system, one
still in use by some rhetoricians today. Other writers propose broader
or narrower schemes of text types: literature and nonliterature; narrative and nonnarrative; narrative, exposition, argument, description; the
lyric, the sonnet; the Petrarchan sonnet. Whether called genres, subgenres, or modes, whether comprehensive or selective, whether generally accepted or disputed, these systems for classifying texts keep genre
focused on static products.[1]

Classifications are the effects of genre but not the extent of genre.
To study genre as a rhetorical concept, one need not necessarily agree
upon or even respond to many of the questions that have been raised
about generic classifications—such as how many genres there are,
whether x is a subgenre of y, whether this text is an instance of genre y
or genre z. Tzvetan Todorov rather breezily claims, "We do not know
just how many types of discourse there are, but we shall readily agree
that there are more than one" (9). Though interesting in particular contexts, such classificatory questions reflect the particular purposes underlying particular classification schemes rather than the nature of genre
itself. Groupings of complex items like texts are more like metaphors

than equations: how texts are grouped depends on which features the classifier has selected to observe—common prosody, organization, tone, aim, or effect on the reader, for example. Daniel Defoe's *Moll Flanders,* for example, can be classified as a narrative, an episodic novel, a pseudo-autobiography, or an eighteenth-century novel, depending on the classifier's interests. Even less transitional works can be classified in multiple ways: a memorandum from a departmental chair can be classified as business correspondence, memoranda, internal correspondence, or academic writing, depending on the classifier's perspective. An article in the *New York Times Book Review* can be classified as a review, an essay, a review essay, a magazine article, or journalism. Each of these works could also be classified in other ways, as purpose and interest dictate. Which of these labels are "actually" genres, which the "right" genre labels? Such classificatory questions may be interesting for the questions they raise about the nature of journalism today, the business side of academic life, or the development of the novel, but they do not define the essence of genre. As Heather Dubrow points out in her history of literary genre theory, the problem with defining genre based on *genus* (kind) is that what we will call a kind depends on "exactly what we think a genre is and hence what characteristics we take into account when deciding whether to grant that label to a given literary type" (5). Defining genre as a kind of text becomes circular, since what we call a kind of text depends on what we think a genre is.

That conundrum does not mean that genres do not involve classification nor that devising a classification scheme is necessarily a waste of time. There are purposes for which classification systems are helpful. After all, we do not reject classifications of biological species just because they reflect a principle of selection. Anne Freadman, in her classic 1987 article on genre, "Anyone for Tennis?," lists filing systems, library classification systems, and disciplinary divisions within a university as examples of helpful classification systems (106). Similarly helpful, Aristotle's systems of classification clarified the purposes of literature and of rhetoric. The classification system that is the modes may have been created, according to Robert Connors's research, to ease the teaching of writing. Classifying texts has enabled scholars to clarify their arguments and discover new understandings, and that kind of genre work may still accomplish some purposes for literary and rhetorical scholars. But no one classification scheme delineates all genres. Genre scholars have long recognized that different classification systems serve different purposes. For a particular project, I might want to group all texts into one of three categories, comedy, tragedy, or tragicomedy; for another project, I might want to use four categories, narration, exposition, description, and argumentation; for another, just two categories, literature and nonliterature. For a project that involves working with texts in a more limited context, as in an accounting firm, for example, the classification scheme would cut smaller pieces of the world: say, letters to clients, research memoranda, internal memoranda, and sales letters. The particular labels that scholars give to genres will vary for different scholarly purposes. Rather than making the concept so broad as to be useless, as some have argued, allowing such flexibility in the definition of genre for scholars keeps the concept fluid and dynamic, able to respond to scholars' changing needs over time.

So far, I have been discussing the genre labels given by scholars and critics, but the most significant genre labels for a rhetorical definition of genre—and the classifications of most concern to rhetorical genre scholars—are the labels given by the people who use the genres. In addition to being named by analysts after the fact, genres are named as people use them, and texts are classified as they are being used. Concerned citizens write letters to their editors, students write essay examinations, teachers write syllabi, and doctors write prescriptions. Using other channels, presidents give inaugural addresses, artists paint portraits, and musicians play country songs. Most current rhetorical genre scholars base their analyses of genre not on the classifications of critics and analysts but on the ways people classify texts into genres as they use them. Carolyn Miller argues for analyzing the everyday genres that people use, and by 1997 David Russell takes as a given that participants' recognition of a genre is what rightly determines whether one genre is distinct from another ("Rethinking" 518). Genre has been redefined, then, from a classification created by critics to a classification that people make as they use symbols to get along in the world.

The cognitive origins of these common genre classifications are not well established. Of course, people classify many things, not just genres. All of language is based on classification, as words classify unique items into linguistic classes: each chair is a unique construction of materials, shapes, and designs, for example, but people call all manner of things they sit on "chair." Genre labels, too, classify unique items, but they classify symbolic actions rather than just types of texts, as I will explain further below. "Genre" itself is a label that scholars have put on one kind of classification, cutting the complexity of human cognition and of the world into this one part. Whether genres are a particular manner of classification or the same kind as all human classification is a question deserving examination by neurologists, cognitive psychologists, and psycholinguists. What we know is that language users perceive genres without being taught them apart from learning language (once they know the words, they describe themselves as telling "jokes" or "stories," for example), and different groups develop new words to describe the different genres they use. People classify unique actions under common labels, and we scholars call those labels "genres."

That the concept of genre has a reality for language users adds significance to the scholar's study of genres: studying genre is studying how people use language to make their way in the world. Examining genres as defined by language users rather than by scholars and critics gives us quite different answers to such questions as which classificatory systems are best and how many genres there are. This basis in user recognition underlies such claims as Carolyn Miller's that "the number of genres current in any society is indeterminate and depends upon the complexity and diversity of the society" (163). With a user-based classification system for defining genre, the scholar's role in determining the proper classificatory system is replaced by another role, described by Miller as "ethnomethodological; it seeks to explicate the knowledge that practice creates" (155). Marie-Laure Ryan earlier notes the importance of such an ethnomethodological enterprise: "The significance of generic categories thus resides in their cognitive and cultural value, and the purpose of genre theory is to lay out the implicit knowledge of the users of genres" (112). I would add that literary and rhetorical critics are themselves people who use genres, and explicating their implicit knowledge reveals the literary and rhetorical values of our culture. Where earlier genre scholars were most interested in literary genres as defined by critics, today's rhetorical genre scholars are more often interested in everyday genres as named by their everyday users. Defining genre according to those common classifications reveals not only "something theoretically important about discourse," as Miller points out (155) but also something important about how people think and how people act, as Miller, Ryan, and others point out. The classificatory nature of genre is an essential part of understanding genre and its significance, but such classification is defined rhetorically rather than critically, by the people who use it, for their purposes of operating in the everyday world.

Genre as Form

Although the classifications named by genre labels would seem to be based on common formal patterns, form alone cannot define genres.

Theoretically, equating genre with form is tenable only within a container model of meaning, for it requires a separation of generic form from a particular text's context. Denying the container metaphor, J. R. Martin et al. write, "It is very important to recognize that genres make meaning; they are not simply a set of formal structures into which meanings are poured" (64). Similarly, I. R. Titunik summarizes P. N. Medvedev's ideas about literary genre: "Genre is not that which is determined and defined by the components of a literary work or by sets of literary works, but that which, in effect, determines and defines them" (175). The problem of circularity also arises for form as it did for classification: A genre is named because of its formal markers; the formal markers can be identified because a genre has been named. The formal regularities we can observe in genres do not alone create the genres; they result from the genres.

On one level, genres do originate in repeated textual patterns, in forms. Readers and listeners recognize formal markers of a particular genre and identify the genre accordingly. "Once upon a time" begins some fairy tales, and "Have you heard the one about" marks some jokes. Business letters follow particular formats for inside addresses and even envelopes, and sonnets have fourteen lines. More complex discourse forms mark genres as well: contracts use a specified legal language and terminology, lab reports include required sections, tragedies follow a rise and fall of action. Such discourse markers have traditionally defined genres for many scholars and critics, and there is no doubting that certain textual forms identify certain genres. As Richard Coe argues in "An Apology for Form," the formal elements of genres are significant and meaningful, and studying the formal elements can offer insights about genres.

Practically, though, identifying reliable formal features of some genres has proven troublesome (consider the diverse forms of the novel, for example, or the essay). The formal features of some genres are at best minimal. Peter Medway has described a genre, called the architect's notebook, that students at his university write. The notebook is a particular kind of notebook physically, of a particular size, color, and material. Those studying to be architects carry the notebooks with them, and they refer to what they write as architects' notebooks. Medway's examination of the insides of these notebooks, however, revealed no common textual traits among the notebooks. Some included pictures, some did not; some used full sentences and paragraphs, some did not; some wrote about architecture, some did not. Such a "baggy genre," as Medway calls it, has little in the way of formal features to define it as a genre.[2] One response would be to deny genre status to kinds of texts that do not have clear formal markers, and in fact some have argued against the existence of a novel or essay genre on the basis of the looseness of its textual characteristics. To deny generic labels to genres identified as such by their users, however, would seem presumptuous, especially in a rhetorical theory of genre that emphasizes the users and uses of genres. Readers say they have read a novel, and writers say they are writing essays. Architecture students say they are writing an architect's notebook.

Historically, too, identifying genres with formal features proves troublesome, for the formal characteristics of genres change over time but the users' labels of the genres do not necessarily change. Trying to solve this analytic problem by distinguishing definitive from insignificant forms has generally been unsuccessful, at best possible only after the fact and only for one historical period at a time. Rather than denying the validity of the users' genre recognition or trying to narrow it to a few forms, the task of the genre scholar is to identify what it is that makes users recognize these as genres.

Comparing genre labels to other words again may help clarify the relation of form to genre: studies of language show that speakers do not select words to classify items solely according to formal properties, that a speaker calls this rocker a "chair" not because of any formal properties of the rocker (though the rocker does indeed have a flat surface connected to an upright surface) but rather because of the speaker's perception of the rocker's function for that speaker at that time. People call a container a "cup" when they drink from it; they call a similarly shaped object a "bowl" when they spoon soup from it. Even more obviously, an emotion is not labeled "love" because of its association with heart rate or skin temperature but because of the speaker's perception of the emotion's meaning. Similarly, people do not label a particular story as a joke solely because of formal features but rather because of their perception of the rhetorical action that is occurring. At most, then, genres are associated with but not defined by textual form. The rhetorical and linguistic scholarship argues that formal features physically mark some genres, act as traces, and hence may be quite revealing. But those formal traces do not *define* or *constitute* the genre. The fact that genre is reflected in formal features does not mean that genre *is* those formal features.

To examine the relationship between form and genre, Karlyn Kohrs Campbell and Kathleen Hall Jamieson in 1978 reviewed substantial criticisms from rhetorical scholarship and concluded that "rhetorical forms that establish genres are stylistic and substantive responses to perceived situational demands" ("Form" 19). Any form, they note, may appear in isolation in other genres, but the "constellation" of forms in a genre, "bound together by an internal dynamic," fuses the elements so that "a unique kind of rhetorical act is created" ("Form" 20, 21, 25). That "unique kind of rhetorical act" is a genre, an action performed beyond any particular formal features. Carolyn Miller delineates Campbell and Jamieson's fusion further, describing a fusion of form with substance to create symbolically meaningful action ("Genre" 159–61). Campbell and Jamieson, Miller, and many genre scholars since look then not to patterns of form to define genre but to patterns of action. To understand those actions requires understanding the contexts within which they occur, contexts that in rhetorical scholarship have been called rhetorical situations.

Genre as Response to Recurring Situation

Although devising classification schemes and delineating formal traces of genres still have value in genre studies, those classifications and forms will not be fully understood without examining the rhetorical situations behind the genres being examined. Part of what architecture students recognize in their architects' notebooks is the situation of being an architecture student, a situation that requires keeping an architect's notebook. Part of what all readers and writers recognize when they recognize genres are the roles they are to play, the roles being played by other people, what they can gain from the discourse, and what the discourses are about. Picking up a text, readers not only classify it and expect a certain form, but also make assumptions about the text's purposes, its subject matter, its writer, and its expected reader. If I open an envelope and find a letter from a friend, I understand immediately a friendly purpose of sharing news and maintaining a relationship, I enter the role of friend and see the writer as friend, and I respond-read accordingly. If, in a different scenario, I open an envelope and recognize a sales letter in my hand, I understand that a company will make a pitch for its product and want me to buy it. Once I recognize that genre, I will throw the letter away or scan it for the product it is selling—hence the many sales pitches that now arrive in our mailboxes disguised as personal letters or important government messages. Such attempts to use form to mislead us about the actual genre again indicate the separability of formal features from the essence of a genre. What I understand about each of these letters and reflect in my response to them is much more than a set of formal features or textual conventions. A rhetorical theory of genre, therefore, must look beyond and behind particular classifications (which are only the indicators of genres and change as our purposes change) and forms (which may trace but do not constitute genre). As recent theory has it, genre entails purposes, participants, and themes, so understanding genre entails understanding a rhetorical situation and its social context.

One major strain of recent genre theory that connects genre to purposes, participants, and themes derives from the notion of genre as typified response to recurring rhetorical situation. Campbell and Jamieson trace the idea's roots to a 1965 discussion of genre by Edwin Black, in which he describes genres as responding to types of situations that recur ("Form" 14). Carolyn Miller's definition, developing out of the body of rhetorical scholarship that followed, defines genres as "typified rhetorical actions based in recurrent situations" (159). Much of North American genre scholarship in composition and rhetoric has followed Miller's definition. While drawing on various theoretical groundings, other scholars acknowledge Miller's definition in delineating their own: David Russell uses Vygotskian activity theory to define genre as "typified ways of purposefully interacting in and among some activity system(s)" ("Rethinking" 513); Carol Berkenkotter and Thomas N. Huckin use Giddens's structuration theory to define genres as "dynamic rhetorical forms that are developed from actors' responses to recurrent situations and that serve to stabilize experience and give it coherence and meaning" (4); and I elsewhere followed Miller, Halliday, and Bakhtin in defining genre as "a dynamic response to and construction of recurring situation" ("Generalizing" 580). Although these scholars use quite different theories to articulate and elaborate their definitions in important ways, they all echo Miller and her rhetorical antecedents in including some common elements of a genre definition: that genre is action, that genre is typified action, that typification comes from recurring conditions, and that those conditions involve a social context. None of these assertions is simple, as these scholars and others have demonstrated in elaborating their theories at length. To reduce those complex theories to common elements, I had to generalize verbs and use possibly objectionable broad concepts, like social context. But these common elements do capture the essence of a reconceived genre theory, even as they must be complicated by those scholars and in the rest of this book to capture the theoretical complexity of genre.

To say that genres are actions is in part to say that genres are not classifications nor forms, as argued in the previous sections. Genres help people do things in the world. They are also both social and rhetorical actions, operating as people interact with others in purposeful ways. To say that genres are typified actions is in part to say that genres are classifications but classifications made by people as they act symbolically rather than by analysts as they examine products. To examine the nature of this typification further and to elaborate the nature of recurring conditions and social context and their interactions with genre, I will first trace the relationships between social context and genre that others have proposed, leading to my own characterization of that relationship.

Miller's definition of genre, "typified rhetorical actions based in recurrent situations" (159), has been considerably complicated over the years by Miller and others, but it remains an oft-cited mantra for many genre scholars. Although also deriving from Aristotle and Burke, the connection of genre to situation has been most frequently drawn from the 1968 work of Lloyd Bitzer. In his elaborate exploration of rhetorical situation, Bitzer refers to what happens when situations recur:

> Due to either the nature of things or convention, or both, some situations recur. The courtroom is the locus for several kinds of situations generating the speech of accusation, the speech of defense, the charge to the jury. From day to day, year to year, comparable situations occur, prompting comparable responses; hence rhetorical forms are born and a special vocabulary, grammar, and style are established. This is true also of the situation which invites the inaugural address of a President. The situation recurs and, because we experience situations and the rhetorical response to them, a form of discourse is not only established but comes to have a power of its own—the tradition itself tends to function as a constraint upon any new response in the form. (13)

According to this model, these "rhetorical forms" (though never called "genres" by Bitzer) develop because they respond appropriately to situations that speakers and writers encounter repeatedly. In principle, that is, language users first respond in fitting ways and hence similarly to recurring situations; then the similarities among those appropriate responses become established as generic conventions.

That texts respond to situations is a conception found also in the work of Kenneth Burke, who asserts that "[c]ritical and imaginative works are answers to questions posed by the situation in which they arose" (1). In Burke's model, writers develop strategies for "encompassing" situations, strategies that "size up" situations in ways that have "public content." Burke notes that similar situations enable us to see "poetic acts" as relevant, and I would add (and will expand later) that similar strategies for encompassing those situations, public as they are, are also visible and may appear as relevant to our similar situations. This combination in discourse acts of situation and strategy (a bifurcation that Burke claims is the precursor of his five-part dramatic act) thus enables us to see genres as strategies that have commonly been used to answer situations.

That generic features suit their situations appears clearly in a relatively fixed genre like the lab report: its particular purposes and reader's needs can be met well by its formal features—such as a quick statement of purpose, separate methods and results sections, and clear section headings that allow the reader to skip to results and check methods only if something looks wrong in the results. If all writers of lab reports use these forms, then all lab reports will respond in some appropriate ways to the needs of their situation. Even a more loosely defined genre reveals the appropriateness of generic conventions to situation. The opening of a letter to a friend, for example, just like all our everyday greetings, signals affection and maintains contact, whether the standard "Hi! How are you?" or a more original nod to the relationship. The features that genres develop (at least at first) respond appropriately to their situations.

Such critics as Scott Consigny and Richard Vatz, however, note how deterministic such a connection of genre to situation can be. In fact, of course, multiple genres can respond to a situation, and speakers and writers can choose fitting responses that are not generically determined. As Carolyn Miller points out, the language of demand and response invites an externalized and deterministic view of situations and genre ("Genre" 155–56). In practice, as well, the genre a writer needs for a particular situation often already exists and hence already guides responses to that situation (an idea that I will say more about later in this chapter). If each writing problem were to require a completely new assessment of how to respond, writing would be slowed considerably, but once a writer recognizes a recurring situation, a situation that others have responded to in the past, the writer's response to that situation can be guided by past responses. Genre, thus, depends heavily on the intertextuality of discourse. As Bakhtin points out in his important essay on speech genres, a speaker "is not, after all, the first speaker, the one who disturbs the eternal silence of the universe" ("Problem" 69). The fact that others have responded to similar situations in the past in similar ways—the fact that genres exist—enables writers and readers to respond more easily and more appropriately themselves. This initial insight—that genres respond appropriately to their rhetorical situations—reveals the rhetorical nature of generic forms and provides the basis of a newly rhetorical theory of genre. Knowing the genre, therefore, means knowing such rhetorical aspects as appropriate subject matter, level of detail, tone, and approach as well as the expected layout and organization. Miller concentrates on what genre reveals about purpose, object, and motive, and she concludes that "what we learn when we learn a genre is not just a pattern of forms or even a method of achieving our own ends. We learn, more importantly, what ends we may have" ("Genre" 165). Knowing the genre means not only, or even most of all, knowing how to conform to generic conventions but, more importantly, knowing one way of responding appropriately to a given situation.[3]

Connecting genres to situation provides genre with an essentially rhetorical nature. It helps explain how language users know to take particular reader and writer roles, how they select a particular genre when they have a particular purpose, and why certain genres are most commonly used within particular groups. Certain people commonly encounter certain situations, so they need ways of responding to those situations and they learn what is appropriate in those situations. As "situations are shorthand terms for motives" (Burke, "Permanence and Change, qtd. in C. Miller, "Genre" 158), genres are shorthand terms for situations.

This relationship of situation to genre has formed the basis of a current rhetorical genre theory, but it needs to be elaborated to comprehend more complex views of both genre and situation. One problem is how to define situation. Bitzer offers one of the most fully detailed definitions of what he calls rhetorical situation:

> Rhetorical situation may be defined as a complex of persons, events, objects, and relations presenting an actual or potential exigence which can be completely or partially removed if discourse, introduced into the situation, can so constrain human decision or action as to bring about the significant modification of the exigence. . . . Any *exigence* is an imperfection marked by urgency; it is a defect, an obstacle, something waiting to be done, a thing which is other than it should be. . . . An exigence which cannot be modified is not rhetorical. . . . Further, an exigence which can be modified only by means other than discourse is not rhetorical. . . . An exigence is rhetorical when it is capable of positive modification and

when positive modification requires discourse or can be as-
sisted by discourse. (6–7)

Bitzer's article explains and exemplifies this definition of rhetorical situation and its essential component, rhetorical exigence, at some length.
Other theorists, notably again Richard Vatz and Scott Consigny, have
criticized Bitzer's definition not only for being too deterministic, requiring that there be only one fitting response to any situation, but also for
requiring a narrowly defined rhetorical exigence that excludes many
kinds of writing and speaking. Since Bitzer limits rhetorical situation to
only those situations with rhetorical exigencies that require discourse
action, Bitzer's definition of rhetorical situation is too narrow for the
wide range of discourse for which genre theorists need to account.

For a broader inclusion of language behavior and a shift away from
rhetorical exigence to function, many genre theorists, including Burke
(111), have turned to B. Malinowski's concepts of context of situation
and context of culture, especially as developed later by M. A. K. Halliday
and others. Context of situation, as Halliday defines it, consists of a field
(roughly, what is happening, purposes), a tenor (who is involved, their
roles), and a mode (what role language is playing) (31–35). Those components of situation predict what Halliday calls "register." He defines
register as "the configuration of semantic resources that the member of
a culture typically associates with a situation type. It is the meaning
potential that is accessible in a given social context" (111). Significantly,
like genre, register is a semantic concept, not a formal one. Halliday most
often lists genre as part of mode, a textual part of situation rather than
an overall response to the situation (143–45). In this respect, Halliday's
social semiotic definition of situation will not adequately capture the
complexity of genre that I am attempting here to establish. Yet at other
times Halliday describes generic structure as being at a higher level of
semiotic structure, one of three factors (along with textual structure and
cohesion) that constitute text. This notion of generic structure, Halliday
writes somewhat vaguely, "can be brought within the general framework
of the concept of register" (134).

Perhaps because of Halliday's willingness to include generic structure at this higher semiotic level, and surely because of the similarity of
Halliday's description of register to others' notions of genre, Hasan,
Martin, and other followers of Halliday have taken what Halliday says
to be true of register to be true of genre as well, even equating Hallidayan
register with their genre. Genres thus become the semantic resources

associated with situation types, the meaning potential in given social contexts. To the extent that register represents semantic resources associated with situation types, it seems a concept closely parallel to new definitions of genre, and it enables us to broaden beyond rhetorical exigencies and Bitzer's more narrowly defined rhetorical situation. All texts participate in contexts of situation, according to Halliday, and all participate in registers, so all texts participate in genres. To the extent that register represents the meaning potential available in a given social context, however, Halliday's concept of register seems much broader than genre. Registers appear to be the broadest associations of language and context, the language used by a mother at play with her child or a lawyer in discussion with her client rather than the more specific generic situation of playing house or conducting an initial interview. Definitions of genre that genre scholars derive from Halliday's broad notions of context of situation and corresponding functions seem similarly large, as in Martin, Christie, and Rothery's definition of genre as "a staged, goal oriented social process" (58), a definition that seems to encompass much more than typified genre. While Halliday's notion of context of situation thus broadens rhetorical situation so that it can be associated with a wide range of genres, it needs narrowing again to apply more specifically to genre as distinct from register or other social actions.

In a 1997 article on "Rethinking Genre in School and Society: An Activity Theory Analysis," David Russell attempts to broaden the level of analysis to include nonlinguistic actions and to capture better the multiple, collective, and interactive social nature of those actions. He uses activity theory in part to avoid a dualism that can come from separating context and text, dealing with an activity system instead of a context. Reminiscent of Halliday's field, tenor, and mode, Russell's analysis breaks an activity system into subject(s), object/motive, and mediational means (510). Activity systems have the benefit over rhetorical situations of encompassing much more than narrowly defined rhetorical exigencies, including even the nonlinguistic, and much more than the immediate situation, including cultural values and other, interacting activity systems. In some ways, it collapses Malinowski's context of situation and context of culture into one activity system. As a result, it shares some of the problem of breadth of Halliday's context of situation and may even less provide a way to distinguish genre from other social actions. Both Halliday's and Russell's theories do, however, move away from the notion of genre as a unidirectional *response* to context of situation or activity system. Simply defining situation differently will not eliminate problems

remaining with the notion of genre as response, with the nature of recurrence of situation, and with missing components of context. What
is needed is a more dynamic and interactive view of the relationship
between genre and whatever the surrounding conditions may be.

Constructing Genre and Situation

An initial problem with defining the surrounding conditions of genres
can be seen by trying to specify what a concept of context must include.
Not everything about the surrounding environment (the temperature,
what is happening in the next block) is relevant for the language use
being considered, and some things outside the surrounding environment
(potential readers, previous texts) are relevant. It is in this sense that
situations cannot be strictly material.[4] The very notion of context "surrounding" genre gives it a separation from discourse and yet a physical
materiality that reinforce a container model of meaning, with artificially
separated text and context, to which many have rightly objected. Yet, if
the context of situation is not simply a physical fact of the surrounding
environment, as it clearly is not, where does it come from? One answer
has been that writers and readers construct it, that people's actions around
discourse delineate what is relevant and not, what constitutes the situation. Carolyn Miller writes, "Situations are social constructs that are the
result, not of 'perception,' but of 'definition.'" ("Genre" 156). Semiotic
structures similarly result from human definition, and Halliday and
Hasan also describe situation as constructed:

> Any piece of text, long or short, spoken or written, will carry
> with it indications of its context. . . . This means that we
> reconstruct from the text certain aspects of the situation,
> certain features of the field, the tenor, and the mode. Given
> the text, we construct the situation from it. (38)

Similarly, Russell explains that activity systems are "mutually (re)con-
structed by participants historically" so that he "treats context not as a
separate set of variables but as an ongoing, dynamic accomplishment
of people acting together with shared tools, including—most powerfully—writing" ("Rethinking" 510, 508–509). The activity system, context of situation, or rhetorical situation is created by people through their
use of discourse.

Neither the construction of situation nor, even more clearly, the recurrence of situation can be simply a material fact but instead must be
rather what Miller calls "an intersubjective phenomenon, a social oc-

currence" ("Genre" 156). Situations cannot recur, Miller concludes from
the work of Robert A. Stebbins and others. No two situations are identical, in either their material or constructed reality. Even the most closely
allied situations will vary from one another, as performances of the same
play vary from one another. Applying performance theory to genre, in-
triguingly, might offer ways of describing the singularity and yet generic
commonality of each symbolic act, each discourse performance, an idea
worthy of fuller elaboration than space in this chapter allows. Each
performance of a play repeats the play with variations and is a distinct
act. While maintaining much commonality with all other performances
of the same play, the actors and audience differ, the sets, props, costumes,
sound, and lights differ, the blocking and staging differ, the interpretation of its meaning differs. (I will explore this inherent variation and
creativity in chapter 5.) Yet promoters advertise that the same play is
being performed, call it by the same name, and audiences expect to see
the same play. The variations of the particular performance are, in fact,
what is appreciated, why the audience attends the play rather than reading the script. The parallels with discourse and genres seem to me fairly
substantial. Each text varies in details, in who the participants are, what
language is used, what meanings are achieved, yet readers and writers
identify that the texts are of a common genre. The play and genre recur,
even though the specific performance (artistic or linguistic) varies in
substantial ways.

Carolyn Miller traces such recurrence to socially construed types
based on Alfred Schuts's notion of a common "stock of knowledge." This
"social construct, or semiotic structure," in Miller's terms, develops from
existing typifications, which develop from "the recognition of relevant
similarities" ("Genre" 156–57). If stocks of knowledge and types equal
genre, then Miller is arguing, as would I, that people construct the recurring situation through their knowledge and use of genres. They recognize similarities of one discourse to another because they already have
a typified stock of knowledge or a socially created set of genres (a term
I will develop in the next chapter). If this is so, then the significance of
that preexisting set of genres may not have been sufficiently acknowledged in current genre theory. Preexisting genres are part of what enable individuals to move from their unique experiences and perceptions
to a shared construction of recurring situation and genre. Miller dismisses
subjective perception as the source of what recurs, for perception is
"unique from moment to moment and person to person" ("Genre" 156).
Yet I would argue that individual perception must be the source of re-

currence, for discourse exists only through the actions of individuals. All discourse is situated in unique experiences, changing from moment to moment and person to person. Discourse exists only when individuals act, and their actions will always be grounded in their uniqueness as well as their social experience. If genre is based on recurrence at all, it must be a recurrence perceived by the individuals who use genres. Existing genres, as part of individual knowledge as well as social typifications, can bridge the unique and the social, so they must play a significant role in people's perceiving similarities. A writer or reader recognizes recurrence because she or he recognizes an existing genre. But for existing genres to exist at all, people must have perceived similarities among disparate situations. Paradoxically, then, people recognize recurring situations because they know genres, yet genres exist only because people have acted as though situations have recurred.

This paradox works, I propose, because people construct genre through situation and situation through genre; their relationship is reciprocal and dynamic. If genre responds to recurring situation, then a particular text's reflection of genre reflects that genre's situation. Thus the act of constructing the genre—of classifying a text as similar to other texts—is also the act of constructing the situation. As mentioned earlier, when readers recognize the genre of a particular text, they recognize, through the genre, its situation. When, for example, readers recognize that they are reading a freshman theme, they recognize simultaneously the writer's and reader's roles. Like readers, writers also construct situation by constructing genre. A writer faced with a writing task confronts multiple contexts and must define a specific context in relation to that task. Writers must determine their persona, their audience, their purposes. By selecting a genre to write in, or by beginning to write within a genre, the writer has selected the situation entailed in that genre. A teacher's assignment may ask for a letter to the editor, but the student writer who begins with an inverted-triangle introduction common in freshman themes is still writing a school essay for the teacher, is still constructing his or her role as student filling a school assignment rather than as citizen trying to persuade fellow citizens. Acting with genres creates the contextual situation. "Thus context is an ongoing accomplishment," in Russell's pithy phrase, "not a container for actions or texts" (513).

This relationship between genre and situation, as constructed by readers and writers, listeners and speakers, is not unidirectional but must be reciprocal. About poetic acts, Burke suggested thinking of situation and strategy, or scene and act, as "each possessing its own genius, but

the two fields interwoven" (64). Situation and genre are so tightly interwoven as to be interlocked. People construct situations through
genres, but they also construct genres through situations. The letter to
the editor written for an assignment in a writing class may be a different genre from the letter to the editor written out of concern for a local
issue. The genre is constructed differently because the situation is constructed differently. Cases where the genre is chosen rather than assigned
make explicit the role of situation in constructing genre: people identify the situation in order to choose an appropriate genre. Once the genre
is chosen, however, the genre reciprocally acts to shape the situation.
Writing a letter to the editor entails certain roles for the writer and reader,
leads readers to expect certain types of subject matter, and lends itself
to particular types of purposes. If the writer defines the situation differently, the writer must work to alter that given situation in the particular letter; if successful, the text may lead readers to construct the situation differently, opening the way for constructing the genre differently.
Letters to the editor in my hometown newspaper, for example, sometimes plead with thieves to return items stolen from the writer's prop-
erty, overlaying onto the usual purpose of persuading a mass audience
to action a different purpose of persuading a single person to action.
Writers and readers in this case must use this genre to construct a different situation from the usual, and they use the situation to construct
the genre differently from the usual. Situations construct genres, genres
construct situations.

   In fact, such cases where writers and readers are violating, challenging, or changing the connection of a genre to a situation can be most
revealing of their integration and interdependence. Consider, for example, what happens when writers and readers match genre and situation differently. Suppose a writer of a formal scholarly article tried to
vary the *situation*—say by changing the relationship of the writer and
reader and treating the audience as a friend. What readers will likely note
is a problem of *genre*, either noting a flawed text that violates the genre
or concluding that the writer is trying to change the genre (the interpretation probably depending on whether the writer is a student or an established scholar, part of the cultural context to be discussed below).
Conversely, a writer who mixes or shifts *genre* in the middle of a text
causes confusion for the reader, not because the reader cannot label the
genre but because the reader cannot be sure of the writer's purpose or
the reader's role—cannot be sure of the *situation*. In watching *Twin
Peaks*, a television series blending mystery, fantasy, and more, viewers

asked not "Is this a murder mystery or is this a fantasy?" but rather "Am I supposed to believe this?" and "Aren't they going to tell me who did it?" For a final example, a reader who "misreads" a text's *genre*—who reads "A Modest Proposal" as a serious proposal, say—most significantly misreads the *situation* as well. Genre and situation are tightly interwoven, as genre theory has long recognized, but it is genre that determines situation as well as situation that determines genre. To say that genre *responds* to situation not only is deterministic but also oversimplifies their reciprocal relationship.

As I will discuss further in chapters 4 and 5 and as many other scholars have noted, people can create and alter genres; that process too reveals the integration and interdependence of genre and situation. Writers can try to vary the matchup of situation and genre. A "change of scene," Burke notes, announces "a new kind of act" (106 note). The scholarly personal essay (or personal scholarly essay) can be seen as an attempt to change the scholarly article's genre, situation, or both. Perhaps writers of such essays wish the scholarly article genre would encompass personal experience; perhaps such writers wish the scholarly situation entailed greater intimacy between colleagues; perhaps writers of such essays wish that the scholarly situation called for a personal genre. Similar interpretations of both situation and genre can be offered for *ecriture feminine* and other alternate, diverse styles of discourse. To alter the situation, the genre must be altered, and to alter the genre, the situation must be altered.

To reunite some of the more complex threads of this developing rhetorical theory of genre, and to suggest some of the implications, I would like to extend an example that Russell gives of going grocery shopping with his daughter. In my much-reduced version of Russell's narrative, they make a grocery list, discover that it helps them in their goal of getting food for the household, so they begin making a grocery list every week and modify as needed over time (516–17). The situation called for the genre. Yet, following Miller's and other's arguments described in this chapter, I would point out that their second trip to the grocery store could not possibly have been identical to the first trip to the store. To define it as the same, they must have ignored the fact that the day or time was different from their first trip or that they were wearing different clothes, for example, and acted as though the situation was a recurrence of their first grocery shopping situation. Even as they adapted their grocery list to changing details of each unique shopping trip—including different items that the household needed or shopping at a different store—they defined the situation as the same as other grocery shopping trips and used the same genre of the grocery list to help structure the situation. So the situation of needing food led to using the genre of the grocery list, which is defined by and takes particular shapes as it is constructed by the situation. Simultaneously, the act of choosing the genre of the grocery list constructed their situation—writing and posting for the rest of the household a grocery list created for them the roles of grocery shoppers, created an expectation that they would gather food at a regular interval, and structured what they would buy and how they would proceed through the store. In addition, using the grocery list created a recurring action and situation where one had not necessarily existed. Russell points out that they could have gathered food by going to a farmer's market or growing their own food. I would add that they could shop at a grocery store in a different way, with different household members shopping each week, picking up only what occurs to them, and moving randomly through the store. The prior existence of grocery lists encourages them to behave in certain ways; it shapes their individual perceptions toward a socially typified way of acting in their unique situation. Using the grocery list meant that they defined the need for food as calling for the same action each week, defined the situation as recurring: the same participants (the two of them must go grocery shopping), the same purpose (they must gather all the items their household members request), and the same process (they must shop in an orderly, planned way through the store). Keeping a grocery list each week entails assuming all that similarity in what could be a different experience each week with only the need for food in common. Keeping a grocery list each week creates the sense of recurring situation. Keeping a grocery list makes the situation recur.

So far in this chapter, I have sketched some basic principles of a rhetorical theory of genre that develops from Miller's definition of genre, explaining and sometimes extending what it means for a genre to be typified social action in response to recurring rhetorical situation. (The issue of social action is being left largely for complicating in the next chapter.) The definition of one component, rhetorical situation, has been broadened from Bitzer's to encompass all kinds of discourse situations, involving Halliday's field, tenor, and mode, though such a broadly defined situation still does not adequately distinguish genre from register. The nature of genre as response has been clarified, for the relationship is not deterministic but rather messily reciprocal, with genres responding to situations and situations responding to genres. In fact, the genres themselves define and create the situations as much as the situations create the genres, for people construct situations through their use of genres. Finally, rhetorical situations never actually recur, for each situation is unique. Thus, the recurrence of rhetorical situation must also be constructed as people use genres, a matter of what people define as similar, whether similar in genre or similar in situation. Genre and situation are reciprocal, mutually constructed, and integrally interrelated.

Genre as Nexus of Situation, Culture, and Other Genres

Even mutually constructed and integrally interrelated, situation and genre do not capture all of the action, however. Later in Russell's story of grocery shopping with his daughter, he notes that he had appropriated the grocery list from his mother and was passing it on to his daughter ("Rethinking" 517). He and his daughter did not invent the grocery list as a genre to help with their grocery shopping task in the activity system of grocery shopping. Rather, they followed the actions defined by their predecessors and learned from interacting with others. The sense of the past and the transmission of cultural values implied in Russell's learning the genre from his mother is inadequately acknowledged in connecting genre to rhetorical situation, context of situation, or even activity system. Even more absent from those versions of context is the existence of genres other than the one being studied, the always already existing genres that are also a significant part of context. To reintegrate these contexts with context of situation and to recognize their role in genre action, I propose adding two elements to the essential components of a genre definition: culture and other genres.

Culture (loosely defined as a shared set of material contexts and learned behaviors, values, beliefs, and templates) influences how situation is constructed and how it is seen as recurring in genres. In part, culture defines what situations and genres are possible or likely. Miller and others have noted the cultural significance of genres, that genres may reveal our culture's values and, in Miller's words, "help constitute the substance of our cultural life" ("Genre" 163). Miller also recognizes culture as a level in her hierarchy of meaning ("Genre" 162), part of what gives significance to human actions. Her hierarchy, above the level of genre, includes "form of life" (following Wittgenstein's term), culture, and human nature, and she notes that "genres are provided interpretive context by form-of-life patterns" ("Genre" 161) and, I would presume, by culture and human nature. I am arguing for culture as more than an interpretive context for genre but as an element in the dynamic construction of genre. Although one might see the effects of culture as implicit in Miller's hierarchy, Miller's semiotic fusion of substance and form and her hierarchy of meaning emphasize how "lower" levels constitute and construct higher levels but encourage less attention than I think necessary to how the higher levels simultaneously constitute and construct the lower levels.

Russell argues for doing away altogether with the "macro-micro distinction" inherent in such levels, and he proposes a blend of activity and genre systems to enable analysis of "the macro-level social and political structures (*forces*) that affect the micro-level actions" of people in education activity systems ("Rethinking" 509, 505). Russell also notes the difficulties of a Bakhtinian conversational model of context, limited as it is to the verbal, the dyad, and the local. Russell instead treats context (and perhaps culture?) "not as a separate set of variables but as an ongoing, dynamic accomplishment of people acting together with shared tools" (508–9). Although I will object in chapter 2 to Russell's treatment of writing and genre as tools, here I endorse his attempt to undermine the separation of context from actions or text. Yet Russell himself finds it necessary to separate the macro from micro level in his analysis (e.g., discussing "micro-level interactions" [512] and "macro-level contradictions" [532]). The attempt to fuse the macro and micro may in fact disguise too much the impact of each. Russell treats elements of objects and power (what I would consider part of ideological culture) as something that develops within activity systems and that may conflict across systems, creating double binds for individuals. With the concept of activity system including such apparently diverse and yet equally important activity systems as a cell biology course and a research university, it may be difficult to locate the material and ideological contexts that I wish to analyze and which I believe would often overlap multiple activity systems. On the other hand, the emphasis on the activity systems within which people operate makes it difficult to see the individuals, the people whose actions construct these systems. Although applauding Russell's move to see context in text, I think that the emphasis on systems too easily loses sight of the messy, the lived experience, the intensely local and micro-level construction of those systems by people, even as it makes it difficult to analyze cultural constructions that may extend over multiple activity systems.

What I wish to capture by adding the concept of culture to our genre definition are the ways that existing ideological and material contexts, contexts beyond the more immediate context of situation of a particular genre, partially construct what genres are and are in turn constructed (reproduced) by people performing genre actions. Extending Russell's example again, the grocery list genre exists in part because of the material fact that large grocery stores are common in Russell's culture. His use of the grocery list reflects the common cultural expectation that people in cities in the United States buy their food rather than grow it. And the existence and structure of the grocery list reflects a common cultural valuing of order and efficiency. Catherine Schryer points out that genres encompass orientations to time and space, orientations that seem to me ideological and cultural more than situational ("Genre" 81). Burke, too, notes the "material interests" engaged in verbal action and describes how this cultural context affects the "idiom" in which one speaks (111–12). The effect of culture on defining genre appears also in a study of readers of romances by Janice Radway. Radway describes how cultural values and ideologies place women in situations in which they are more likely to read romances than other genres. She also describes the material cultural context of placing romances in grocery stores and its effects on spreading the reading of romances. One effect is that readers can easily identify the genre: books placed in a particular section of the grocery store will be the kind of books the women want to read, that is, romances, thereby increasing their purchase. The material and ideological culture partly constructs the situation (as women become housewives) and the genre (as romances become the books found in grocery stores). This (what I will term, following Malinowski) "context of culture" has profound effects on situation and genre that seem readily apparent and will become even more so through the social and historical studies in the rest of this book. The ways that genres also construct or reproduce the culture, in the reciprocal relationship so essential to genre, will be examined further in the next two chapters. Though the cultural context has perhaps been the least investigated until recently, a definition of genre that includes a distinct context of culture provides a source for explaining significant facets of genre.

The second element I wish to integrate into the definition of genre is the influence of other genres. Its effects on the identification of situations and cultures may be less readily apparent, though it stems directly from the constructive nature of genre already described. As noted earlier and by others, one never writes or speaks in a void. What fills that void is not only cultural context (ideological and material baggage surrounding our every action) and situational context (the people, languages, and purposes involved in every action) but also generic context, the existing genres we have read or written or that others say we should read or write. The "context of genres" that I propose includes all the existing genres in that society, the individual genres and sets of genres, the relatively stagnant and the changing genres, the genres commonly used and those not used. While the existence of other genres has certainly been acknowledged by many others, including context of genres in my definition emphasizes the fact that genres are always already existing, emphasizes the past in the present. Adding a context of genres to genre theory acknowledges that the existence of genres influences people's uses of genres, that writers and speakers do not create genres in a generic void, that people's knowledge and experience of genres in the past shape their experience with any particular discourse and any particular genre at any particular time. The context of genres is distinct from the theoretical concept of genre that I am trying to explain and elaborate in this chapter. As opposed to an abstract concept of genre, the context of genres is the existence of particular genres, the already existing textual classifications and forms already established and being established within a given culture, the set of typified rhetorical actions already constructed by participants in a society.

This context of genres influences each symbolic act, sometimes more visibly than others. Jamieson has demonstrated how existing genres constitute antecedent genres when people must construct new genres for new situations and cultural contexts, an idea explored more fully in chapter 4. Many teachers are familiar with how students draw from known genres, like narratives or personal experience essays or plot summaries, when asked to write unfamiliar genres, like critical analyses. The existence of prior known genres shapes the development of new or newly learned genres. A similar influence of existing genres operates on all language users all the time. Let me extend Russell's example one more time. Russell uses the genre of the grocery list because it already exists in his repertoire, as learned from his mother. He may have learned it easily, and his daughter may have picked it up easily, because each already knew related genres, other types of lists, for example. Russell's daughter now knows the grocery list genre because it already existed in the world, her father's world, and was taught to her. As she continues to use it in later years and even to change it with her use (perhaps adapting it to online grocery shopping), the genre will continue to resonate with her past experiences of making lists with her father, a resonance that itself resonates with her father's past experience with the genre and his mother's past experience before that. Genres are always already existing. People interpret situations, select genres, and function culturally within a context of existing genres that brings the past perpetually into the present.

Thus context of situation, context of culture, and context of genres all influence the actions of writers and readers, speakers and listeners, and they do it partly through genre. Each kind of context has both a material and a constructed reality, for what makes them "contexts" is the extent to which people give them significance, as described in the preceding section for context of situation. All three contexts interact, and at the nexus of that interaction lies genre. A genre constructs and is constructed by a notion of recurring situation, entailing participant roles, purposes, and uses of language. A genre constructs and is constructed by cultural values, beliefs, and norms as well as by material culture. A genre constructs and is constructed by the set of existing genres surrounding it, genres used and not used by fellow participants in the society. These contexts of situation, culture, and genres act simultaneously and interactively within a genre, and genre sits at the nexus of such interactions, for genre is what Bakhtin calls "the *whole* of the utterance," a unity and a unifier ("Problem" 60).

This nexus is similar to the nexus of contexts that Burke sees coming together in the individual, in whom all the "social idioms" are incorporated to "build ourselves" (112).[5] Miller and Russell, too, like other genre scholars, place genre between the textual and the contextual, the individual action and the social system. Contexts for Burke become incorporated within an individual. Seeing contexts incorporated instead within genre, as I do, helps give writers access to the variety of changing situations, cultures, and generic contexts without being overtaken by them. A language user operates within the contexts of culture, situation, and genres as they inhabit the genre of the discourse. Since people use many genres, people can participate in multiple contexts just as they do multiple activity systems, experiencing the similarities, the contradictions, and the double binds as they go. The layers of contexts—of situation, culture, and other genres—create other places for such double binds or concurrence to occur. Writing an academic lab report entails adopting scientific "objectivity" as well as academic subservience to teacher authority (culture), encourages defining the situation as student reporting to teacher on what was done and what the teacher already knows (situation), and draws on the writer's experience with other lab reports and academic papers and the teacher's experience with other scientific genres. Because genre encompasses these contexts and individual discourses encompass genre, when we examine a genre, we have access to all three contexts; when we examine a particular discourse through the lens of genre, we have access to these contexts and to the unique situation of that discourse, how this discourse varies from and works within those generic expectations. In studying genre, thus, we can study the concrete and local as well as the abstract and general. Not as removed as situation or activity system, genre mediates between text and context. Not as general as meaning, genre mediates between form and content. Genre allows us to particularize context while generalizing individual action.

Reluctant as I am to reduce this reciprocal, constructed, and individually situated theory to a formula, I offer figure 1.1 to try to clarify the angles of analysis and the interacting elements. I hope that this visual representation, while not nearly as theoretically elaborated as Miller's or Russell's graphics, provides some clarity that can prove useful for studying genres in later chapters and for others who may find it helpful. While this figure roughly represents the distinctions I am proposing between the contexts, the mediating genre, and the individual action, this flat figure falsely implies static levels and cannot begin to represent

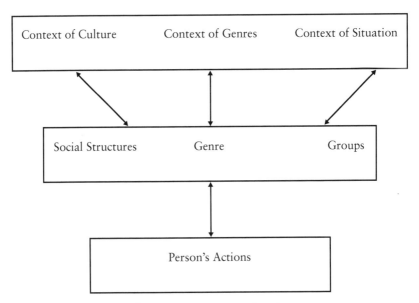

Fig 1.1. Interactions of contexts, genre, and action

the interactions of the three contexts with one another and through a genre, a dynamic perhaps better represented by a set of overlays, overlapping circles, three-dimensional cones, and moving waves rather than boxes and arrows. The contexts of situation, culture, and genres interact amongst themselves, with the context of situation in part specified by the contexts of culture and genres, the context of culture in part specified by the contexts of situation and genres, and the context of genres in part specified by the context of situation and culture, all operating simultaneously and dynamically. Partially undercutting the micro-macro distinction necessary for analysis, each one of the three contexts captures a different level of social context: the context of culture draws attention to the macro level of context, the context of situation draws attention to the micro level of particular situations, and the context of genres resists such dualism and draws attention to a level between the macro and micro levels. The context of genres encompasses the already typified situations, so it is a level above the particular context of situation, but it also encompasses the specific ideological and material conditions of the existing multiple genres, a level more particularized than the context of culture.

I propose, then, that genre be seen not as a response to recurring situation but as a nexus between an individual's actions and a socially defined context. Genre is a reciprocal dynamic within which individuals' actions construct and are constructed by recurring context of situation, context of culture, and context of genres. Genre is visible in classification and form, relationships and patterns that develop when language users identify different tasks as being similar. But genre exists through people's individual rhetorical actions at the nexus of the contexts of situation, culture, and genres.

Although this reconception of genre is theoretically complex, I want to be careful not to simplify the definition and relation of genre and contexts. Many areas of genre theory still need further research and exploration. For example, not all genres allow a simple matchup with a particular set of contexts; some might interact with multiple contexts. Not all contexts that people define as recurring produce recognized genres, and some may produce more than one genre. People may, of course, mix genres and mix contexts, and they may use genres badly. Genres may be unsuccessful, fail, or die out. Genre is too rich a subject to be mined completely in just one volume, though I hope the chapters that follow will dig deeply.

One of the great appeals of studying genre, to me, is that genre is based on what people already know and do. People recognize genres, and people are the ones who define whether a genre exists. Shania Twain understands that everybody has to be something, everything participates in genre. Only by ignoring what language users themselves know can we ignore the significance of genre. It is the intriguing job of genre scholars to figure out what lies behind what everyone already knows.

2
An Analysis of Genres in Social Settings

Explanation entails simplification; and any simplification is
open to the charge of "oversimplification."
—Kenneth Burke, "Philosophy of Literary Form"

Describing the social significance of genre is at once necessary and impossible. As complex as society is, so is genre's working within that society. As we complicate our understandings of society, its relationships
and workings, we must similarly complicate our understandings of genre
and how it works, for genre develops within, embodies, and establishes
society's values, relationships, and functions. In the preceding chapter,
I explored genre's relationship to situation and genre's rhetorical power,
and I distinguished three kinds of contexts: contexts of situation, of culture, and of genres. In this chapter, I deepen the examination of genre's
rhetorical contexts by exploring genre's relationship to the particular
social structures and groups with which it reciprocally interacts. In terms
of figure 1.1, this chapter examines especially the mediating level between
contexts and individual actions. Groups, social structures, and genres
translate contexts into socially specific settings, and they transform individual actions into contextually meaningful social actions.

Genres operate socially, as what Miller calls social actions. But what
makes genre inherently social? First of all, genres require multiplicity,
multiple actions by multiple people. All discourse is predicated on two
people, a writer and reader or speaker and listener (though one could
debate whether one person can play both roles or whether discourse
makes a sound if it falls in an empty forest). But genre is predicated on
more than two people, on multiple people acting repeatedly, thus creating the perception of recurrence. The social nature of genres involves
more than simple multiplicity, though, for that perception of recurrence

comes from socially developed understandings of situations. People recognize grocery lists, to use an example from the last chapter, because they
have participated in supermarket shopping trips. Students come to learn
lab reports as they come to learn the particular expectations of science
courses. Lawyers learn briefs as they are trained in law school and practice to use briefs. The multiple actions that comprise genres are constituted and interpreted within particular social structures and particular
groups. That genres are always imbricated socially is a claim assumed
and demonstrated by many genre theorists (Berkenkotter and Huckin;
Bazerman, *Shaping*; Swales; and C. Miller, "Genre"). One common way
of describing genre's social involvement is to claim that genres function
for a group of language users to fulfill the group's needs. The rhetorical
situation to which a genre is related arises from the functional needs of
a particular group; hence those who encounter that situation are those
who need and use that genre. Genres function for people in their interactions with one another in groups and through social structures; they
are social actions.

Social function has thus been used to explain genres' purposes and
to elucidate their features. Explanations based on social function can clarify genres' features and their functioning, but they have a danger of focusing too heavily on the group and too little on the social structures. Because they mediate contexts, the particular social structures and groups
encompass contexts of culture as well as situation. Genre analyses in the
past have sometimes been primarily situational (examining local purposes, participants, and settings) and insufficiently cultural.[1] Because
genres operate within society, they are enmeshed in the complex relationships that are society, including such issues as power differentials and
ideological identities. Consider a few simple examples of the interaction
of situational and cultural contexts, social structures, and genres. The
school lab report fulfills the social function of demonstrating that an
experiment has been conducted and results achieved; the people involved
in such a situation are teachers and students, the genre users. Many of
the features of the lab report can be explained through this attention to
social group and situation. To understand fully the genre of school lab
report, however, the analysis must also recognize the social structures
involving all teachers and students in science courses, the complex relationships of teachers to students in North American schools, and the
epistemology of science and its belief in observable data. Understanding the social setting requires also understanding the cultural setting.
Consider another example: the request-for-proposals genre fulfills the

need to specify purposes and criteria for grants, but it also reflects more broadly the power relationship between institutional grant givers and institutional grant receivers, and it reflects and reinforces the ideology of the grant-giving institution. Since social structures and groups mediate contexts, to examine the social setting of genres is also to examine their cultural embeddedness.

I will explore how genre functions socially and culturally in this chapter by proposing and explaining six basic principles. Stating such basic principles risks stating what to some might seem obvious, but I hope to show that none of these principles is simple. Stating basic principles also has the benefit of opening them to scrutiny and clarifying assumptions that need further research, as Berkenkotter and Huckin demonstrate in their first chapter of *Genre Knowledge in Disciplinary Communication,* in which they lay out five principles of how genre functions as situated cognition, a model to which this chapter is indebted. To avoid becoming too removed from situated practice, however, I will follow the theoretical discussion of principles in this chapter with an examination in the next chapter of how they work out in a specific case, the case of writing done by tax accountants.

Genres Within Different Kinds of Groups

The social nature of discourse, and of genre, has been one of the most fruitful rediscoveries of textual study. Bakhtin states broadly that "verbal discourse is a social phenomenon—social throughout its entire range and in each and every one of its factors, from the sound image to the furthest reaches of abstract meaning" ("Discourse" 259). Further, Volosinov writes that all forms of "little speech genres" "operate in extremely close connection with the conditions of the social situation in which they occur and exhibit an extraordinary sensitivity to all fluctuations in the social atmosphere" (20). Historically, too, genres connect to social groups, for "[e]ach period and each social group has had and has its own repertoire of speech forms for ideological communication in human behavior" (Volosinov 20). The connection of genre to a group's activities and needs has been argued strongly in all major schools of genre theory.[2] Followers of Halliday in the Australian school emphasize generic function for particular groups. Scholars in the fields of English for specific purposes and English for academic purposes emphasize the relation of generic textual traits to communicative purposes for disciplinary groups. Finally, new rhetoricians have concentrated on the genres of professional communities and the social structures with which genres interact.

The heart of genre's social nature is its embeddedness in groups and hence social structures. Rhetorical situations are likely to be perceived as recurring by the same group of people, whose experiences are similar enough and repeated in similar enough ways to be perceived as recurring situations. It is also groups of people who are in a position to pass genres on to new participants, who form the groups with which new members interact. The genres that develop from a group's interactions, then, reciprocally reinforce the group's identity and nature by operating collectively rather than individually. It is no logical leap to argue that genres, which reflect and construct recurring rhetorical situations, also reflect and construct a group of people. To extend Bitzer's well-known example, the speeches of prosecution and of defense evolve from the recurring rhetorical situation of a trial with its rhetorical exigencies to charge and defend. That rhetorical situation also involves a recurring social setting, that of the legal system and lawyers, and even the cultural context of American notions of justice. The genre of defense speech interacts not only with its immediate rhetorical situation but also with the social structure of the legal system and the judges and lawyers who inhabit that system. Clearly, genres need to be understood in terms of their social structures and groups.

Beyond Discourse Communities

For many scholars, that social setting is described in terms of its inhabitants, the members of the social group, although those members, like situation and genre, are both the creators of the group and created by the group, constructing and constructed, as I will discuss more fully in the next section. One common label for such a group is "discourse community." The concept of discourse community developed usefully in composition theory for several purposes, among them to help specify the overly vague abstraction of "context" and to call attention to the social nature of texts (e.g., Bizzell). The considerable discussion over the past fifteen or more years includes some telling criticism of discourse community as an idealistic and naive concept (e.g., Harris, "Idea"). Since genre has so often been closely tied to the concept of discourse community, I wish briefly to review the initial concept and its modifications before suggesting modifications of my own.

The connection of discourse community to genre has been explored most fully by John Swales in his 1990 book *Genre Analysis: English in Academic and Research Settings*. Echoing Martin and other functionalists' emphasis on communicative purpose but applying it to writing for academic purposes, Swales states the social embeddedness of genre for many genre theorists: "Established members of discourse communities employ genres to realize communicatively the goals of their communities" (52). Deriving from the linguistic notion of speech community, the concept of discourse community has provided a way of defining relevant groups of language users, and the establishment of community through discourse has proven useful for genre theorists. Swales initially defines discourse communities as "sociorhetorical networks that form in order to work towards sets of common goals" (9). He then describes six defining characteristics that identify a discourse community:

1. A discourse community has a broadly agreed set of common public goals. . . .
2. A discourse community has mechanisms of intercommunication among its members. . . .
3. A discourse community uses its participatory mechanisms primarily to provide information and feedback. . . .
4. A discourse community utilizes and hence possesses one or more genres in the communicative furtherance of its aim. . . .
5. In addition to owning genres, a discourse community has acquired some specific lexis. . . .
6. A discourse community has a threshold level of members with a suitable degree of relevant content and discoursal expertise.

(24–27)

Swales defines genre by connecting genre to one component of rhetorical situation—purpose—and then connecting purpose to discourse community:

A genre comprises a class of communicative events, the members of which share some set of communicative purposes. These purposes are recognized by the expert members of the parent discourse community, and thereby constitute the rationale for the genre. This rationale shapes the schematic structure of the discourse and influences and constrains choice of content and style. (58)

The "communicative events" that genre comprises also have social force, in Swales's terms, for he defines such events as "comprising not only the discourse itself and its participants, but also the role of that discourse and the environment of its production and reception, including its historical and cultural associations" (46). Genre, then, is shaped by a rationale determined by a discourse community and operates within a historical and cultural environment.

The problems with discourse community as the definer of genre's social nature are several, many of which Swales has recognized. Swales himself has described the criticisms of idealism and circularity and the problems of definition that he and others have pointed out (*Other Floors* 21–22, 196–204). Also, Swales's original emphasis on the "expert" or "established" members of the community disguises the heterogeneity of actual communities, with members at various stages of expertise, some on the periphery of the community, and all with different degrees and kinds of power within the community. Joseph Harris, in *A Teaching Subject,* has suggested the metaphor of city rather than community to reveal the diversity of membership, among other things. People also participate in multiple communities, so the borders of a discourse community are not as distinct as Swales's original criteria might make them appear. People move in and out of and among multiple groups, leaving communities more fluid and dynamic than the concept of discourse community has tended to capture.

I also find it counterintuitive to define groups according to the discourse they use, though doing so solves several problems of group identification and is convenient for scholars of discourse. Privileging discourse in this way does reveal that discourse helps to establish the community, though Swales cites studies by Dwight Atkinson and Yu-Ying Chang in concluding that

> [t]he discourse community concept was thus more useful for *validating* the existence of groupings that already shared a complex of ideas and sentiments, and less useful for seeing how such groupings were initiated and nurtured, or for assessing the precise characteristics of any purported collectivity. (*Other Floors* 21, emphasis in original)

On the basis of his own research, Swales concludes that a redefined conception of discourse community remains a viable and helpful approach to genres and his method of textography, one especially appropriate for rhetoricians and discourse analysts. Others, too, have redefined and refined the concept to solve various problems and respond to different criticisms (e.g., Killingsworth and Gilbertson, Porter). I find, though, that defining communities in terms of their discourse, while convenient for discourse analysts, has two significant and related problems that make any further refinement of the definition of discourse community irrelevant: the concept of discourse community privileges discourse above other group activities, motives, and purposes; and it disguises the social collectivity that shapes the very nature of the group and of its discourse (and its genres). As a result, it emphasizes too heavily the role of discourse in constructing groups and not enough the role of groups in constructing discourse.

It seems odd that lawyers and judges, for example, should be defined primarily as a community who share discourse, though of course discourse is central to the functioning of their community. Rather, what lawyers and judges have in common underlies the discourse they share. Speech communities in linguistics, on which the concept of discourse community is partially based, are grounded in the idea that people who share experiences tend to speak in similar ways. Usually, a speech community has been identified by its shared experiences, by its common demographic and social identity: middle-aged, upper-class white men in Philadelphia, for example, or teenaged working-class Latinas in Los Angeles. In those instances when speech communities are discovered through their common speech characteristics instead, sociolinguists seek underlying commonalities of identity. In the classic study of the speech among residents of Martha's Vineyard, for example, William Labov found different pronunciations among what would appear to be a homogeneous social group. What revealed the pattern of those different pronunciations and explained their basis was the difference in whether the young speakers planned to remain on the island or planned to move to the mainland. Those who planned to remain had pronunciations different from other young people and more similar to the pronunciations of older residents of the island. Two speech communities within the group of young people developed through different underlying loyalties, different identities. Transferred to the concept of discourse community, the concept of speech community shows that common traits of written discourse are significant to the extent that they reveal underlying commonalities of identity or values; they are not meaningful in themselves, just as saying "dog" rather than "chien" is not meaningful in itself. Recognizing common genres within a group, therefore, is but the first step in recognizing a community. The definer of that community must be some nondiscourse commonality that the common genres reflect and perform. Communities thus are better defined by their common goals, values, or identities than by their common discourse or genres.[3]

Lawyers and judges, then, share common goals, values, and identities, a fact to which their common genres attest and which their common genres promote. Of course, those common genres also attest to the fact that lawyers and judges communicate with one another often, that they have shared experiences. The young speakers on Martha's Vineyard must have not only identified with the older speakers on the island but also had contact with them, the basic insight of dialectology from which sociolinguistics and the concept of speech community developed. People must speak with one another, even indirectly, in order to speak like one another. Similarly, people who share genres must have contact with one another. It seems an obvious statement, but its implications extend beyond the obvious. People have different kinds of contact with different people. Some people are nodding acquaintances, some are colleagues, some are friends, some are family members. People know some people through a single shared interest, others through daily common endeavors. Contact with some people is voluntary; with others it is required to accomplish particular goals, perhaps even required to keep a job or an intact family. Linguists have long known that the degree and type of contact influence the degree of influence on people's speech. The same can be argued for communities and genres. There are different types of groups who develop genres, and those different types may produce genres with different relationships to the groups.

The kinds of groups that Swales and many other genre scholars most often describe are professional or disciplinary communities, especially ones that have frequent, work-related contact. In his recent study of the groups working on three floors of a building at the University of Michigan, Swales refines Porter's concept of a "place discourse community" to capture "a group of people who regularly work together" and whose members "have a settled (if evolving) sense of their aggregation's roles and purposes" (*Other Floors* 204). He goes on to add definitional criteria, including the existence of common genres, so that he can distinguish such communities from other groupings of people. As a result of his narrowed criteria, Swales concludes that one of the groups he studied, the Computing Resource Site, does not constitute a place discourse community. Its high turnover of staff (participants in the group), its participants' resulting weak sense of history, and the relatively low number of texts produced at that site, among other things, counteract its distinctive ethos among some participants, its consensus about the relationship between theory and practice, and its appearance as a working group, leading Swales to eliminate it from place discourse community status

(205). Attempting to establish defining criteria for discourse communities leads Swales to eliminate from consideration one group that clearly operates as a group, that has frequent daily contact around common endeavors. The other two groups Swales does classify as place discourse communities, though one, the Herbarium, clearly fits the criteria while the other, the English Language Institute, has one criterial problem.

Rather than refining the criteria to establish narrower definitions of types of discourse communities, to exclude some groups from further examination, I would prefer to see all three groups as interesting for discourse and genre analysts and as differing in their characteristics, both in kind and degree, in ways that might well relate to the differences in their discourse and genres. The fact that the English Language Institute contains two groups with potentially clashing cultures, rather than posing a problem for discourse community researchers, could create a rich area for research into how people negotiate ideologies through discourse when conflicting ideologies are present within the same working group. The fact that the Computing Resource Site has high turnover and relatively few texts produced within the group could present an opportunity to study how coherence is established (or not) within a rapidly changing group and what role discourse from outside the group plays. By making the Herbarium the model of a place discourse community, Swales and others who privilege traditional professional groups determine that the social contexts will be of particular kinds, limiting as well the range of genres examined. Swales, for example, would not examine weather forecasts, a category of discourse that people identify with a generic name (*Other Floors* 198).

In order to include the whole range of genres, with all their multifarious ways of operating within groups, I would prefer to begin with the whole range of groups, with all the multifarious ways that people gather and that social structures organize those people. I would prefer to step back, to look at larger definitions of ways that people group themselves, and to see what kinds of discourse are used by these generally different groupings of people. In advocating a return to such vague "terms of art," as Swales calls them, I am advocating a return to a broader understanding of the interaction of society and genres. Perhaps renewed research can examine how genres interact with multiple kinds of groups rather than primarily with the kinds of groups most distinct and most based in discourse. Such research as Peter Medway's on architecture students' use of architects' notebooks, with his discovery of what he calls "baggy genres" that I described in chapter 1, illustrates how different the genres might be that exist in different kinds of groups. Such research might eventually reveal patterns of relationships among groups and genres, guiding further research. Until enough research into a wider range of groups and genres has established those patterns, however, beginning with some "baggy" types of groups can serve to provide some focus without overly restricting our perspective. I propose beginning with three types of groups: communities, collectives, and networks.[4]

Communities, Collectives, and Networks

Groups of people who share substantial amounts of time together in common endeavors would seem most clearly to merit the label *community*. Such relatively homogeneous communities would include Swales's place discourse communities but also the Computer Resource Site, academic departments, professional organizations with active publications and meetings (perhaps including an electronic discussion list), work groups or businesses, and social organizations with frequent contact like sororities or fraternities. Although homogeneous compared with more diffuse social groups to be discussed below, these communities, like physical communities, still contain the heterogeneity of multiple cultures and of diverse people, experts and novices, powerful and peripheral members, sycophants and rebels. Even though these communities pervade people's lives, people still participate in multiple communities and move among them, sometimes easily and sometimes with conflict. While I agree with Swales that "[h]uman beings are not chameleons" (*Other Floors* 202) and that participation in some groups is more significant for constructing people's identity than participation in other groups, people do indeed participate in multiple groups and shift identity and motives from one group to the next. I am a member of an academic English department but also of a university and of the Conference on College Composition and Communication and of the American Dialect Society. (Notice that each of these communities is also easily named.) My presence in each of these communities helps to shape them and shapes me, and my participation in these multiple communities affects each of the communities and at times causes conflicts (though to different degrees, depending on how central a member I am). Each of these communities also has genres through which participants act to fulfill the goals of that community, as many genre scholars have described. My department uses such written genres as memoranda, ballots, minutes of meetings, bylaws, teaching manuals, course descriptions, syllabi, writing assignments, and grade sheets. The university shares the genres of grade sheets and memoranda but has its own genres of handbooks, policies, and a variety of forms. Both professional organizations work through the genres of conference abstracts, conference papers, journal articles, and subscription notices, but one also acts through committee reports, winter workshop announcements, and mailing lists, while the other acts through an electronic discussion list, a newsletter, and word lists. Though unlikely, it is possible that a community exists that uses no written genres in its actions, though spoken genres are surely necessary for any communication to occur within the community.

In the next chapter, I will examine more closely how genres operate within one community in an extended example of writing by tax accountants. Much research within genre study examines such communities, including Thomas Huckin's study of proposals for the Conference on College Composition and Communication, Graham Smart's study of writing at the Federal Bank of Canada, and Catherine Schryer's study of veterinary records, among many other studies of professional communities. Such groups fit my label of community because of their common endeavors, the closeness and frequency of their interaction, and the distinctness of their identification (the ability to name them), as well as the existence of shared genres. The genres of such communities would also seem to be functionally specific and well defined, yet they must be flexible enough to enable participants to act in complex ways in multiple and complex contexts.

The borders of communities are not rigid or static, for people not usually participating in a community enter and leave at specific times for specific purposes. A trial, for example, operates within the legal community, but it draws into that community people who do not usually participate in the legal community—defendants, witnesses, and jury members, for example. The fact that a community "owns" that activity (as early Swales in *Genre* and Berkenkotter and Huckin might put it), however, is evident in the comfort of some participants (lawyers, judges) with its purposes and methods, purposes and methods with which other participants (first-time defendants, witnesses, and jury members) are less familiar. Similarly, student representatives may join departmental or university committees, but the subtexts and procedures of committee meetings "belong" more to some committee members than others, committee members who regularly participate in the department community. Particular kinds of activities, with their attendant ways of acting through genres, can be seen as operating within, "belonging to," particular communities, though still communities with permeable borders.

Such distinct communities are not the only kind of group, however, for people organize themselves in diverse ways. Some groups form around a single repeated interest, without the frequency or intensity of contact of a community. These *collectives* would include interest or volunteer groups, hobby clubs, task forces that cross communities, and academic classes such as an English composition class.[5] Either for a short time (as in an academic class or task force) or at infrequent intervals (as in a club or interest group), these collectives act for a shared purpose that is often singular and focused. Political committees form to get their candidate elected, task forces are charged with suggesting solutions, volunteers gather to organize a book sale, or students and teachers join a class to fulfill a requirement, to offer certification, or to learn or teach something. Although they usually are, such collectives need not be physically together, something that might be required for the closeness of a community. For example, the on-line auction service eBay unites sellers and bidders electronically, who submit item descriptions and pictures, bids, and evaluations of completed sales. Users of eBay form what one journalist called "an instant community of like-minded souls united by common interests" (*Kansas* I4). Research that examines the writing in a particular course would fall into this category, but relatively little of genre research has investigated the genres of such collectives. Collectives have a clarity of focus and purpose that does not exist at the other levels I am proposing, for they lack the complexity of purpose and relationships of communities while maintaining still a definable goal. Their genres, similarly, develop for specific functions—flyers, reports, newsletters, advertisements, syllabi, examinations, and research papers.[6]

Some genres develop within groups that are loosely linked *networks*. The concept of social network, developed in sociology, has been extended by Lesley Milroy and James Milroy in linguistics to explain relationships among people and their speech that are not as tightly knit as that of a speech community and that may reflect more urbanized settings. Social networks are the connections made by one person knowing another person, who knows another person, who knows another person (like the linking made popular by the play *Six Degrees of Separation*). Social networks often form the basis of networking, making contact with someone who knows someone one knows. Social networks are common but often unrecognized in discourse study. A few genres that would seem to come from a social network include wedding invitations, weather forecasts, catalogues, and e-mail spam. One place social networks have become more visible is in electronic mail, in the address lines of an electronic message. People often receive jokes through e-mail, for example, with address and copy lines filled with long lists of e-mail addresses, the set of people who form the sender's social network for jokes. People in that network may never have met one another, but they are receiving common discourse. As the recipients of that joke forward the message to their own social networks of joke lovers, the original social network expands. Similar networks are made apparent through chain letters, but social networks exist for all people in less visible ways as people link one to another through all their contacts in a society. The interactions and influences of such social networks are less easily traced than those within tighter communities, but they exist nonetheless, as Lesley Milroy's work has more fully demonstrated.

Some e-mail genres, like e-mail jokes, I would argue, are developing through just such social networks. In e-mail messages, genres exist that many people created relatively recently through adapting existing genres to the new context of electronic mail. The form of e-mail messages looks most like a memorandum, as Orlikowski and Yates point out (554–55), yet the technology is used for communications external to as well as internal to the organization. Since people call the discourse "e-mail" or an "e-mail message," it seems so far to be perceived as a single genre. Over time, though, I would expect the different kinds of messages to gain labels reflecting different genres. Already, e-mails from friends are taking on different forms from e-mails from colleagues, both reflecting their different situations. The different kinds of relationships and the different nature of the groups, in particular, seem to be distinguishing one potential e-mail genre from another. Although sharing some common traits, e-mail messages now can reflect quite different situations: I receive messages from my departmental chair announcing a lecture, from my dean requesting budget figures, from an editor discussing a textbook proposal, from my friend in Duluth keeping in touch, from the dozens of cousins who copy each other with bits of news on their cousin network, and from my mother, who just got her first computer. Right now, my address book represents a loosely connected network of e-mail correspondents, all of us linked through e-mail. As the technology continues to be integrated within different social groups, only some kinds of messages, like jokes, will continue to reside within networks. Others, like discussion lists and professional correspondence, will clearly be positioned within collectives or communities.

Although only more research can uncover the nature of genres within social networks, it makes sense that a genre that might develop from a social network would be different from a genre that develops from a closer community. People have reasons to communicate with one another in a social network; that communication is what establishes a social network. But that communication may be unidirectional, is more infrequent or sporadic, and may be more variable in its purposes, participants, and contexts. With such infrequency and such variation in context of situation, actions might recur less often than in genres from collectives or communities. The resulting genres surely reflect those differences but not necessarily in predictable ways. Since a genre within a social network may occur only occasionally, it might develop less particular or firm expectations. On the other hand, such an infrequent genre need not adapt to as many different or complex situations as do genres within a community, so it might develop a simple and relatively fixed set of expectations. Wedding invitations are quite specifically defined, but jokes allow a range of approach. Weather forecasts fall somewhere in between. More research into genres that are attached loosely to social networks rather than intimately to communities is necessary to sort out such distinctions and to discover further factors influencing their nature and development.

Swales's insight that genres function within groups to fulfill their communicative goals remains critical to an understanding of the social nature of genres. The diverse nature of those groups and their participants, however, may affect their genres and so requires further investigation. The three types of groups I propose—communities, collectives, and social networks—may be redefined as more research examines how genres operate in different kinds of societies, but the differing ways people gather, however they are defined, will surely influence the genres people use to achieve their purposes. Thus I propose a first principle of the social nature of genres:

1. *Genres usually develop through the actions of many people, in groups. A genre operates within a group of language users, but the nature of that group and hence of its genres varies, from communities (people who share substantial amounts of time together in common endeavors) to collectives (people who gather around a single repeated interest, without the frequency or intensity of contact of a community) to social networks (people who are connected once—or more—removed, through having common contact with another person or organization).*

Genres Through Human Action

Remaining difficulties with examining genres in terms of the groups that create them are the issues of the fluidity of groups' borders and memberships and the nature of how genres are "used" within those communities. One way to resolve the problems is to stop defining genre's social nature in terms of the groups of people for whom they operate, to stop equating socialness with group inhabitants. Social structures rather than social groups can be described and examined. Such an approach has been taken by structuration theory and activity theory, and both have been applied to genre theory.

One approach that moves sharply away from discourse communities while maintaining a social communicative purpose is to define genre as a tool within an activity system. Activity theory, as explained by Russell and based in Engestrom's development of Vygotsky, avoids the reduction of defining the group in terms of its discourse, for it sees that "collectives" have "long-term objectives and motives beyond conversation," and "some shared object and long-term motive of the collective to do some things to, and some things with, some other things beyond discourse" ("Rethinking" 507). The object of study in activity theory is the activity system, "any ongoing, object-directed, historically conditioned, dialectically structured, tool-mediated human interaction" (510). Both individuals and groups operate within activity systems, using tools to accomplish their social actions. A genre, according to activity theory, is "the typified use of material tools of many types by an activity system" (513). Genres are routinized, common operations, what Russell shorthands as "operationalized social action" (516 and elsewhere).

Activity theory recognizes that people participate in multiple collectives, for people move in and out of activity systems. It also builds in the interactive nature of collectives, including that activity systems interact with one another. As an attempt, too, to bridge the macro and micro levels of analysis, activity theory discourages simple dialogism in favor of multiple voices and undercuts rigid dualities, as Russell argues well. For genre theory, however, it leaves two related difficulties: it analyzes genre more as a tool than as an action, and it diminishes the role of people in creating and using genres.

In spite of Russell's calling genres "action," activity theory appears to emphasize the nature of genres as tools. They are analyzed not at the level of activity system or action but only at the level of operation (table 1, 515), and they are most often associated with mediational means (tools) rather than with the two other components of an activity system, subjects or objects-motives. "[A]ctivity systems are made up of specific goal-directed, time-bound, conscious actions," according to Russell, "which are, in turn, operationalized by *variable mediational means* (choices of tools, including genres)" (514, emphasis in original). To include genres as "choices of tools" and to define genre as the routinized use of tools is to remove genre from the level of social action, especially from motives and outcomes, which are separate components of activity systems. It is not a far step from equating genre with the use of tools to equating genre with form; nor is it a far step from equating genre with "a routine operation, usually unconscious" (515) to equating genre with formula. To the extent that genre becomes a tool, it loses its rhetorical nature. Communicative purpose remains an integral part of collective action but not an integral part of genre.

One might argue that genre is a common way of using tools rather than the tools themselves, keeping it an action in at least some sense, but such treatment would raise an issue of level of analysis: genre is somehow not part of one component of an activity system—not a mediational means—yet it is also not the activity system itself. A related difficulty is the interaction between genres and people. Russell defines genre, again, as "the typified use of material tools of many types *by an activity system*" (513, emphasis added). Genre is used not by people but by an activity system. The use of tools, which when operationalized becomes a genre, "mediates the behavior of people in activity systems in specific and objective ways," according to Russell's interpretation of Leont'ev (511). People move in and out of activity systems with the systems apparently existing separately from them. Although the prior existence of genres (what I called the context of genres in chapter 1) does affect how people perform their social actions and achieve their communicative and social purposes, this version of activity theory would seem to make genre an agent acting on its own, through the actions of an equally inhuman activity system.

The identification of genre as either tool or agent is one of the most central assumptions underlying many theories of genre, seen among other ways in scholars' choice of subjects ("people use genres" [tool] *versus* "genres perform these acts" [agent]). For genre to be a tool alone is to reduce its force, as I just described, to limit the nature of genre to formal formulae, a preexisting, static, material object that people can pick up and use or just as easily set aside. For genre to act as agent independent of human operators is to magnify its force too much, to enlarge the nature of genre to material action that makes people do things or that does things without working through people. It is instead the nature of genre both to be created by people and to influence people's actions, to help people achieve their goals and to encourage people to act in certain ways, to be both-and. Genres never operate independently of the actions of people, but the actions of some people influence the actions of other people through genres.

Such a reciprocal interaction of human action and genre is similar to the interaction of contexts and genres that I explored in chapter 1. People construct genres, but then genres construct people, especially the identity or roles of people, as Russell among others recognizes. Once genres are established by people, they exist institutionally and collectively and have the force of other social expectations and social structures. Since people do not exist in a world without preexisting genres, people are always already operating within a context of genres, a context of genres that originates in the actions of people.

The concept of duality of structure, taken from Anthony Giddens's social theory, captures further the reciprocal, constitutive relationship of people and their social structures, including genres.[7] As explained by Yates and Orlikowski in their study of how organizational genres changed in response to technological changes,

> social institutions . . . are enacted through individuals' use of social rules. These rules shape the action taken by individuals in organizations; at the same time, by regularly drawing on the rules, individuals reaffirm or modify the social institutions in an ongoing recursive interaction. ("Genres" 299–300)

Thus, people who "follow the rules" are operated on by those rules, and their actions in following the rules reproduce (reinforce and recreate) those rules. On the basis of Yates and Orlikowski's research, Berken-kotter and Huckin "paraphrase Giddens . . . paraphrasing Marx" in concluding, "it is the social actors that are the agents of change . . . , but not through conditions of their own making" (21).[8]

With the help of the concept of duality of structure, perhaps genre, in its role as a social structure, can be seen as both tool and agent, both constructed and constructing, always constructed by people but not always by the same people who are acting with it at that moment. Duality of structure helps to explain also all of the interaction of people and their contexts—context of culture and situation as well as context of genres. Cultures and situations, like genres, are constructed by humans responding to material conditions and perceiving similarities. As people interact with cultures, situations, and genres, they are shaped by those contexts and reaffirm those contexts. Even as people use a particular genre to mediate between context and text, they both operate within and recreate that genre. Genre's mediation between the macro and micro levels defies that dualism, for it reproduces the macro in the micro and alters the macro through its creation in the micro. Or, that is, *people, through genres, mediate, defy, reproduce, alter, and create.*

Genre is inherently social because people are inherently social and people act through genres. Thus I propose a second principle of the social nature of genres:

2. Genres do not exist independent of people, though the generic actions of some people influence the actions of other people. To say that genre is a social action is to say that people take action through their conceptions of genres; genre is a human construct, not a material tool nor an agent.

Genres and Social Function

Having cautioned that genres must always remain connected to people and not be disembodied, I return to Swales's basic insight, that genres function within groups to fulfill their communicative goals, for understanding the functions of genres for groups remains critical to an understanding of the social nature of genres. The group and functional connections of some genres are quite obvious, especially in the spheres of business, law, science, and other spheres that we tend to view as highly pragmatic. Certain tasks must be accomplished in a trial, for example; to fulfill those tasks, different genres have developed. Briefs are written to make arguments to the judge before the trial begins, saving time and laying the groundwork for the trial's arguments. Judges' decisions are handed down to settle legal issues and establish justification. Questioning of the witnesses and cross-examination serve to establish and counter the "facts" of the case. Summation speeches on both sides argue each side's position, reviewing the conflict. Jury instructions define the relevant law and direct juries' actions. The jury's verdict concludes the debate, designating the "winner" and "loser." The judge's sentencing determines the action to be taken (prior to appeals). These genres do the work of the trial. The lawyers, judges, and juries have certain tasks to accomplish. The genres help that group of people accomplish those tasks.

The difference between this claim—that genres function for a group—and that of the preceding chapter—that genres reflect and construct recurring rhetorical situations and contexts—is one of perspective, not of definition. Obviously, in the trial example, each genre is reflecting a rhetorical situation, answering the situation's question, in Burke's terms, meeting a rhetorical exigence, in Bitzer's terms, and adapting to a field, mode, and tenor, in Halliday's terms. Each genre in the trial is operating within the contexts of culture and genres as well as situation. Shifting from a more local situational perspective to a cultural perspective, however, reveals not only how that genre fulfills a purpose for the participants but also how that genre interacts with other genres, other purposes, and other situations to fulfill the more general needs of groups. In this case, the group needs to conduct a trial, which itself is needed to determine guilt, which derives from the legal system's raison d'être. The social workers' case report is another clear example, as are most kinds of business memoranda and letters and the genres of tax accountants, to be discussed at length in the next chapter. Most academic genres function to test one skill or another that the disciplinary or university community has been charged with certifying: the research paper for research skills and incorporation of a field's epistemology, the lab report for scientific method, the freshman theme for literacy and basic coherence of thinking, the essay examination for comprehension of essential concepts, and so on. As these academic examples suggest, functions are not simple nor usually singular, especially not in the genres through which communities, rather than collectives or networks, achieve their goals, and functions are often ideological as well as practical. A genre might be describable in terms of one primary function, but most will have others as well. Generic functions must not be confused with discourse modes or aims, which attempt to reduce the complexity of all discourse to single characteristics. Instead, generic functions must remain complex and multiple and socially embedded. Explaining genres' functions discourages equating genre with category and encourages embedding genre within both rhetorical purpose and social contexts. As complex and multiple as groups are, so are the goals they have and the genres through which they achieve those goals. As ideological as groups are, so are the functions of their genres, as will be discussed more in principle 6 below. Genres help people to fulfill the group's complex needs and fulfill its complex purposes. Those social and group functions affect the constitution and construction of the genre.

The functional nature of genres can be overstated if genres are reduced to "taking care of business" in an uncomplicated, mechanistic manner, as I believe Martin et al. come dangerously near to when they state, "Genres represent the most efficient ways cultures have at a given point in time of going about their business. It is in this sense that genres are functional" (62). As rhetorical acts, genres cannot be transparent and purely efficient uses of language or they would not be able to adapt to the particularities of each communicative event.[9] Elsewhere, Martin takes a more moderate stance that more appropriately describes the functional nature of genres: "Genres are how things get done, when language is used to accomplish them" (1985, qtd. in Swales, *Genre* 26).

Do all groups have their own genres, as Swales in *Genre Analysis* claims in his fourth characteristic of discourse communities? The problem with this question is its potential circularity. If a group does not have its own genre, according to Swales, then it is not yet a discourse community. Borrowing genres from other communities is not sufficient, yet according to the argument about classification offered in chapter 1, whether the analyst says two communities have the same or different genres will depend largely on the analyst's purposes. Are all business memoranda a single genre? Are all research papers? If so, multiple communities use them. Of course, an analyst can find differences between the research paper in psychology and that in history, so they can be claimed as different genres. But quibbling over such classifications, as I argued in chapter 1, is beside the essential point of genre. Requiring all groups to have their own genres unnecessarily raises such classificatory questions. As Russell says, groups have multiple goals, some of which are not communicative. Yet it is difficult to imagine how groups will achieve their goals without communication of some sort, since it is in the very nature of groups that individuals must cooperate and cooperation requires communication. Although it seems a philosophical possibility that groups could achieve goals without genres, it seems an unlikely reality, though a genre may not be unique to a particular group.

Do all genres function always within groups? Although all genres certainly develop through group action (one person doth not a genre make), that claim must at least be complicated to apply beyond the more obviously pragmatic genres. What is the group that provides the rationale for poetry? novels? letters to friends? grocery lists? Having expanded the conception of groups to include collectives and networks as well as communities makes possible a group function for some genres that might otherwise not seem attached to a group. I discuss the group functions of literary genres more in chapter 6. Such genres as letters and grocery lists may develop, like e-mail messages, from the social networks within a culture, while more specific types of letters and lists might develop within communities of families and intimates. Do all genres serve some function for a group of people? That claim may be upheld. Novel readers pick up a novel for a purpose, a purpose that the genre of novel fulfills (again, I discuss literary genres more in chapter 6). Letters to friends serve important purposes of bonding and cementing relationships for the friends. Grocery lists enable the shopper and the keeper of the inventory to perform their tasks most efficiently, even when the two roles are filled by the same person. Even poetry may be seen, from a social view, to have a function for those who write and read it (and today, writers and readers of poetry may even be becoming a tightly knit and exclusive community). Without a doubt, the functions for a group are more significant for some genres than others, but the complex social functioning of genres within groups is central for understanding many genres and may be enlightening even for those genres where social function is less transparent. Thus I propose a third principle of the social nature of genres:

3. *Genres function for groups, though those functions are typically multiple and ideological as well as situational.*

Interpreting Social Function Through Discourse

Since genre is a concept that mediates between texts and contexts, discourse will typically show marks of its genres and of the contexts with which the genre interacts. Since genres function socially for groups, discourse will typically show traces of those social functions. In simple terms, discourse typically has traits that make sense because of the genre's functions for its group. Such an obvious statement is worth making because it, too, needs to be elaborated. Much of hermeneutics and rhetorical criticism is based on interpreting the meaning of discourse features. Generic traits can be interpreted situationally, as discussed in chapter 1, and they can be interpreted culturally. Lab reports are structured as they are, for example, not only to serve the immediate situation most appropriately (clearly labeled sections, fixed order, and so on) but also to embody the scientific method representative of the group's ideology. Interpreting discourse features thus requires not only situational but also cultural astuteness. Because ideologies, values, assumptions, and epistemologies are rarely explicit, however, those participating in the group with the genres being examined are the most reliable interpreters of the discourse's cultural as well as situational meaning. It is difficult for those who have not acted through the genres to recognize the full meaning and significance of textual features. Just as users of the genres are the most reliable definers of a genre, they are also the most reliable interpreters of that genre. On the other hand, people are shaped by their contexts and genres, and no one can be fully aware of the complexities of a group or its genres or fully conscious of their ideological effects. To some extent, interpretations are always informed guesses colored by ideological frames, and, if our understanding is to advance, there must always be analysts-critics as well as users-participants. Genres and their social meanings can be interpreted through discourse, though cautiously. Thus my fourth principle:

4. A genre commonly reveals its social functions with characteristic discourse features, but interpreting those features may require active participation with the genre and can never be complete.

Genre Sets

Rarely does a group accomplish all of its purposes with a single genre. More often, as I argued in my study of tax accountants' writing, a set of genres functions for the group, and the interactions among those genres affect the functioning of each genre ("Intertextuality").

Todorov describes the largest set of genres when he writes, "the choice a society makes among all the possible codifications of discourse determines what is called its *system of genres*" (10, emphasis in original). Todorov's system of genres describes what I have called in chapter 1 the *context of genres,* the set of all existing genres in a society or culture. Speaking of it as a system, however, as Todorov does, implies a tighter, more static structure than I believe the context of genres involves. The context of genres must remain flexible and dynamic, for the society from which genres develop is always changing, as Bakhtin notes:

> The wealth and diversity of speech genres are boundless because the various possibilities of human activity are inexhaustible, and because each sphere of activity contains an entire repertoire of speech genres that differentiate and grow as the particular sphere develops and becomes more complex. ("Problem" 60)

What Bakhtin describes as the "repertoire" of genres (a term Orlikowski and Yates also adopt) is more particular than the context of genres. It is the set of genres that exists within a particular "sphere of activity" or group. As Bakhtin notes, the genre set develops as the group develops, still serving the group's needs. Thus, the genre set of the legal community may long have included the genres involved in a trial but may more recently have developed genres involved in arbitration. As the needs of the group change, the genre set changes to reflect those needs, thereby also changing the larger context of genres.

Acknowledging the significance of genre sets emphasizes the significance of intertextuality to genre. Intertextuality plays an important role in individual genres as well as genre sets, of course, for the development of a genre always requires at least two actions for recurrence and typification to be perceived. Kristeva's intertextuality and Bakhtin's dialogic theories would argue that all discourse contains such exchange among texts. In genre theory, Anne Freadman offers a comparable dialogic analysis of genre in her unusual and insightful article "Anyone for Tennis?" In this article, Freadman argues that genre is best described as a game and one that requires at least two texts related dialogically (97–98), an interaction that she later describes in terms of "uptakes" ("Uptake"). No genre exists without at least two texts, for no class can contain only one member. The notion of genre set extends this intertextuality across genres. Extended to genre sets, the concepts of intertextuality and dialogue allow us to see the inherent relatedness of genres within the same social group and its actions. Within the legal community, the genre set that operates within a trial again offers a clear example. Achieving a trial's purposes requires a charge, which requires a plea; opening statements and summations, which respond to each other; witness questioning, which results in cross-examinations; and, with increasing frequency, a verdict requiring sentencing, which is responded to in an appeal. Of course, trials are set up as debates, so their intertextual nature is pronounced, but they represent the less obvious intertextuality of all genres. A memo announcing a meeting is related to minutes of that meeting; both may be related to proposals, regulations, or other documents that result from the purpose of that meeting. A single letter, business or personal, often results in a series of letters. A marriage proposal is tied to wedding invitations, cards of congratulations, guest books, marriage vows, thank you notes. Understanding the marriage proposal requires understanding all the other genres that it entails.

In examining genre sets, there is some benefit to connecting genre sets to activity systems as well as to groups, whether communities, collectives, or networks. The trial is clearly an activity system, and its genres interact essentially and functionally. The participants in a trial, as I noted earlier, include defendants, witnesses, and jury members as well as the usual participants in the legal community, lawyers and judges. Using activity system as the unit of analysis, therefore, enables a clearer depiction of diverse participants and roles, of an overarching purpose for multiple genres, and of multiple genres as the means of achieving that purpose in a trial. Genre sets operating within activity systems that are similarly distinct might likewise benefit from an activity system analysis. There also exist, however, different kinds of genre sets that do not fit so neatly into an activity system as defined apart from its group. Lawyers act within many genres that are not contained in the activity system of a trial: all their work that does not result in litigation. The genre set of this and other professional communities operates to achieve the multiple functions of such a group without a distinct overarching activity. Some genre sets are used in multiple systems and communities as well. Yates and Orlikowski ("Genre") describe what they call the meeting, collaborative authoring, and collaborative repository genre systems that develop from a commonly used networking program. These genre sets transform as well as reinforce the interactions of the team they studied, an effect presumably present in other activity systems and other communities that use the same program. Genre sets help the community to cohere and define itself, among other functions, and are more clearly viewed, I would argue, from the perspective of the community's operations than from the notion of activity system, which I argued earlier is too easily removed from human enactment.

The difference, I propose, can be captured by complicating our conception of genre set to encompass different kinds of genre sets, more kinds than even the two just described. Some genres work together to perform different roles in achieving a common purpose, like the genres directly involved in a trial. This set of genres interacting to achieve an overarching function within an activity system I would call a *genre system* (a term Bazerman in "Systems" has adopted for all of what I have termed genre sets). Larger ideological purposes that analysts might identify, such as helping a group cohere, will come into play for other kinds of genre sets; the term *genre system* I would reserve for a genre set identifiable by those who use it that has clearly linked genres with a common purpose. Calling such genre sets "systems" implies more potential rigidity than they actually have, but the term does capture the regularity and often rule-governed nature of the interaction of genres within a distinct activity. Other genre sets that might be considered genre systems would include those genres involved in assigning grants or bids (requests for proposals or bids, proposals or bids, granting documents, reports, requests for grant extensions, etc.); those genres involved in a job search (job advertisements, resumes or curricula vitae, application or cover letters, invitations to interview, thank you notes, rejections, job offers); those genres involved in writing class assignments (writing prompt, student drafts, teacher commentary, possibly extending to revised papers, and grades); or those genres surrounding a wedding (proposal, acceptance or rejection, invitations, RSVP's, bridal registries, gift cards, thank you notes, vows, marriage certificates, toasts, etc.). Each genre system can be described in terms of a particular activity it accomplishes. As the close linking and necessary ordering of these last examples show, a genre system might also be called a genre sequence, though genre system might better capture the complexity of interaction in more complex activities like trials. As the last two examples also suggest, a genre system is still flexible, for not all genres in the system must be used for the purpose to be achieved and there are alternate genres for achieving the same ends.

More often discussed as genre sets since my depiction of the sets of tax accountants are what I would now call *genre repertoires,* following the term of Bakhtin and the general use of Yates and Orlikowski. A genre repertoire is the set of genres that a group owns, acting through which a group achieves all of its purposes, not just those connected to a particular activity. The genre systems of a particular activity could be part of a larger genre repertoire, as the trial genre system would be part of the legal genre repertoire. *Repertoire* is an especially helpful term for this set, for it connotes not only a set of interacting genres but also a set from which participants choose, a definer of the possibilities available to the group. The genre set that I described for tax accountants I would now call a genre repertoire. Most professional communities, if not all (a matter for research), have genre repertoires, though they might or might not contain genre systems. The genres within a repertoire do interact, though often in less obvious ways, with less clear-cut sequencing and more indirect connections than exist in a genre system.

I would expect research also to show that genre sets differ in different kinds of groups. The genre repertoires of communities define the work of a relatively coherent group, people with complex goals and often well-developed or long-standing ways of achieving those goals. People in collectives also have genre sets that help to define their work, though they may less often have the complexity of a genre repertoire. For example, task forces have a genre set including the charge, minutes, and reports, but they rarely have a range of functions to fulfill or a repertoire of genres to choose among. Volunteers organizing a book sale have established ways of advertising, organizing, and enacting the donations and selling of books, though their genres might less often be written. For these more loosely defined sets of genres, associated through the activities and functions of a collective but defining only a limited range of actions, I would retain the term *genre set.* Some collectives certainly might have a genre repertoire, if a single-interest group has a long history and has developed more complex functions. Some collectives certainly do have genre systems, especially those with a single, well-delineated activity as their reason for being. The participants in the eBay online auction that I mentioned earlier, for example, have a distinct system of item descriptions, bids, notifications of sales, and evaluation of transactions that have a specified sequence and work together to achieve a common task, the sale of items, yet they form a group, a collective, only for that task. Genre systems may more likely operate with collectives, since collectives more often have single, well-defined tasks. Networks, on the other hand, may more often have no genre sets at all but rather only single genres that reflect their connectedness. The network of people who receive e-mail jokes, after all, may connect those people as a group only through that one address heading. Again, research is needed to explore how the types of genre sets operate in different types of groups. My first hypothesis would be that communities more often operate through genre repertoires, collectives more often through genre systems or genre sets, and networks more often through single genres interacting with other genres only in the largest context of genres.

Genres may interact with one another in more particular relationships as well. Yates and Orlikowski note that some genres overlap in function and situation, so the term *overlapping genres* might also prove useful for the analysis of how genres interact. Some genres would seem to fit a *call and response* pattern, as a request for information results in a letter giving information. Some genres would seem to serve as *supergenres* for other genres, providing the basis of and reference point for other genres, as tax regulations operate for other tax genres, scriptures for religious genres, laws for legal genres. Janet Giltrow has explored genres that describe or proscribe other genres, what she terms *metagenres,* such as guidelines or proscriptions. Research will continue to reveal other ways that genres interact with one another as scholars increasingly examine relations among genres.

If a group of people does share more than one genre, that set of genres as a unit will serve that group's needs and will have a functional significance beyond the significance of each part.

5. A group usually operates through a set of genres to achieve the group's purposes, but the nature of that genre set varies among different types of groups. Genres interact with one another in the context of genres and in genre repertoires, genre sets, genre systems, overlapping genres, call and response genres, supergenres, and other possible relationships that further research will uncover.

Ideologies Through Genres

Because people in groups develop genres, genres reflect what the group believes and how it views the world. As Todorov writes, "Like any other institution, genres bring to light the constitutive features of the society to which they belong" (19). A genre and a genre set, like any other artifacts of a society, reveal those who use them. Somewhat statically, Volosinov again describes the enmeshing of genre with its social context:

> Each situation, fixed and sustained by social custom, commands a particular kind of organization of audience and, hence, a particular repertoire of little behavioral genres. The behavioral genre fits everywhere into the channel of social intercourse assigned to it and functions as an ideological reflection of its type, structure, goal, and social composition. The behavioral genre is a fact of the social milieu: of holiday, leisure time, and of social contact in the parlor, the workshop, etc. It meshes with that milieu and is delimited and defined by it in all its internal aspects. (97)

Pierre Bourdieu expresses this social situatedness of genre more broadly, as Thompson explains in his introduction, seeing every linguistic exchange as

> situated encounters between agents endowed with socially structured resources and competencies, in such a way that every linguistic interaction, however personal and insignificant it may seem, bears the traces of the social structure that it both expresses and helps to reproduce. (2)

The kinds of social facts that genre reflects are many, but some stand out as common to and significant for most genres and their groups. Freadman describes those social facts in terms of the rules of the game, who can do and say certain things, when, and where ("Anyone" 113). Bizzell describes them, for the academic community, as "characteristic ways of interacting with the world" (229). Bourdieu concentrates on their reflection of power. Berkenkotter and Huckin list "norms, epistemology, ideology, and social ontology" (21). Frequently noted by many are a group's ideology, epistemology, assumptions, beliefs, and values. Encompassing several of these descriptions, I would describe genre as reflecting especially and commonly a group's values, epistemology, and power relationships—its ideology.

Although the extended example of tax accountants' genres will clarify this principle more fully, a few relatively obvious examples may help. Dorothy A. Winsor found that the genre of the work order helped to maintain existing hierarchical social structures. The trial genre system, to continue an example, reflects the power relationships among judges and lawyers in many ways: objections are addressed to the judge, the judge is the only one permitted to "rule." Defendants seem especially powerless in the trial genre system, for they are not even permitted to speak except in response to the lawyers' questions. In fact, their ability to choose silence may be at times their only real power. The legal community's epistemology, its ways of knowing truth, are everywhere evident in the trial genre system: witnesses must be "expert" or "material" to testify, their stories must withstand cross-examination, each utterance of witness, lawyer, or judge must be supported by the legally defined "facts," and the final truth comes from common consensus in the form of the jury verdict, which the judge could still overturn on the basis of the law. The values of the legal community, as a remaining catchall, appear in many conventions: such values as explicit courtesy ("if it please the court") and the right of the defendant to have the last word (the sequencing of the two summations). These values, epistemology, and power relationships are reflected in many other aspects of the trial (clothing and seating assignments, for example), but each genre and the genre system also reflect them in ways that may be less easily recognized.

The generic acts of objecting, ruling, testifying, and cross-examining, however, also act to reinforce the ideology in which they were created. Addressing objections to the judge gives the judge the power to rule. Describing witness expertise in testimony tells the jury that expertise matters. Cross-examining keeps the truth from ever having only one side. Genres not only reflect but also reinforce the ideology of the group whose purposes they serve. In some significant ways, the group's beliefs constitute the genre and the genre constitutes the group's beliefs. This shift from simple reflection to reflection and construction is represented in Berkenkotter and Huckin's shift (conscious or not) from describing how genres "signal" a group's values to stating that genres "instantiate" those values (21–23). Once genres are established that, as we have just seen, reflect the group's values, epistemology, and power relationships, the existence and continued use of those genres reaffirm those very values, epistemology, and power relationships. If genre is "a zone and a field of valorized perception, . . . a mode for representing the world," as Bakhtin writes ("Epic" 28), then using that genre reinforces that perception, that representation of the world.

This reciprocal relationship between the group's ideologies and its genres is characterized well by Giddens's concept of duality of structure, a concept I described earlier in this chapter and that Yates and Orlikowski and Berkenkotter and Huckin discuss more fully. Berkenkotter and Huckin summarize the idea: "As we draw on genre rules to engage in professional activities, we *constitute* social structures (in professional, institutional, and organizational contexts) and simultaneously *reproduce* these structures" (4). Using the verb *reproduce* to describe this reciprocal relationship also calls up the specter of the Sapir-Whorf hypothesis of linguistic relativity, for our view of the influence of language upon thought or perception will determine how rigidly defining we consider this cycle to be. My view here is *not* that the genre determines how its users view the world; rather, I would argue only that the use of a genre privileges one way of viewing the world, the view of the group from which it stems. Early work by Bakhtin suggests a similar perspective, where genres represent multiple perspectives:

> [A]ll languages of heteroglossia [including language of genres], whatever the principle underlying them and making each unique, are specific points of view on the world, forms for conceptualizing the world in words, specific world views, each characterized by its own objects, meanings and values. ("Discourse" 291–92)

Later work by Volosinov, however, is more deterministic, with world view being inescapable (e.g., 85). Ongstad, too, argues for the constructivist turn back from the genre to the group, though he edges toward the deterministic in spots:

> The socialization *to* genres implies socialization *through* genres. This means that the genres carry a world picture (Whorf), an *ideology* (Bakhtin/Volosinov), a doxa (Barthes) or a tacit culture which is forced upon the user through the communication. . . . The genres *are* or *constitute* the experienced kind of community which are often associated with the term "society." . . . The genres which constitute the groups, the language or the sign systems as a whole in a given society *are* that society. . . . We think that genre community in a modern society might be more significant as social dimension

than general terms like class, social-economic groups, strata.
(23–24)

Leslie Olsen, reviewing the research on discourse communities, states a
more moderate and reciprocal view that not only do the context and
values of the community affect the content and form of the document
but "a few of the studies also suggest that there is sometimes an effect
of the content and form of a document on its context, including helping to define the sense of community and to project its set of values and
attitudes" (188–89).

Many scholars have examined particular genres for their ideologies
and have demonstrated that the genre encourages a particular ideology
(Yates and Orlikowski; Bazerman, *Shaping;* Schryer, "Records"; among
dozens of others). As Winsor concludes, "As a textual tool used to accomplish work, genre is a profoundly political force" ("Ordering" 181).
Prince goes even further in examining what happens when people learn
to use genres different from those they already know, and he argues that
learning those genres requires that they learn new epistemologies and
values as well. He cites Whately as having seen that

> an institutionally sanctioned genre—here the school declama-
> tion—imposes a specific interpretation of what counts as
> knowledge. The habitual composition of such a form changes
> thought and character, creates a youth who is self-alienated,
> frigid, empty, artificial, "dressed up in the garb, and absurdly
> aping the demeanor of an elderly man!" (732)

Similarly, he points to his three-year-old child's experiences and those
studied by Scollon and Scollon of the Athabaskans, indigenous peoples
of Alaska:

> For the Athabaskans, learning to write essays was not sim-
> ply a matter of acquiring a few new verbal skills (e.g. profi-
> ciency in forming a thesis, organizing paragraphs, and so on).
> Rather, the new genre implied cultural and personal values
> that conflicted with pre-existing patterns of thought and
> behavior. . . . In each case the discourse to which they have
> been habituated to a great extent determines the nature and
> direction of intellectual development. (741)

Although I do not want to argue that using a genre "determines the
nature and direction of intellectual development" (and I will, in chap-

ter 5, deal directly with the issue of individual choice and variation within a genre's ideology), it does seem evident that the relation of group and genre is reciprocal, that the group's values, epistemology, and power relationships shape the genres and that acting through those genres in turn then maintains those same values, epistemology, and power relationships, though it is such actions that also must construct that ideology.

How this principle interacts with the differences of types of groups and genre sets that I have proposed is an interesting area for speculation. It would not surprise me if further research discovered that genre repertoires reproduce communities' ideologies more forcefully than do the genre sets of collectives. The very closeness of a community, including the frequency of its participants' interactions, would suggest that it has more deeply entrenched ideologies that its genres promote. A community repertoire also contains more genres to reinforce its ideology. On the other hand, the complexity of a community requires more flexibility in its genres, to enable them to adapt to local situations; the narrower expectations of a collective's genre system might retain tighter control over variations from the group's procedures and hence its ideology. Research is needed here as well to complicate our understanding of how genres, groups, and ideologies interact.

6. *A genre reflects, constructs, and reinforces the values, epistemology, and power relationships of the group from which it developed and for which it functions, though the forcefulness of that reinforcement might vary in different kinds of groups and in different kinds of genre sets.*

Summary of Six Principles of the Social Nature of Genre

Altogether, the six principles I have sketched here characterize the social nature of genres, how they interact with one another, how they develop and operate within group settings, and how their use in turn affects their groups and social structures.

1. *Genres usually develop through the actions of many people, in groups. A genre operates within a group of language users, but the nature of that group and hence of its genres varies, from communities (people who share substantial amounts of time together in common endeavors) to collectives (people who gather around a single repeated interest, without the frequency or intensity of contact of a community) to social networks (people who are connected once—or more—removed, through having common contact with another person or organization).*

2. Genres do not exist independent of people, though the generic actions of some people influence the actions of other people. To say that genre is a social action is to say that people take action through their conceptions of genres; genre is a human construct, not a material tool nor an agent.

3. Genres function for groups, though those functions are typically multiple and ideological as well as situational.

4. A genre commonly reveals its social functions with characteristic discourse features, but interpreting those features may require active participation with the genre and can never be complete.

5. A group usually operates through a set of genres to achieve the group's purposes, but the nature of that genre set varies in different types of groups. Genres interact with one another in the context of genres and in genre repertoires, genre sets, genre systems, overlapping genres, call and response genres, supergenres, and other possible relationships that further research will uncover.

6. A genre reflects, constructs, and reinforces the values, epistemology, and power relationships of the group from which it developed and for which it functions, though the forcefulness of that reinforcement might vary in different kinds of groups and in different kinds of genre sets.

These six principles do not capture all there is to say about the social nature of genres, nor will they all remain unaltered by other scholars and future research. What they do attempt to capture is some of the complexity of society as it is reflected in the complexity of genre.

Such general proposals suggest avenues of further research, including that into the particularities of language users acting through genres. Do genres differ in significant ways in different kinds of groups, whether those groups are defined as communities, collectives, and networks, or defined as some other configuration? What kinds of relationships do genres privilege over others? How do the different kinds of people in groups differently influence the formation and modification of genres? How do people gain the conceptions of genres cognitively? How do groups deal with conflicting functions of genres? Which kinds of discourse features are most consistently revealing of generic ideologies? What other kinds of intergeneric relationships exist? How do those relationships affect genres' operations within groups? Do some groups and genre types reproduce ideology more fully than do others? What various forms do the interaction of group, genre, genre set, and ideology take?

Because I have tried in this chapter to outline general principles and describe the most essential aspects of how genres operate in society, the chapter necessarily omits the rich, local situatedness of actual writing, the particularities that such generalizations overlook. Examining the particular writer writing particular texts exposes different realities, as evidenced, for example, in a work such as Swales's recent study described in *Other Floors, Other Voices: A Textography of a Small University Building* and, I hope, evidenced in the next chapter. Proposing, examining, and illustrating general principles exposes other realities, in this case how people with common experiences share common perceptions and actions. Whether viewed at the theoretical level or examined in a particular situation, genres are part of our cultural heritage and our social context; hence we can use them both to enable and to constrain. Understanding genres can enlighten our understanding of discourse, communities, and cultures—and of ourselves.

3
A Study of Genres in Context, a Theoretical Intermezzo

> We struggle more with getting the facts than we do deciding what to do with the facts once we have them.
> —tax accountant, in an interview

The real complexity of genres, as of societies, can best be suggested in examining actual genres in actual settings. To demonstrate some of that complexity, to interrogate the six principles I proposed in the preceding chapter, and to illustrate the definition of genre I propose in the first chapter, I will examine in this chapter the genres used in a professional community, the genres used by tax accountants. In 1986, I investigated the writing done by tax accountants in the so-called Big Eight accounting firms (later merged to a Big Six and later Big Three). Among other results, I discovered a profession highly dependent on texts, one whose work was the production of texts and whose epistemology was grounded in the authority of texts.[1] One part of the original study focused on the genres through which tax accountants performed their work, for how texts shaped the work of tax accountants varied according to genre. To describe the interaction of genres within the community and how they together represented the accountants' work, epistemology, and values, I used the term *genre set*. The original depiction of the tax accounting community and its genre set, in my original article, helped to establish how genres help professionals do their work, but that depiction now needs to be elaborated in order to capture the complexity of a community enmeshed in genres. Examining the community of tax accountants provides a useful example of the rhetorical and social significance of genres. My study of the genres used by tax accountants further complicates the basic principles, as, I suspect, does every study of specific practice. Finally, to complicate the theoretical principles one step further, I will briefly indicate the ways in which these generalizations, even when situated in a particular case, disguise individual variation and situatedness.

Methods and Sources

The 1986 study solicited sample texts, analyzed those texts, and conducted interviews with members of tax accounting firms. To solicit sample texts, I contacted the managing partner of a regional office of each of the (then) Big Eight accounting firms and asked him to send me at least three samples of every kind of writing done in his tax accounting department. Six of the eight firms responded by sending me samples of between five and seven different types of texts. Of most relevance to the purposes of this book, I examined these sample texts to determine the comparability of the genres named by the six firms, to identify their rhetorical situations, and to discover some of their linguistic features.

These textual analyses contributed to the formation of interview questions. Interviews of at least one hour each were conducted with eight different accountants from the six firms. These accountants ranged in experience from two to eighteen years and ranged in rank from "Senior" accountants (one step up from "Staff" or entry-level accountants) to "Managers" and "Partners." Each interview included discourse-based questions (Odell, Goswami, and Herrington), some based on the generic linguistic features discerned, and open-ended questions, including questions about the types of texts written, who writes and reviews them, and how they are used.

From this research, the discoveries focused on here involve the constitution and definition of genres within the tax accounting community, how each genre reflects some work the community must accomplish, the cooperation and intertextuality of genres within genre sets, and the reflection and perpetuation of the community's epistemology and ideology in those genres.

Defining Genres, Defining Communities

The social significance of the genres becomes apparent early on with the naming of the community's genres. There are many ways of grouping texts, depending on the analyst's purposes (as argued in chapter 1), but when considering genres within their contexts, the generic classification that matters most must be the classification recognized by the users of those genres (as Bazerman argues in *Shaping Written Knowledge*). How do the members of the community group their texts? Which groupings do they recognize without instruction? If our task is ethnomethodological, to describe actual practice, then the genre users should be the ones to identify the genres.

In this study, the tax accountants were the ones to identify their genres, and all six accounting departments shared a common classification of texts, common genres. In response to my prompt to send me samples of the kinds of writing they did in their department, representatives of the six departments were remarkably similar in their selection of genres. That is not to say that all six sent exactly the same set of genres. As is so often the case when asking others to identify writing, firms differed in what texts they considered important enough to count as a kind of writing in which I would be interested. Only two of the six, for example, sent samples of engagement letters, although when asked directly, the other four all acknowledged that they commonly produce what they would call engagement letters but had not considered them important enough to send. Adding in those that informants readily acknowledged but did not volunteer, I identified five genres that were given similar names by all six accounting departments: nontechnical correspondence, administrative memoranda, transmittal letters, engagement letters, and proposals. Another four genres were also recognized in all six departments and volunteered by many but were sometimes grouped together into larger genres: some participants identified two genres, memoranda for the files and research memoranda, where others identified only a single genre of memoranda for the files that encompassed both; and some separated tax protests from other letters to taxing authorities. In all six departments, though, informants recognized and acknowledged the differences among those four separate genres—memoranda for the files, research memoranda, tax protests, and other letters to taxing authorities. These nine genres, then, represent distinctive classifications of texts for all the tax accountants.

Another important type of text for tax accountants raises some complications but may be most suggestive of how communities reveal themselves through their generic classifications. All six accounting departments sent samples of letters to clients. Letters to clients were the only genre, in fact, sent initially by all six firms (again, some recognized and sent samples of other genres when prompted to do so). Yet different participants grouped these letters differently, and follow-up interviews did not reconcile these differences. To some, there are three distinct types of letters to clients: promotional, opinion, and response letters. To others, one of those three types might be recognized but the others not distinguished. To still others, letters to clients is a single genre. All six firms, though, recognize the larger genre of letters to clients. I could clearly separate, however, the three types of letters by distinct linguistic features as well as rhetorical situations. The analyst saw three distinct genres where the participants sometimes saw only one. Are they, therefore, three genres?

There are, at times, inconvenient conflicts between the analyst's perception and that of users of the genre. Ellen Barton discovered, when she analyzed personal essays for medical residencies, that what she saw as critical parts rhetorically were not similarly revered by selection committees. In the case of letters to clients of accounting firms, I need not select either my analysis into three genres nor some accountant's naming of one genre. Both can be accurate, as I argued in chapter 1, since classifications differ for different purposes. Using the community's recognition as the test, letters to clients would seem to be one genre while the three different types might be treated as subgenres. After all, many in the community did not recognize the three types, even with prompting, though the three types must be recognized tacitly, since they reveal distinctive textual traits. Within a community, then, a defining criterion for genre status might be recognition of that genre by all expert members of that community. Subgenre status might be a useful distinction to maintain, defined as a type of text that some but not all expert members recognize and that has some distinctive linguistic and rhetorical features. Significantly, however, one subgenre appears to represent the prototype of that genre. As a sample of letters to clients, all six departments sent an opinion letter. One of the subgenres thus may have privileged status as the unmarked form or prototype of that genre for that community.

While such distinctions among genres, subgenres, and prototype genres help to characterize how the tax accounting community classified and identified its genres, such a compromise position, designed to admit the expertise of all the participants, may yet mask further distinctions within the community itself. The community of tax accountants is not as homogeneous as this master list of common genres might suggest. First of all, I reduced the larger community of tax accountants down to those working in Big Eight accounting firms, omitting tax accountants in private practice, in government or corporate jobs, or in smaller accounting firms. Second, I gathered information from those Big Eight tax accountants working in the firm's offices in Kansas City. While one might expect that the genres would be the same for tax accountants in such firms whether they are working in Kansas City or in New York, since they probably communicate amongst themselves across city lines, the local situation surely alters their genres in some ways because it alters their contexts. So what I called the community of tax accountants is at best the community of Big Eight tax accountants in Kansas City in 1986. The genres they identified, which form the basis of my classification, may or may not be the genres of other tax accountants, if genre definition is to be determined by the recognition of its users.

Even within this narrowed community, the disagreement over how to classify letters to clients reveals that the six accounting departments do not form a single community with a single set of genres. All see themselves as writing letters to clients, and, judging by the samples sent in, all see themselves as offering formal opinions to their clients in those letters. But the firms differ in how they see their relations to clients in more particular terms. For most firms, promotion was not something they were involved in to any notable extent. Some pointed out that the national office sometimes wrote promotions that the regional offices simply mailed out to their clients; others did not see themselves as ever conducting self-promotion apart from other tasks. A similar difference of self-perception might connect to the difference between opinion and response letters. To those for whom there is a difference, the opinion letter explains the firm's interpretation of the tax rules on a specific client issue, taking an official and legally liable stand on how a client's taxes should be treated. The response letter, on the other hand, explains what the tax regulations say about a tax issue in a general way, without taking a stand on how the regulations would apply to the client's specific case. To those for whom there is a difference, the difference between these two subgenres is significant, a difference of legal liability most of all. They see themselves as serving their clients in two distinct ways. To those for whom there is no difference between opinion and response letter, for whom there is only one genre of letters to clients, their service to their clients is always legally liable and always relates the regulations to the client's specific case, although it may be more or less general in a given letter.

A difference in how genres are named, then, reveals a difference in how the community perceives its work and its relations to others. The firms differ in whether they see themselves as sources of more general information for clients as well as sources of legal opinions on clients' particular cases, and they differ in whether they see themselves as needing to promote their services to their clients. They differ in the genres they recognize in their repertoire. In fact, one other genre, tax provision reviews, was named by only two of the firms. Two of the six firms did not use the genre at all, according to the participants, and participants in the remaining two firms recognized the genre only hesitantly with my prompting. It would seem to be a genre that exists for some accountants and not others, reflecting perhaps the different experiences two of the firms have had and the differing emphasis they place on one kind of activity. As these generic differences show, the larger community of tax accountants contains within it smaller communities with diverse experiences and ideologies—and diverse genres. As noted in the previous chapter, communities are not so neatly circumscribed nor so homogeneous.

The differences among the firms should not obscure the fact, however, that almost all of the genres were identified similarly in all of the tax accounting departments. The genres alone provide strong evidence that tax accountants in Big Eight firms do indeed constitute a community, no matter which firm and no matter whether the participants are in Kansas City or New York. The participants share a common genre repertoire upon which they all agree. The ten genres, including the common genre of letters to clients, that tax accountants share are listed in Table 3.1 along with the number of firms who volunteered each genre and the number of samples of each sent. I have included in the table the subgenres of letters to clients that some participants identified, in order to acknowledge the existence of the subgenres textually in the samples sent from all six firms.

Table 3.1

Tax Accounting Genre Repertoire

Genres	No. of Firms That Sent Samples	No. of Samples Received
Nontechnical correspondence	3	5
Administrative memoranda	4	17
Transmittal letters	5	20
Engagement letters	2	4
Proposals	1	3
Memoranda for the files	4	9
Research memoranda	5	18
Letters to clients: promotional	2	6
Letters to clients: opinion	6	11
Letters to clients: response	4	10
Letters to taxing authorities	5	14
Tax protests	3	5

While this list shows the genre repertoire as the participants identified it, tax accountants actually use a much wider range of genres than these, but they are genres that the accountants themselves do not think of as genres or as types of texts. Because the informants did not think of them as writing or as texts, even with my prompting, I do not include here the many documents tax accountants write in preparing income taxes: tax returns, schedules, amended returns, and so on. In considering how the genres accomplish the tax accounting department's work, however, we must certainly include these various tax documents. Similarly, tax accountants act through many spoken genres, though I did not conduct the kind of ethnographic study needed to collect samples of such spoken genres. The list of ten genres represents, then, what the participants in the community perceive as the written genres they use to accomplish their work. Although the list does not reflect differences among participants or between firms, and it does not capture the genres of all tax accountants at all times, it does represent a remarkable coherence of perception across different firms, reflective of the coherence of a professional community with an established genre repertoire.

The Functions of Genres Within Community Needs

The genres of a community function for that community and are functions of that community, both situationally and culturally. The community of tax accountants recognizes the primacy of function for their genre repertoire, evident in the fact that they named their genres primarily according to their functions. A quick description of the task of each is offered here to help define the ten genres being discussed and illustrate their task orientation.

Nontechnical correspondence includes all letters that maintain external relations and accomplish external business but that are not distinctive to tax accountants. Similarly, administrative memoranda are the internal correspondence necessary to the maintenance of internal relations and running of the organization. Together, these two genres are the correspondence that in many studies of business writing would be all the writing examined but which, for tax accountants, become two broad types of necessary but routine writing. (Again, many genres in one context may become two in another context, since genre definition comes from the purpose and the user, not a fixed definition or classification scheme.)

The functions of some of the tax accountants' genres are obvious: transmittal letters to identify the purpose and context of transmitting another document, for example; engagement letters to document a new accountant-client relationship; and proposals to propose work for the department. Memoranda for the files record any activity that did not occur in writing: advice given in a phone conversation, an agreement reached in a meeting, and so on. Research memoranda summarize Internal Revenue Service (IRS) statements on a tax question or issue to direct and support the firm's position taken in a client's case. They may, for example, provide the technical support for the opinion offered in a letter to a client. Letters to clients solicit a client's business, respond to a client's questions about general tax issues, or offer specific opinions on a client's case. Letters to taxing authorities (that is, the IRS and its agents) respond to notices or assessments received by clients and attempt to negotiate with the agent an action favorable to the client. When negotiations fail, a tax protest is written arguing on legal and formal grounds for a client's or the firm's position on an issue.

Each of these genres fulfills an important purpose in accomplishing the work of the tax accounting department. Their actions are often explicit in what they are called: transmittal letters transmit; engagement letters engage; proposals propose; research memoranda research; tax protests protest. The five genres whose names do not contain an action contain instead a situational label: correspondence that is nontechnical in subject, memoranda that serve administrative purposes, memoranda that are to be filed, letters that have client audiences, and letters that have taxing authorities as audiences. In each genre, the tax accounting department's need and the genre's function are apparent. Each genre fulfills a distinct task for the tax accounting community.

Interactions among a Community's Genres

Not only does each genre in isolation accomplish a needed task for the tax accounting community, but also all of the genres together interact and cooperate to accomplish all of the community's work and to define what is possible to do within the community. These interacting and cooperating genres within a single community constitute the community's genre repertoire.

At some level, each genre depends on other genres just as, or even because, each task that an accountant must perform depends on other tasks being performed as well. Take for example what the Partners described to me as a common scenario. A Partner receives a letter from a client asking about the tax treatment of a particular "fact pattern" that differs in some way from the usual case; he (all the partners I interviewed were male) asks a Senior accountant to prepare a research memorandum on the relevant issue for the client's particular case. The Senior accountant studies the Tax Codes and various Regulations and decisions (genres I will return to in a moment) and writes a research memorandum, appending to that memorandum photocopies of relevant pages from the Codes and Regulations. The Partner, after reading the Senior's research memorandum, writes an opinion letter to the client. The task and genre sequence may go even further if the client follows the Partner's advice and the IRS later questions that tax treatment in a letter to that client, in which case the accountant may then produce a letter to the IRS and, if necessary, a tax protest. The genre sequence may also be traced back further if the client's initial letter is prompted by a promotional letter or if we view the client's letter as the eventual result of a proposal and engagement letter.

The many texts involved in this one scenario instantiate multiple genres, each genre helping the accountant to accomplish a task that interacts with other tasks instantiating other genres. The essential intertextuality (intergenre-ality?) of generic action appears in several forms. In its simplest dialogic form, the letter from a client requesting an opinion and the letter from the accountant giving that opinion act as call and response. Another form of intertextuality among these genres occurs when the text of one genre is incorporated into the text of another genre, as usually happens when the text of the Tax Codes and Regulations is copied directly into a research memorandum. Bakhtin might describe this latter relationship as one of primary to secondary genres, since secondary genres like novels contain within them other, primary genres, but in the case of tax accounting the primary genre carries a different status from other genres. The Tax Codes and Regulations are the law to the tax accountants; they are the genre which must be obeyed. All of their work refers to those laws, though to different degrees, and most of their work depends on those laws for their existence.[2] Letters to taxing authorities exist because differing interpretations of the Codes and Regulations are possible, letters to clients and research memoranda exist because taxpayer actions must accord with the Codes and Regulations, and tax accountants exist because taxes must be paid in amounts and forms specified by the Codes and Regulations. The Tax Codes and Regulations stand in relation to the other genres in the tax accountants' community as what I have called a supergenre, a genre that serves as the basis of and reference point for other genres. The kind of incorporation of one genre by another that occurs when genres incorporate the Tax Codes and Regulations, then, is different from primary to secondary incorporation, where one does not define the other. The Tax Codes and Regulations, like scriptures for religions, underlie, overarch, and connect most of the tax accountants' genres; they serve as a supergenre.

A different kind of supergenre might also exist for tax accountants, one that also defines and delimits the tax accountants' work: the genre of the client's complete file. Every action taken for or with a client, from a phone call to a tax protest, is to be recorded on paper and placed in the client's file. Every action taken for a client is to be taken only after consulting the client's file. The client's file is a genre that comprises many texts of other genres. While it exists materially in the form of a particular client's file, it exists as a genre to the extent that the accountants conceive of all those texts together as a single type of text. They understand that they are supposed to consult the client's file regularly. A similarly comprehensive but not regulatory supergenre was created in one firm when a Partner asked that every document written in the department be compiled periodically into a single bound text and reviewed by all Managers and Partners in the firm. While that genre developed only in the one firm, in that one firm the bound collection of texts was developing as a genre that fulfilled a specific function and acted as a supergenre to the other genres in that firm.

A relatively minor kind of intertextuality across genres occurs when text from one genre other than the Codes and Regulations is copied into another genre. Most commonly, such copying occurs when a Partner copies text directly from a research memorandum into an opinion letter to a client. Different from the supergenre, these genres are more lateral and the copying of one into another is more a question of ease than of definition. The copying is a relation among genres, though, rather than just among individual texts, for only some kinds of texts are copied into other kinds of texts. Such relations between two genres might simply be described as *incorporation*.

In the described scenario, the genres of research memorandum, opinion letter, letter to the IRS, tax protest, and promotional and engagement letters all serve as part of the accountant's genre repertoire, the set of genres through which accountants accomplish their work and which define their work. The genre repertoire describes the kinds of actions that tax accountants typically will take. A letter from a client could conceivably prompt many kinds of actions, including phoning the client, delegating it to another worker, giving it to a boss to review or advise, calling the client in for a meeting, contacting an IRS agent for an opinion, throwing the letter away, or filing the letter and ignoring it. Any one of these actions might be reasonable under some circumstances in some communities, but none of them represents typical or expected action for a tax accountant. When a tax accountant receives a letter from a client, the accountant writes an opinion letter to the client. If the answer is not obvious or the particularities of the case are unclear, a tax accountant assigns an associate to research the issues and present conclusions in a research memorandum, after which a tax accountant writes the client an opinion letter. Taking that action reflects how other tax accountants have acted in the past, and it reinforces the "rightness" of that action for tax accountants in the future.

New accountants entering the firm learn what actions are expected in part through learning the genres that are expected. The Seniors I interviewed spend considerable time writing research memoranda. In the process of learning how to write that genre, they learn the values of the community, to be discussed below, but more essentially, they learn what actions are considered appropriate and how situations are perceived. A letter from a client requesting information that needs research is to be recognized as a common, recurring situation in spite of the particularities of that client's fact pattern. As they described it, the same actions occur no matter what the client's case, for they have learned how to reduce the particularities to cases (hence the expression "fact *pattern*") in order to conduct the kind of research the Manager or Partner expects. From that research, they draw certain kinds of conclusions that can be presented in the first part of a research memorandum and follow that with their summary of what they have learned to see as relevant laws and decisions. By learning the research memorandum, novice accountants are trained not just in a genre but in the kinds of actions considered appropriate.

Although the genre of the research memorandum may be most obvious, since it is one that novices write, all the genres have similar effects of defining the actions of the tax accountants. In my earlier account of this research, I concluded,

> This genre set not only reflects the profession's situations; it may also help to define and stabilize those situations. The mere existence of an established genre may encourage its continued use, and hence the continuation of the activities and relations associated with that genre. (340–41)

The Partner knows not to throw away the letter from a client but rather to write an opinion letter. Writing a letter to a taxing authority leads the accountant to cite Tax Codes and Regulations and argue facts rather than to argue the client's neediness or good intentions. Each genre encourages some actions and not others, so the set of genres together, the accountants' genre repertoire, encourages a limited range of actions and excludes as insignificant or inappropriate other kinds of actions that are not part of the genre repertoire. In theory, expanding the genre repertoire to include the oral genres as well—phone calls and meetings of various kinds—and the written genres that the accountants did not consider as writing—the tax forms of various kinds—would enable all of the tax accountant's work to be accomplished through the genre repertoire. The tax accountant's tasks and the work of the tax accounting department are achieved through instantiations of this genre repertoire. One genre alone cannot do it; all the genres working in isolation cannot do it; only all the genres interacting and cooperating as a set can fulfill the tax accounting department's needs. As I concluded in my earlier work from this study, the set of genres interacts "to accomplish the work of the tax department. In examining the genre set of a community, we are examining the community's situations, its recurring activities and relationships. The genre set accomplishes its work" (340).

While the genre repertoire is the set of genres through which accountants act, I would now add that they operate within a genre set that is larger than their genre repertoire, a genre set that includes also the genres they read (reading, of course, also being an action). A full understanding of the tax accountants' work and genre repertoire would have to include the genres that they read as well as those they write, especially the letters from clients and from taxing authorities, the client's file, and the Tax Codes, Regulations, and decisions that constitute the supergenre for tax accountants.

In the end, defining the genre set of a group reveals once again the fluidity of groups and the necessary flexibility of its definition. Some of the genres important to their work are written by people other than tax accountants (Tax Codes and Regulations, letters from clients and taxing authorities). Yet that very importance, common across different people in different firms, attests to the coherence of a tax accounting community, as does the similar identification of common genres. The genre set of a group and its genre repertoire create and define the group even as they are created and defined to fill the goals of the group. To act through the group's genre repertoire is to act as a member of the group.

Reflections and Reinforcement of the Community in Its Genres

Examining the genre repertoire of the tax accounting community reveals much about the community itself, its values and beliefs, its members and their relationships. As described in the preceding two sections, the work of the department is apparent in its genre repertoire; the genres can tell an outsider what accountants do. Different aspects of those genres can also tell what accountants believe, for genres, as discussed in the second chapter, reflect and reinforce the community's values, epistemology, and power relationships.

Because a genre develops from the actions of the people in the group in the context of a perceived situation, the genre will show how most people in the group act or are expected to act and what most of its members believe, behave as if they believe, or think they should believe. It is this mixture of behavior and expectations that I mean when I characterize "a group's values, epistemology, and power relationships." If a group values personal experience, for a simple example, the genre will incorporate personal experience; if a group values emotional appeals, the genre will use emotional appeals in trying to respond effectively. Virtually any aspect of a genre might be interpreted in terms of a group's beliefs. An organizational pattern reflects the group's sense of importance and logic; a persona reflects the group's attention to individuality or distance; a relative balance of complex or compound sentences reflects the group's belief in directness or sophistication. Once the stance is adopted that such generic rhetorical features can be interpreted in terms of the group, then seeing such connections depends largely on the skill of the interpreter and the awareness of the participant informants, much as the ability to see rhetorical strategies depends on the skill of the rhetorical analyst.

In the case of the tax accounting genres, some generic aspects stand out as more indicative of the community than others. The research memorandum, for example, appears to be a genre representative of the epistemology of tax accounting. As documenter of the support for any position taken by the firm, the research memorandum requires a clear line of analytic reasoning and, most of all, substantial and frequent citation and quotation of the Tax Codes and Regulations. The "truth," according to this genre of tax accounting, comes from logic and textual authority. The way that textual authority is presented reveals that individual interpretation of textual authority is to be minimized, that the texts should speak for themselves, for the relevant passages of the tax laws are frequently copied directly into the research memorandum, with no paraphrasing and, significantly, no quotation marks. This unmarked quotation, according to my informants, allows the research memorandum to maintain the precision of the Tax Code. There is, in other words, no room for interpretation at this level.

The lack of interpretation permitted at this level reveals also the power relationships involved in a tax accounting department. The Managers or Partners are allowed, even required, to interpret the tax codes, but the Senior and Staff accountants, those who write research memoranda, are not. Interpretation of the text requires expertise and experience, according to the tax accountants interviewed; the Senior merely provides the text for the Partner to interpret. Some Seniors take this role so rigidly that they even photocopy the relevant passages from the Tax Code and attach them to their research memoranda, ensuring that the Partner can sort out any possible interpretation that the Senior's write-up in the memorandum might have introduced. Some Partners approve of such literalness and deference from the Seniors.

Although Seniors are not allowed to interpret text, they are allowed, even required, to draw conclusions from the text. Research memoranda always begin with a conclusion, a judgment based on the tax codes, an answer to the Partner's specific question. Those conclusions may be hemmed with qualifiers and hedges, but they specifically judge what interpretations the Tax Codes allow in the given case. In fact, then, the Seniors are given the power to suggest interpretations. They are not, though, given the power to make the judgment alone: after the answer to the question must come pages of detailed textual support for that answer. The Partner need not accept the Senior's judgment without deciding for himself. It is significant that individual relationships, rather than community-established roles, may counteract the power accorded by the genre: one Partner pointed out that if he knew the individual Senior and had enough experience to trust the Senior's judgment, he might act on the Senior's conclusion without reading the supporting evidence, knowing that the Senior would have provided sufficient support (though he would still expect the supporting evidence to be included). The ideology of the community, its power relationships, and the expectations of the genre do not determine the accountants' actions: an individual can still decide to act contrary to the norm on the basis of his or her individual experience and needs. As always, what the genre and community establish is only a frame; the individual uses that frame in a particular instance. Nonetheless, the genre's statement about the community is clear: specific textual authority is sufficient and necessary authority; that authority resides in the word *verbatim* and should be interpreted only with experience and expertise; the judgments of Seniors must be subordinated to that of Managers and Partners.

The research memorandum exemplifies other community values as well, but these examples should be enough to illustrate the point. They also illustrate the correlate, that the genres not only reflect but also reinforce the values and beliefs of the community. The Partner who trusts the judgment of a particular Senior still requests that the Senior write a research memorandum, and that research memorandum still requires that the Senior quote the texts directly, not interpret the texts, and subordinate the Senior's judgment to that of the Partner. Even though recent theories of interpretation might question the ability of any writer to cite support without interpretation, the tax accounting community is not likely to shift to that belief easily as long as the research memorandum requires compilation of verbatim text. The community creates a genre from its beliefs, and using that genre in turn reinforces its beliefs.

That reinforcement of beliefs is especially true for the novices in a community, the entry-level and Senior accountants in the case of tax accounting. Although genres are always created by people, they are not often created by the least powerful in a group. The reality for novices especially, then, is that the already existing genre repertoire defines and delimits their actions and enforces the group's ideology. Seniors described to me learning how to write research memoranda by asking others how to do it, by studying research memoranda others had written, and by revising their first attempts on the basis of feedback from those above them. Many understood the rhetorical reasons for various aspects of that genre, but they reported gaining that understanding only later, after they had learned to write the genre more formulaically (for more discussion of formulaic genre learning and its ideological effects, see chapter 7). In fact, being able to explain the rationale for a genre requires incorporating the ideology that lies behind that genre. By the time Seniors can report the reasons for copying Tax Code language exactly in their research memorandum, for example, they have learned that their interpretations of that language are not to be trusted and must be checked by their "superiors"; by the time they can explain why they begin the research memorandum with a direct answer to the question, they have learned that the end goal is always the "right" answer and that the Partner's time is valuable (more valuable than theirs). In following the genre that others have created, then, novices learn to follow the values, epistemology, and power relationships of the group, thereby constructing that ideology themselves. The same effect holds for experts in the group, as genres reinforce the ideology of those who came before them, but those with more power are more capable of altering both the ideology and the genres of the group.

Even less powerful than novices to effect change in the ideology or genres of a group are those who enter the group's realm only occasionally or who remain on the periphery. In the case of tax accounting, the most obvious such groups are the clients and the taxing authorities. Clients, of course, must be served or they will take their business elsewhere, but their lack of knowledge and their dependence on the experts to stay out of jail (or suffer similar dire consequences) make them unlikely to interfere with the group's established actions. The taxing authorities, though quite powerful in some ways, remain on the periphery of the tax accounting firms. The actions of IRS agents and others certainly affect the work of the tax accountants, and they probably could affect directly the genres that are addressed to them. If they began asking accountants to testify to the character of their clients, for example, the client's character would surely become more highly valued and the letters to taxing authorities would cite more human qualities and fewer Tax Regulations. Yet such change is unlikely to happen, for the taxing authorities, though not in the community of the tax accounting firms, share the larger community of those involved with the taxation system in the United States. Their common reliance on the Tax Codes and Regulations, their common respect for and use of the same supergenre, places them within a common ideology. Groups overlap and interact, so being on the periphery of one group does not necessarily make one on the periphery of that group's ideology or its genres. The genres that most concern taxing authorities developed to serve the needs of both tax accountants and tax agents; it reflects the ideology of both.

That mutuality is less true for the letters to clients. Even though the client's needs must figure into the opinion letters to clients, for example, the letters are often dense with specialist reference and jargon, including exact citation of specific regulations, and they are often filled with such qualifiers that the client might not know how to proceed. When asked the reason for using specialist language and references, tax accountants explained that their first priority is to protect themselves from legal liability, to ensure that taxing authorities would find their written opinions accurate if challenged, and to ensure that they cannot be seen as advising a client to do anything that might be in violation of tax law. Secondarily, they want to offer their clients the information or advice they requested. One part of the community's ideology—the need to protect from legal liability—thus conflicts with another part—the need to serve clients and guide them to appropriate actions. The need to please possible future taxing authorities is clearly stronger than the need to please existing clients (or perhaps more accurately, the need to please clients in the long term depends on pleasing taxing authorities). Taxing authorities would seem in fact to have the most power in this community, even as they sit on the periphery. The genres reflect that conflict and reveal that genres do not develop only transparently efficient responses to transparent situations but involve more complex values and relationships of power.

Individual Variation Within Social Generality

Examining the genres of tax accountants in light of the basic principles of how genre operates in society has, I hope, proven enlightening in some respects. It has enabled me to examine the functions, interactions, and ideologies of genres in ways that reveal how and why a group acts through writing. I have attempted to complicate the simple notion that texts reflect their rhetorical situations by contextualizing those texts in their cultural settings, and I have attempted to complicate the simple notion that texts reflect their social uses and settings by proposing different kinds of groups and multiple uses. Yet the picture of genre's social functioning that I have outlined so far is still incomplete, for it cannot capture the complexity of society nor hence of its genres. Even as I have attempted to note the different kinds of groups and multiple people who constitute a group, the very basis of a social perspective in human collectives means that individual variation will be inadequately recognized. Similarly, the very treatment of texts as instantiations of genres means that variation across texts will be neglected. Although those simplifications are necessary results of a social examination, I cannot wait until the chapters on standards, creativity, and literary genres to rectify that incompleteness, and I cannot leave this chapter and the tax accounting example without recognizing the greater complexity that writers and texts have beyond any statement of basic principles of societies and genres.

A genre is not completely monovocal, nor are genres within a genre set or repertoire completely coherent and unified in their values and beliefs. Within a single genre, not everything is restricted or specified. The overall organization may be quite specified in readers' expectations, but the organization within sections may be unspecified. A certain level of technical lexicon may be expected, but the simplicity or complexity of syntax may vary widely from one writer to another. Even the most rigid of genres—say, the school lab report—allows some variation, or else each A-level lab report resulting from a given assignment would be identical to every other A-level lab report (that is assuming that some judged not of "A" quality might be deficient in some generic aspects). Even so-called generic literature encompasses considerable variation: the hero of a mystery novel must be clever, but the hero may be male (Travis McGee) or female (V. I. Warshawski), obviously clever (Holmes) or stumblingly clever (Columbo), young (Nancy Drew) or old (Miss Marple). To the extent that any one of my parenthetical examples seems not to fit the genre to a particular reader (for example, a reader may exclude children's mysteries), that reader is defining the genre with more restrictive criteria for his or her own reading purposes. But no one can restrict the criteria for a genre so tightly that no variation exists: a genre by definition must include more than one text, and any two texts will include differences as well as similarities.

Those differences across individual texts are largely ignored in my study of the writing of tax accountants, but they exist nonetheless. All the research memoranda began with direct answers to the questions asked followed by detailed recitations of relevant Tax Codes and Regulations, but some were longer than others, some attached photocopies and some did not, and each described different sections of the codes in different orders. All opinion letters to clients cited the codes and regulations, but some did so more frequently than others, some surrounded those citations with more details about the client's case than did others, and some began with more personal greetings than did others. The patterns I detected and described held for different texts labeled as instantiating the same genre, but there are always more ways that texts differ one from another than ways they are the same.

Every instance of a genre is different from every other instance of that genre. Genres group texts that are similar in some significant ways, but that grouping requires abstraction from the many differences in those texts. Variation, then, is as inherent in genres as is conformity, a notion to be discussed at length in chapter 5.

Looking at genre sets reveals that genres also vary in the values and beliefs of the group that they reflect. As Harris, among others, has pointed out, a community is not completely homogeneous. Neither, then, are its genres. Different genres within a group may reflect and reinforce different beliefs of the group, theoretically even apparently conflicting beliefs. Because each genre reflects and constructs a different rhetorical situation and fulfills a different function, each genre will potentially be attached to different values, epistemologies, and power relationships existing within the community.

It may be that the more tightly knit the community, the more coherent are its genres. The tax accountants I interviewed, for example, were remarkably consistent in their responses to my questions, differing in degree rather than in kind. One might find paraphrase of the Tax Codes and Regulations more acceptable a bit more often than another, for example, but both agreed it was usually inadvisable. The genres of tax accountants appear similarly consistent in the beliefs and values they represent. One genre might use paraphrase more often than another, suggesting less dependence on and belief in the Tax Codes as a verbatim authority, but the difference is one of degree rather than kind: both genres use the Tax Codes as their primary authority and both quote those Codes. The one place where the sense of a single community most broke down was in the definition of the genre of letter to clients. The fact that participants in one firm saw three genres whereas participants in another firm saw only one genre certainly suggests that the community is not completely coherent. The differences in their perceptions of those genres in fact appeared to reflect a difference in how they viewed their clients and how concerned they were about legal liability and about self-promotion. In a less tightly knit (or less narrowly defined) community, the genres and their representative beliefs may be even less consistent. The academic community, for example, to the extent that it exists, is rather loosely held together in some ways, with different disciplines holding different beliefs. Their genres hence may exhibit more of the variety that is the point of this section. Surely the sciences' lab report reflects an epistemology different from that of the humanities' personal response paper or argumentative essay. Even within a department, the traditional critic's literary interpretation reveals a different epistemology and value from those of the cultural studies scholar's thick description or the composition teacher's idea for the classroom. The research paper shows such variety within itself, for a research paper in a literature class, requiring support from authorities and from textual citation, differs considerably in epistemology from a research paper in psychology, which might require support from experimental data as well as authority.[3]

Even within an apparently tightly knit community of tax accountants, though, there are conflicts and differences in the ideology represented by their genres. The opinion letter to clients appears to encompass two conflicting values: providing helpful advice to clients, and protecting the firm from legal liability. The research memorandum requires less expert accountants to limit their own interpretations of the particular tax law, yet it also requires them to take a stand in the very first section on their interpretation of the meaning of the law for a particular case. All of their reliance on the Tax Codes and Regulations as a supergenre treats it as transparent text to be taken literally, but many of the genres exist in order to offer interpretations of that text, as if it were in fact ambiguous. Further examination would surely reveal other potential conflicts and differences across genres in this one community, differences that seem to come not from different individuals within the group but rather from the very nature of groups and genres, that their ideology is not completely coherent or consistent. Swales's account of the conflicting cultures in the English Language Institute shows a similar clash within what still seems a coherent community *(Other Floors)*.

The ideology of the genre and group also varies in its enactment from one individual to the next. Individual writers, again, take the admonition against interpreting Tax Code more seriously than do others, for some in research memoranda paraphrase sometimes, some always quote exactly, and some also attach photocopies. Some Partners in opinion letters cite the fewest Regulations possible, others as many as possible. Individual relationships also supersede expected power relationships. One Partner used the answers given in research memoranda without reviewing the actual Tax Code when those memoranda were written by a particular Senior, for his experience with that individual had taught him that the individual Senior's answers were reliable. Although the Partner retained the power to make that decision, his lack of review of the Code in the rest of the memorandum violated the expected relationship of a Partner to a Senior. Any accountant can choose to act differently, even choosing not to document or to destroy documents, following motivations less apparent in the existing genres. As will be discussed theoretically in chapter 5, the individual still acts, though within a society and a genre, and that action may take unpredictable turns.

Variation may exist within a genre set, allowing different genres to reflect different community values and beliefs. Variation surely exists within a genre, allowing each instantiation of that genre to be both similar and different from all other instantiations of that genre. And variation surely exists in how individuals are encompassed by or operate within those genres. In reflecting and reinforcing the complexity of society, genres reinforce conformity but they also require choice. This political aspect of the social nature of genre perhaps deserves a few comments on its own, briefly here before a more extended discussion in chapters 4 and 5.

The encouragement of conformity among its participants is a fact of genre, for genres provide an expected way of acting. Like expectations for dress, manners, or "proper English," generic expectations encourage and reinforce one way of behaving over another. People who choose not to meet those expectations meet varying responses, depending on their status and social setting. To refuse to write *whom* in formal settings is to risk being judged inadequately educated, but it is also to risk being judged friendlier or more personable.[4] The reaction to breaking generic expectations can be similarly two-sided. One who refuses to lay out a resume in a standard format risks being rejected for the job, but the risk may also result in getting the job if the employer seeks explicit creativity or independent thinking. A dramatist who breaks "the fourth wall" and makes the playwriting visible risks offending the audience and risks expanding the audience's perceptions. A dramatist who breaks the unities risks Samuel Johnson's ire but also his admiration. There are consequences for violating generic expectations, but those consequences are not always easily predictable.

Much surely has to do with the status in the society of the individual who is breaking the convention, partly because generic conventions serve to mark membership in the group. Those who belong follow the conventions; those who don't follow the conventions don't belong. As a junior tax accountant learns to quote the Tax Code and learns to state the question's answer in the beginning, that writer's research memoranda thus will mark his or her inclusion in the community of tax accountants. English majors learn to cite the text heavily and to use metaphorical language in their critical essays, demonstrating their inclusion in the literary community. Beginning literature students mark their exclusion from that community by citing dictionaries and using simple lexicon—that is, they do not use generically expected evidence or lexicon. As sociolinguists have often noted about conforming to a nonnative dialect, conforming to the genre's conventions represents an acceptance of the community's values, epistemology, and power relationships that those conventions reflect. Having established membership in a group, a writer then can violate expectations with less severe consequences, though even then the consequences are unpredictable. The Partner who trusted the Senior's interpretations of the Tax Code could choose to violate the expectation that he would review the Code before writing an answer to a client; that Partner did not choose to violate the expectation that he would write such a letter, he did not choose to write a letter that gave a direct answer without citing the Code, and he did not choose to write a letter that gave his own opinion without researching it first. The violations of expectations that I witnessed in this study were few and minor, though of course I saw only those texts that the study participants chose to show me. Still it appears that the power of genre to encourage conformity is strong indeed.

Yet that power does not make genres evil or even necessarily politically repressive. Sociolinguistic research demonstrates that all groups and all dialects have common ways of using language that mark membership in that group, the neighborhood as well as the school, the lower as well as the upper classes, the ethnic minorities as well as the ethnic majorities. As Robert Pattison argues for literacy, standards themselves, including generic standards, are not negative; it is how society uses those standards that makes them work for or against people. That there are generic conventions to which readers expect conformity is not negative; that those conventions identify members and nonmembers is not negative. Like other standards, genre is used by society to accomplish its ends. A benevolent society may use those standards, including genre, benevolently; a fascist society may use those standards fascistically. Although we still must examine genres embedded in their society, with whatever social agenda society has integrated into them, it is important to remind ourselves that it is not genre that has agency, not genre that creates a social agenda. Examinations of particular sites such as this study of tax accounting genres illustrate the reciprocal and constant interactions of individuals and groups, genre and genre sets, and situational and cultural contexts.

4

A History of Genres and Genres in History

> Man's yesterday may ne'er be like his morrow;
> Nought may endure but Mutability.
> —Percy Bysshe Shelley, "Mutability"

Genres have long been seen metaphorically as having lives: being born, growing, and sometimes dying. The novel is described as having risen out of the eighteenth century, birthed from travel narratives, episodic sagas, letter manuals, and other parents; some have forecast the novel's death. The periodical essay, along with its forum, died in the eighteenth century; the Petrarchan sonnet was created; free verse emerged; magical realism revived the novel. In the twentieth and twenty-first centuries, we watch as e-mail messages are born, develop, and divide into personal messages, business e-mail, forwarded jokes, and spam. We learn new genres of web pages and web sites, instant messages and voice-mail messages. That genres have such lives has long been recognized metaphorically, and scholarly histories of specific genres abound. But what do those individual lives tell us about the collective concept of genre? Some genre scholars, most notably Ralph Cohen and Kathleen Jamieson, have examined connections between genre and history. What this chapter attempts is to use a few genres and genre sets as case studies to generate some generalizations about how genres develop historically—how they originate, adapt, and change. Drawing these generalizations from existing studies of particular cases, thereby grounding the abstract principles in specific genres, allows me to make explicit what at times may seem obvious in order to open them to further examination and investigation. Finally, the last section of this chapter explores the implications of an earlier quantitative study I conducted of the relationship between genres and language change. This study, demonstrating that language changed differently in different genres over more than a century, allows me to refine the relationships among individual, social, and cultural change. The results offer some insights into how history operates on genres and suggests how genres operate on history.

Genres as Dynamic

Because genres are typified actions, people don't expect the genres they use to change. A sonnet is a sonnet, an editorial is an editorial, a sales letter is a sales letter. On the basis of the understanding of genres examined in the preceding chapters and noted by many genre scholars, however, genres that have persisted over time must have changed, even if that change is not generally visible at the time. Logically, since they reflect their cultural, situational, and generic contexts, and since those contexts change over time, genres, too, must change over time. Since groups of people use genres to suit their purposes, and since those purposes change as the groups change, genres, too, must change in their purposes. Since people use and recognize genres as they go about their daily lives, and since the nature of those daily lives changes over time, genres, too, must change in their daily uses. Since people use genres to construct recurring situations out of variable events, genres, too, must adapt to variation. If they are to survive, genres must change. Logic, theory, and scholarship all lead to the necessity of genre being dynamic. Genres must be flexible synchronically and changeable diachronically.

Genre's synchronic flexibility will largely be addressed in the next chapter, examining how genres at once act as standards and permit variation. A brief summary of some of those ideas is necessary here, though, since that essential flexibility of genres synchronically is what enables genres to change diachronically. Rhetorical situations themselves are not static entities, once and forever fixed. As discussed in chapter 1, each rhetorical situation varies slightly from all other rhetorical situations. So the genre through which people act in that situation and out of which people construct a recurring situation must be capable of adapting to those variations; it must be flexible, never fully stabilized, not even "stabilized for now," in Schryer's term (a point I will argue more fully in chapter 5). In language theory, similar inherent variation in language-in-use contributes over time to language change. That is, language varies as people use it; those variations create the possibilities for changes, as some variations are adopted and, with continued and widespread use, later become recognized as changes in the language. Similarly, in genre theory, the inherent flexibility of genres permits variations and enables them to adapt over time to changes in contexts and uses. Over time, the contexts in which a genre is embedded will change, as the nature of the participants changes or new subjects are dealt with or new forums develop. The genre constructed by and constructing this situation, therefore, will also change.

The changes to which genres adapt include changes in contexts of culture, situation, and genres, the three kinds of context delineated in chapter 1. Since genres are embedded in social and institutional contexts, as discussed in the preceding chapters, cultural and situational changes may be expected to produce generic changes. The nature of society requires it, as Gunther Kress points out:

> If genre is entirely imbricated in other social processes, it follows that unless we view society itself as static, then neither social structures, social processes, nor therefore genres are static. Genres are dynamic, responding to the dynamics of other parts of social systems. Hence genres change historically; hence new genres emerge over time, and hence, too, what appears as "the same" generic form at one level has recognizably distinct forms in differing social groups. (42)

Implicit in the dynamic nature of society and rhetorical situation, then, is the dynamic nature of genre. Even the nature of our world, fluid and inconstant, requires that we understand genre as dynamic. In his discussion of blurred genres, Clifford Geertz sees a contemporary world with what I would call an amorphous context of genres:

> The properties connecting texts with one another, that put them, ontologically anyway, on the same level, are coming to seem as important in characterizing them as those dividing them; and rather than face an array of natural kinds, fixed types divided by sharp qualitative differences, we more and more see ourselves surrounded by a vast, almost continuous field of variously intended and diversely constructed works we can order only practically, relationally, and as our purposes prompt us. It is not that we no longer have conventions of interpretation; we have more than ever, built—often enough jerry-built—to accommodate a situation at once fluid, plural, uncentered, and ineradicably untidy. (20–21)

The fluid world requires fluid genres, categorized differently according to different purposes (as discussed in chapter 1), what Geertz notes as the "vast, almost continuous field of variously intended and diversely constructed works we can order only practically, relationally, and as our purposes prompt us." Geertz sees this context of genres as increasingly blurred; if he is right, this change in the context of genres surely affects the enactment of individual genres. Even if he is not right, changes in any one genre necessarily constitute a change in the context of genres, which in turn changes the context within which individual genres are shaped. Contexts change, so genres change.

Consider how genres adapt to changing contexts of situation, culture, and genres through a brief example of the genre set surrounding weddings in the United States. As the ideology of marriage has changed over time, so, too, have the genres announcing and constituting the marriage changed. Wedding genres (invitations, announcements, vows, registries, toasts, thank you notes, to name a few) have adapted to the weddings of subservient wives and their owner husbands as well as to the weddings of flower children in meadows. Wedding genres have encompassed second-time and older brides and couples with children. Invitations take on new beginnings, vows include new participants, but the genres persist recognizably. New situations and values have also led to the creation of new genres, genres which in turn contribute to new social actions: the existence of gift registries, for example, has changed the way guests select and buy gifts for the bride and groom, and the fact of prenuptial agreements surely influences the attitudes and beliefs of the engaged couple. Yet through all these changes, many wedding genres persist and even continue to be called by the same names. The variation inherent within them and the nature of genres as constructed social actions enable them to adapt and change.

More detailed historical studies of particular genres confirm the dynamic nature of genres and elaborate the processes by which genres develop and change. The next section of this chapter compares the discoveries of several different studies of specific genres and genre sets: of American business communication, presidential genres, the "freshman theme," and the modes. I will pull from studies of each genre set some common ways that genres have seemed to operate historically, using the patterns of one study to elaborate the discoveries of another. Together, these cases allow me to explore how genres originate, how they respond to contextual changes, the role of individuals in genre change, and how genres maintain both flexibility and stability. This method, of course, offers no more than hypotheses, since each case is unique and therefore case studies generate areas for exploration rather than proof. In that respect, these cases also demonstrate what may be the most reliable and perhaps valid general principle about the history of genres: Every genre tells a different story.

The Origins of New Genres

Genres seem to originate often out of other genres. It seems analysts can always point to antecedent genres and antecedent texts, in Jamieson's terms, for any new genre. In the "vast, almost continuous field of variously intended and diversely constructed works" that Geertz describes in the quotation above, many texts will bear relation to many other texts, and analysts after the fact will be able to construct relationships among many kinds of texts, pointing to antecedents and origins in earlier genres. On the basis of theory, we would expect not just analysts but speakers and writers as well to construct texts and genres from preexisting texts and genres. Because speakers and writers do not speak from a void, as discussed in chapter 1, Bakhtin observes that "[a]ny utterance is a link in a very complexly organized chain of other utterances" ("Problem" 69). Every text echoes previous texts in some ways; no text responds to a unique situation; every text is contextual. Similarly, every genre echoes previous genres in some ways, no genre responds to a unique situation, with no previously recurring participants or subjects or forums; no genre develops in what was previously a contextual void. Antecedent texts and antecedent genres serve as powerful sources for and constraints on the development of new genres.

Tracing the history of a genre, then, leads through other genres. "Where do genres come from?" asks Todorov, and he answers, "Quite simply from other genres. A new genre is always the transformation of an earlier one, or of several: by inversion, by displacement, by combination" (15). To Bakhtin in "The Problem of Speech Genres," all secondary (complex) genres develop by absorbing and digesting different primary (simple) genres, which have developed out of "unmediated speech communion" (62).[1] But it is difficult to imagine any "speech communion" unmediated by the context of other genres, and taken to a logical extreme, the search for the origin of genres can become a fruitless search for the mother genre, the antecedent of all other genres. If genre is indeed a nexus of contexts, including a context of genres, then any new genre must emerge from a relationship with the old genres. Tracing the evolution of a genre back to some of its antecedents can reveal the nature of the genre and its situational and cultural origins as well.

At least as important as recognizing antecedents in the context of genres is recognizing cultural and situational antecedents: the developing changes in ideologies, situations, and settings that create the circumstances for a new genre. The case studies of particular genres that I will discuss demonstrate that, though traceable to antecedent genres, "new" genres usually develop to fulfill new functions in changing situations arising from changing cultures, at times to fill widening gaps in existing genre repertoires. The combination of a preexisting context of genres and newly developed, unfulfilled needs enables the construction of newly identified genres.

The role of new genres in fulfilling new functions that develop from new cultural and situational contexts is especially apparent in the case of business communication in the late nineteenth and early twentieth centuries. JoAnne Yates provides a detailed and complex analysis of the changes in American businesses during the late nineteenth and early twentieth centuries and the role of communication in those changes in her book *Control Through Communication*. In a thorough and complex study that goes well beyond the generic pieces I will extract, Yates reveals how American businesses were transformed from small, family-run companies run largely through oral and informal communication to today's large corporations "held together by networks of communication up, down, and across hierarchies" (xv). Changes in management philosophy and technology in particular led to changes in the corporate communication system, according to Yates. One of the results of these changes was the development of new genres and the adaptation of existing genres. I will draw the relevant details about genres from within Yates's much more comprehensive study in order to examine a widespread cultural change that involved several new genres.

From 1850 to 1920, a new philosophy of management, called "systematic management," arose and became popular (Yates, chap. 1). Systematic management stressed system and efficiency. As smaller firms became larger firms, the traditional ad hoc management methods became inefficient, and communications between farther removed managers and their workers and among increasingly divided departments broke down. Systematic management developed as a management theory and technique that would transcend the individual by relying instead on the system. It had two primary principles: "(1) a reliance on systems mandated by top management rather than on individuals, and (2) the need for each level of management to monitor and evaluate performance at lower levels" (10).

A new genre repertoire developed to fulfill new functions in the community deriving from this new view of management. The particular genres that constituted the genre repertoire changed as the community's functions, forums, and relationships changed. Completely new genres (that is, those that may have had antecedents but that appear not to have been perceived generically previously) developed to meet the community's new needs. Among the new genres were circular letters or general orders (issuing specific policies or procedures), routine and special reports, various kinds of forms, manuals (describing the company's systematic procedures), in-house magazines, and managerial meetings. Existing memoranda also evolved, changing the format, style, and even paper used for previous internal correspondence, to be discussed in the next section. Together, all the genres constituted a complex and effective genre repertoire.

Yates points to possible antecedents for the new genres, confirming our expectation that new genres appear to emerge from other genres. Circular letters had three possible antecedents in purpose, form, and audience, according to Yates (66): military orders, advertising circulars, and printed company rules. The manual genre, too, had its antecedents, probably in the railroads' rule books for train movements and circular letters (71). Committee meetings were another new genre, though certainly meetings had been held before 1920, and the meeting genre may trace its antecedent to the owner's oral communication with the foreman (100).

Although Yates finds such antecedents for various aspects of these new genres, each genre of course differs significantly from its antecedents, for it fulfills some newly developed purpose for the business community, purposes that emerge from the significant cultural changes of the time. One new genre thus created was the circular letter. The increasing systematization of work required companies to state the policies employees were to follow and, eventually, to define the responsibilities and procedures involved in every job. Stating the policies subordinates were to follow became the purpose of the general order or circular letter (70). As the entire company became more systematized and each position governed by more policies, the need for a written collection of these policies became more pressing. Philosophically and ideologically, too, systematic management argued for a comprehensive set of rules that would lay out the company's system. This "comprehensive corporate memory," as Yates describes it (71), became the new genre of the manual. The newly developed genre of the manual served an important function for the newly systematized companies, which wished to use the system to transcend the individual (71). A third new genre that developed out of the new functions of systematic management is the form. Forms fulfilled the important function of standardizing and systematizing the daily work of the business, a need that had not been felt previously. Yates describes their new importance:

> In a period during which "system" was the universal catch-word, forms filled an important role in systematizing certain types of downward communication. They conveyed, as economically as possible, specific instructions that would otherwise have been conveyed orally (thus leaving no record) or in an individually composed note (thus taking more time). They were simultaneously mass communication and individual communication. (74)

By 1925, a book had been published on the design and use of forms (80), and a new genre had become an established part of the new genre repertoire.

These three new genres, the manual, the circular letter, and the form, fulfilled some of the new functions required by the shift to systematic management. Resulting in part from such sweeping changes in ideology and culture, new genres resulted as well from changes in the context of situation. The roles of the participants in the community changed during this period, particularly the relationship between managers and subordinates. Rather than the personal, family orientation of the previous relationship between owner-manager and workers, the growth in company size and the dehumanized management philosophy in the late nineteenth century distanced owners and managers from foremen and workers. Workers and managers both resisted this depersonalization of the workplace, and a series of labor problems and strikes beginning in the 1870s brought to a head the need to "reinject a personal element into the workplace" (75). One major result was the development of another new genre, the in-house magazine. To repersonalize the workplace, the in-house magazine included articles about the home and work lives of executives, stories about long-time employees, news of employee clubs and activities (76). The personalizing purpose of the in-house organ was described in an article in 1918:

> "Many shops have outgrown the one-man stage. No longer can the head of the organization interpret his policies person-

ally to the workmen. But a factory house organ, whether it
be a single typewritten sheet or a 24-page magazine, offers
an opportunity to bind personal interest closer in the small
shop and keep management from becoming mechanical in the
large plant." (qtd. in Yates 17)

In reinstilling the human into the system, the in-house magazine responded
to the changed relationship between manager and subordinate and fulfilled the need to repersonalize the company. Yates reminds us, however,
that, as the in-house magazine "improved morale and cooperation," it
indirectly reinforced control (77). While fulfilling the need for improved
relations between management and workers, the new genre also served
the functions of the new company system. The genre reflected its position
as a nexus of both the changing situation and the changing culture.

More explicitly reinforcing the changed roles of participants in the
situation of business communication is the genre of the committee meeting, functioning to assure the cooperation of the managers in particular
(Yates 18–19). The need to gain the cooperation of lower-level managers, whose autonomy under systematic management was considerably
reduced, led to committee meetings in which "[h]igher level managers
solicited suggested improvements in processes and systems from lower level
managers (especially foremen and department heads), at the same time
encouraging cooperation with existing systems" (19). Again, the new genre
responded to the changed relationship among managers at different levels
and fulfilled the function of gaining cooperation with the system, reinforcing both its context of situation and its context of culture.

Yates's history demonstrates how these new genres—circular letters,
manuals, forms, in-house magazines, and meetings—developed out of
the new circumstances of American business in the late nineteenth century. In my terms, they fill gaps in business's genre repertoire that appear as the nature of business changes, fulfilling newly developed functions and reflecting new roles for participants, new situations. Each new
genre adds something a bit different to what exists, each develops out
of different antecedents, even as each develops in a common context.
Together, they indicate the complex interaction of genres and functions,
of how contextual changes lead to perceived needs that are absorbed by
modifying existing genres into newly constructed genres.

In many ways, the detailed history of these genres recounts what I
might have expected as the "typical" origin of a genre: gradual development over time by modifying existing genres, responding to gradu-

ally emerging cultural and situational changes, especially newly perceived functions and changing relationships among participants. Studies of other genres, however, reveal that genres do not always originate so quietly or "naturally." Karlyn Kohrs Campbell and Kathleen Hall Jamieson provide us with a detailed study of part of the genre repertoire used by American presidents.[2] Especially in their book *Deeds Done in Words,* Campbell and Jamieson examine how presidential genres fulfill the functions required by the institution of the presidency, including those genres newly created for the new situations of the newly united states.

Campbell and Jamieson's book follows their work in *Form and Genre* to present a rhetorical theory of genre, work that Carolyn Miller drew from for her writing, and which I have incorporated so their understanding of presidential genres is generally consonant with the understanding of genre I am using in this book. In *Deeds Done in Words,* Campbell and Jamieson thus describe the significant functions of each presidential genre in its situations and how each genre has responded to those functional needs. They write, "Rhetorical types are linked to purposes; that is, they arise to perform certain functions, to accomplish certain ends in certain kinds of situations" (104). In the case of the presidential genres Campbell and Jamieson consider, those purposes and functions were largely and suddenly created by the creation of the new republic in its Constitution. Rather than developing gradually over time, the new presidential genres originate with the new institution of the presidency and are often required by the Constitution, one specified fully, one only generally, and one only by extension. The only genre fully specified by the Constitution is the veto message, but it is specified, as Campbell and Jamieson write, down to "determining its purposes, major lines of argument, predominant strategy, and structure as well as the persona and tone usually adopted by the president" (76). For the state of the union address, not the rhetorical strategies but only the general function is defined by Article 2, section 3 of the Constitution, which requires the president periodically to inform the Congress of the state of the union. As Campbell and Jamieson describe it, that general requirement has resulted rhetorically in an address that includes "(1) public meditations on values, (2) assessments of information and issues, and (3) policy recommendations," structurally organized to link those three processes into an essay (54). The third new genre, the inaugural address, derives from the Constitution only as an extension of the oath of office. It becomes established as a genre because it helps construct a recurring rhetorical situation, a "specific kind of ceremony and occasion," a "rite of passage, of investiture" (33). Each genre, then, develops in response to the functional needs of the recurring rhetorical situations presidents face, but only the inaugural address emerges gradually from evolving functions over time. The veto message and state of the union address are genres that result first from mandate, a mandate that is itself, of course, the result of situational and cultural changes. Interestingly, "recurrence" in these created and mandated genres at first exists only as projected onto future presidents and their expected actions. Although their original creation and identification might have come from mandate, the other part of genre origination—not just the naming but also the development of rhetorical strategies to serve the nexus of contexts—evolves later, as individuals create instances that become precedents for later presidents (to be discussed more fully later in this chapter). The recurrence necessary for genres may be dictated in the Constitution but must still be constructed by individuals through repeated use.

These new presidential genres have antecedent genres, but not always effective ones. Campbell and Jamieson cite the broader genre of epideictic discourse as the general antecedent of the previously nonexistent inaugural address. The first state of the union addresses are less successful in their choice of antecedent. As noted previously, Jamieson in an early study (1975) examines the origin of state of the union addresses and papal encyclicals and finds that "[a]ntecedent genres are capable of imposing powerful constraints" on new genres developing in response to "unprecedented situations" ("Antecedent" 414). The power of antecedent genres to shape new discourse is so powerful that Jamieson concludes, "[I]t is sometimes rhetorical genres and not rhetorical situations that are decisively formative" (406). In these cases, she found that the antecedent genres chosen were not appropriate to the situation, imposing severe constraints and making it difficult for future rhetors to break with the inappropriate tradition. The first presidents had to create their own state of the union addresses in a context of genres as well as situation and culture that moved them toward ineffective rhetorical choices, creating ineffective antecedent texts for later presidents. A key difference between this case and that of business genres appears to be the sudden origin of the genre and its construction by such a few individuals (a circumstance I will discuss further below). Such a situation depends heavily on the first rhetor to choose antecedents wisely. From these two cases—business and presidential genres—it seems that new genres are clearly grounded in old genres as well as in rhetorical situations and cultural contexts, but when new genres develop abruptly they may derive more from the context of genres than from the context of situation.

A third case demonstrates that genres can be consciously created, as were the presidential genres, and yet develop their generic qualities gradually, as did the business genres. What is most unusual about the third case, though, is its function: to constitute a genre set. The third case I will examine in this chapter is the creation of the modes. The modes represent a different kind of genre than I have been considering up to now, for the modes were genres created by analysts to serve the situational and community needs of analysts. Like the presidential genres, the modes were mandated by one group to be written by others—students, in the case of the modes. Together, the modes constitute a genre set, a set of genres that analysts within a community have agreed serves a function (to categorize discourse), but they were created consciously and deliberately over time and their function is to be genres.

The specific set of genres that became what we call the modes were created over time as analysts tried different possibilities for classifying discourse. The history of the modes has been described by Connors ("Rise"), Kitzhaber, and d'Angelo. The first sets were based less on antecedent genres than on philosophical principles and ideas. George Campbell in 1776 created a set of types of discourse based on faculty psychology, a set of four types with each one designed to represent one of the four faculties: ones that "enlightened the understanding, pleased the imagination, moved the passions, influenced the will" (Kitzhaber 121). In 1827, Samuel Newman based his related genre set on "the object, which the writer has primarily and principally in view" (qtd. in Kitzhaber 122), and his set consists of didactic, persuasive, argumentative, descriptive, and narrative. With these invented genre sets now serving as antecedents, other analysts tried other sets: adding the pathetic to Newman's set; explanation, argument, excitation, and persuasion; description, narration, argument, exposition, and speculation; even description, narration, letters, essays, dissertations, orations, arguments, and poetry (Kitzhaber 123). Several genre sets were proposed between 1825 and 1875. In 1866, Alexander Bain proposed a set of five genres: description, narration, exposition, persuasion, and poetry (Kitzhaber 119–20). Four of those were popularized—primarily by Genung, according to Connors ("Rise" 447)—and by 1895 the modes of description, narration, exposition, and persuasion had won out as the genre set used by analysts and teachers alike.

The function of this created genre set was to provide a set of genres that suited the rhetorical abstractions of the time and that was easily taught. Frank d'Angelo argues that the modes were developed to simplify and organize the many kinds of discourse that were described in the nineteenth century. In the textbooks of the time, prose classifications required extended lists of types: for just one example, letters (including letters of business, official letters, letters of friendship, letters of condolence, letters of congratulations, and letters of introduction), narratives, fiction, essays (including editorials, reviews, treatises, tracts, dissertations, and disquisitions), theses, and orations (d'Angelo 32). To the rhetoricians and teachers of the time, the set of four modes offered a neater and more practical classification. Kitzhaber writes,

> The reasons why the four forms became so popular toward 1900 and after were concerned chiefly with the narrowing of rhetorical theory and its increasing rigidity. . . . the prevailing tone of rhetorical theory throughout the nineteenth century had been abstract and almost purely academic. . . . Such convenient abstractions as Unity-Coherence-Emphasis and the forms of discourse were ideally suited to the purposes of instruction in a subject that had been cut off from all vital relations with other subjects in the curriculum and, in a sense, from life itself. They demanded no change in traditional habits of thought, they were few and easily remembered, and if one did not look at them too critically they had an apparent plausibility. (138)

As an invented genre set, the modes had only to serve the needs of those who created them. Since the community of rhetoricians and teachers of rhetoric needed a simpler classification system, the modes served their needs well for a time. The needs of writers outside the classroom were not the central concern. As contexts change over time, Connors most forcefully argues, the modes will fall out of favor, but the rhetoricians and teachers of rhetoric at the time created a genre set that served well the particular nexus of situational, cultural, and generic contexts in which they operated ("Rise").

In all of the three cases outlined here, we can reconstruct a nexus of contexts that the newly created genres operate within. Writers of new genres draw from the existing context of genres, adapting existing genres more or less successfully to new situations. New genres fill gaps in genre repertoires, fulfill new functions of a group, reflect new relationships among participants, and otherwise adapt to the changing needs of the changing people who use them. Some genres are in fact created deliberately and consciously, rather than emerging gradually. Their successful development depends in part on the successful selection of antecedents, but it depends also on the lucky combination of contexts and individuals, as discussion of these same cases in the next section will illustrate.

Contextual Changes and Genre Adaptations

Looking beyond and behind antecedent genres, we can see the history of genres in the individuals, society, and culture that use them. Obversely, we can also see the history of the culture in the genres it uses, for genres can act as a kind of tree ring, with generic changes revealing cultural changes.[3] As Kress argues and as the cases considered below support, genres change as their social and institutional contexts change. Depending on circumstances and our perspective, contextual changes can result in new genres developing, discussed in the previous section, or in old genres developing new qualities. Using Bitzerian demand-response language, Campbell and Jamieson emphasize how genres change in response to new cultural and rhetorical purposes:

> A given type persists only so long as it remains a functional response to exigencies. In effect, any rhetorical type is constantly under pressure, and as conditions or purposes change, and as rhetorical action establishes new precedents, advocates alter and expand existing genres or develop substitute forms better suited to achieve their ends. (*Deeds* 104)

As societies and institutions develop new functions, new genres will be needed, as described in the previous section. These contextual factors will also put pressure on existing genres, on the context of genres that I argued in chapter 1 is reciprocally constructed with situational and cultural contexts. In the cases discussed below, existing genres are influenced by such various social events as government regulations, train accidents, assassinations, and article and textbook publications. The details in each case vary enormously, leaving us with a most general principle: Genres change as their situational and cultural contexts change.

In the case of presidential genres, once the presidential genres are established and their traits conventionalized, the existing genre may serve as a constraint on future instances of that genre, but the genre can still change. The established presidential genres change in response to changes in their context, as Campbell and Jamieson note above. The extended example they discuss is the change in the genre of war rhetoric, which had to adapt to changes in its primary purposes and in the relationships of its primary participants. They define war rhetoric as the discourse justifying the United States' involvement or continued involvement in hostilities (drawing on the language of the War Powers Resolution of 1973) (*Deeds* 101). Originally, the genre developed out of the constitutional specification that Congress has the power to declare war, while the president is commander in chief, with the result that the president cannot declare war himself but must ask Congress to perform that act. Early war rhetoric, therefore, by Madison, Wilson, and McKinley, solemnly requested that Congress consider declaring war. That genre changed, however, as the relationship between the president and Congress changed. As presidents assumed more and more military power and assumed the power to declare war without Congress's prior authorization, the genre of war rhetoric changed from seeking authorization to seeking advice and consent. "As a result, what began as a genre based on reciprocity and cooperation has become a genre crafted to compel congressional approval as well as public support of unilateral executive action," according to Campbell and Jamieson (*Deeds* 118). That change in the cultural and situational context of war rhetoric resulted in change in the genre, particularly in its lines of reasoning and its argumentative warrants. The existing genre adapted to the new relationships and purposes.

This adaptation of existing genres to new contexts appears also in the case of business communication, but the case also emphasizes the role genres play to reinforce context as well as reflect it. The massive changes in American business that Yates describes did require the development of new genres, as discussed in the previous section, thus creating a new context of genres. But existing genres also adapted to the changing contexts of culture and situation. These changes in both new and old genres combine to constitute a new genre repertoire for American business, a repertoire that both reflects and reinforces business's new ideology.

All of the companies examined, according to Yates, changed their internal genre repertoire from an ad hoc oral set of genres to a formal and complex internal communication system, reflecting and revealing the significant changes in the ideology of business that Yates describes. Both the reliance on mandated systems and the upper-level monitoring of lower levels required communication, communication that was both more formal than and of a different kind from what had been usual with ad hoc management. Yates writes,

> Systematic management as it evolved in the late nineteenth and early twentieth centuries was built on an infrastructure of formal communication flows: impersonal policies, procedures, processes, and orders flowed down the hierarchy; information to serve as the basis for analysis and evaluation flowed up the hierarchy; and documentation to coordinate processes crossed the hierarchy. These flows of documents were primary mechanisms of managerial control. (20)

From these new communication demands developed a new communication system. New genres developed to fulfill new functions, and old genres changed to suit their new uses. That genre repertoire (or formal communication system, as Yates frequently calls it) was used to weave the various strands of a company together and, most significantly, to implement its management system and hence reinforce its ideology. While the new genres resulted from this ideological change, the genre repertoire that developed served in turn as a primary tool for managerial control. Reflecting the new cultural context, the new ideology of business, the resulting genre repertoire emphasized information and analysis and placed the system over the individual, the impersonal over the personal.

In this new business climate, existing genres changed. Previously recognized genres, especially reports and memoranda, changed in their purposes and in how and where they were used as well as in their form and style. The purpose of both the report and the memorandum shifted during this period in subtle but significant ways (Yates, chap. 3). Reports had existed before the late nineteenth century (though in form they were not distinct from letters) as sales agents' reports, military reports, and managers' reports to owners (77). With the advent of systematic management, however, reports were used not just to describe information but also to analyze. Where circular letters and manuals were essential to the first principle of systematic management—"a reliance on systems mandated by top management rather than on individuals"—reports were essential to the second principle—"the need for each level of management to monitor and evaluate performance at lower levels" (10). Reports became the main source of data that flowed upward to managers. They had to provide more and different kinds of information than they had provided previously, and over time they increasingly performed some initial analysis of that information. Their change in purpose, therefore, was from descriptive to analytic.

Memoranda also changed in purpose during this period. Before the late nineteenth century, internal correspondence was used to communicate across distances. What developed in the late nineteenth and early twentieth centuries was the use of internal correspondence within a facility, when distance did not make oral communication difficult. That change in the place of the memo genre reflects changes in the purposes of memoranda. Rather than simply providing internal information across distances, the memorandum was serving to document managers' positions and department activity, thereby serving as part of the company's memory. Managers began writing notes to others within the company to record what they had discussed orally, what they had done within their department, or positions they wished to assert. Company growth and systematization had led indirectly to managers feeling the need to "put it in writing." The memorandum evolved to serve that purpose.

Changes in purpose, one major part of the situation, account for changes in many existing genres, but other elements of situation also result in generic changes, and one situational change often leads to another. Genres changed in where they were used—for example, memoranda being used within a facility—and in the participants being asked to produce them—more managers and foremen were being asked to write reports and were voluntarily producing memoranda. As more people produced and requested them and as the system more often required them, the genres of memoranda and report changed necessarily in their frequency of use. More memoranda and reports were being written than ever before, a fact which surely led to some of the changes in form to be described below. As more documents were produced more often, the technology of filing systems developed to handle the paper load; and as the filing systems became more sophisticated, documents became more accessible and hence more documents were produced. The filing systems enabled another kind of generic change, a change in how the genres were being handled and later used, an important aspect of the genre set's intertextuality. Entire filing systems were established in order to make documents more accessible, enabling memoranda and reports to be kept for later reference (and, of course, encouraging the proliferation of memoranda). Because they were more accessible, the genres were used for reference in ways that had not been practical previously. Together, all of the genres, new and old, were gathered into the massive filing systems and constituted a corporate memory, a genre set comparable to that developed by tax accountants today and discussed in the previous chapter.

Necessarily related to these changes in genres' purposes, places, participants, frequency, and later use are what most visibly reveal changes in situations: changes in the genres' forms and style. Yates details the many changes in the form and style of these American business genres (particularly in chapter 3). Here I will take from her rich study just a few to illustrate the kinds of changes that occurred as their situations and culture changed. Many genres, both old and new, changed in layout during this period. Reports and memoranda both began as letters in form but gradually dropped the salutations and addresses in favor of headings and standardized blanks. As the circular letter evolved, it too changed in format from a letter with salutation to a heading. Reports began to incorporate graphs as well as tables into their bodies. Even such details as the size and type of paper to be used changed in different genres during this period, and the company manual developed from a bound set of pages to a loose-leaf notebook that could change one page at a time as the rules changed. The internal organization of these genres must surely have evolved as their purposes and desire for efficiency evolved. The one Yates discusses in detail is the organization of the report. Two basic report organizations competed and eventually coexisted during this period: one that emphasized facts first, then conclusions; and the other that specified the conclusions first, followed by the facts (92–93).

The style changes that occurred in these genres were ones in keeping with systematic management: they were designed to increase precision and efficiency. Discussion of the circular letter specified that the letters must aim for clarity and precision most of all, "to guarantee uniform compliance" (71). Clarity and precision were the stylistic requirements of most of the genres designed to carry out the corporate system, not only circular letters but also manuals, forms, memoranda, and reports. The memorandum and report, deriving from the letter genre, also shifted style over time in another interesting way. In the interest of efficiency, both genres dropped the polite style of the external letter, with not only its polite salutations and signatures but also its use of politeness in requests and indirect statements. Yates writes of the memo, "While custom and courtesy restricted the form and style of external letters, internal correspondence evolved in ways intended to make it more functional to read and to handle" (95). The style of memoranda and reports became impersonal, direct, matter-of-fact, rather than personal, courteous, or cordial. Those amenities did not matter in the new cultural system of efficiency.

Style and form, as the traces of genre, reflected the major cultural changes of the time, as did the entire genre repertoire in Yates's detailed study. These cases also delineate some of the situational changes that affected genres, most notably changes in purpose but also changes in participants and manner of use. Cultural changes appear to affect not only the situations of particular genres but the context of genres as a whole, as they did in creating new presidential genres and in changing business genres from an ad hoc communication set to a formalized communication system. The genre repertoire of a group can change in composition (adding new genres) and in generic interaction (as genres adapt to fulfill different functions for the community).

Even when change in a single genre is considered, its interactions with other genres prove critical to how it will adapt to change, as suggested in studies of another case, the school theme. The status of the theme as a genre is, of course, open to dispute. I will discuss its status and changing nature below when I consider the flexibility and stability of genres. For now, I will justify my treating it as a genre by noting that school teachers continue to use the label "theme" to categorize texts written in school for the purpose of practicing and displaying writing skills. The texts composed in school to practice writing, what I will now call themes, changed in character and scope in the late nineteenth and early twentieth centuries in conjunction with cultural changes in universities. But the history of the theme is a history of its interaction with other genres; the history of the individual genre is still a history of a context of genres.

The theme might have developed a quite different character had the forensic system won out as the model for university writing. According to histories of composition, universities in the late nineteenth century shifted from a liberal curriculum to a more specialized curriculum with electives. According to David Russell, in his extensive study *Writing in the Academic Disciplines, 1870–1990* (esp. 51–64), the system of rhetoricals transformed into the forensic system. The forensic system consisted of a series of college-wide writing requirements, not limited to a particular writing course. Harvard required sophomores to write a theme every four weeks, juniors to write one every three weeks, and seniors to write four forensics (argumentative themes) (52). Columbia College, from 1865 to 1870, attached the college-wide writing requirements to particular courses, requiring freshmen to write monthly compositions in a rhetoric course, sophomores to write monthly compositions in a historical course, juniors to write monthly original declamations in a literature course, and seniors to write weekly philosophical essays in a moral philosophy course (57). Increasing specialization was leading toward more specialized writing requirements—and genres—in particular classes, not the general exhibition rhetorical or theme but the particularized lab report or literary analysis. The cultural emphasis on specialization was leading to a context of specialized genres.

By 1920, however, the forensic system was largely discarded, leaving required courses in rhetoric and composition to assign the practice and display of writing skills in themes. The theme became a genre of one writing course, with its particular situation. The history of the writing class is by now well known (Kitzhaber, Berlin). By 1900–1920, according to Berlin, the required yearlong writing course was "nearly ubiquitous" (55). What was assigned in those writing classes to practice writing skills is what interests me here. In a 1926 survey described by Berlin, students wrote in the average freshman composition course four pages each week, just under two short themes and two longer themes each semester (61). In a 1940 survey, the median requirement was twelve shorter themes and one longer theme each semester (65). Some particular examples illustrate how often students were asked to demonstrate their writing skills. At Harvard around 1900, students wrote daily themes, six each week, and they wrote six longer themes in each semester (37–38). In the 1920s, Harvard students wrote approximately four themes each week and occasional longer themes (68). The average student at Syracuse University in the 1920s wrote a weekly out-of-class theme, a weekly in-class theme, and a longer "research paper" (66). The theme, then, was a common and frequently written genre at least through 1940 and had become defined as a text written to practice and display skills in a writing class.

Changes in the theme at the turn of the century can illustrate how genres can act as the metaphorical tree rings I characterized earlier—signs that some cultural change must have occurred that merits investigation. As has been well documented by Kitzhaber and Connors ("Personal"), the topics of themes and their subtypes changed from the nineteenth century to the twentieth. Teachers shifted from assigning themes with abstract topics to personal topics, and then some began assigning different subgenres in reaction against the personal emphasis. An 1850 composition textbook listed such topics as curiosity; nature; the religious institutions of Egypt, Greece, and Rome; Byron and Ezekiel; and "On the Comparative Prevalence and Strength of the Principle of Loyalty and Independence in Man" (Kitzhaber 59). Topics common from 1850–1880 include "Evanescence of Pleasure"; "Paul at Athens"; "Youth, Mammon,

and Old Age"; and "The Dice of the Gods Are Loaded" (Kitzhaber 104).
The shift to personal topics, according to Kitzhaber and Connors, occurred from the 1890s on. Connors attributes the shift from impersonal
to personal subjects in the freshman theme to the changes in educational
culture that produced students who knew little but their own experience.

> "Write what you know," has been perhaps the most common
> advice given to writers, and the movement toward personal
> writing assignments has been the inevitable result of taking
> the dictum seriously within a culture whose educational in-
> stitutions give most of their clients only a shallow knowledge
> across a broad range of fields. The natural subject to turn
> to—the only subject about which most students know more
> than a few threadbare (or misremembered) facts—is personal
> experience. ("Personal" 179)

Whereas the earlier educational and general culture had emphasized the
liberal curriculum and encouraged teachers to emphasize knowledge of
what great writers and thinkers had said, in such forms as the keeping
of commonplace books, the new culture of specialization and separation of fields (according to Russell's argument) encouraged asking for
more disconnected knowledge of disparate areas. One result was the shift
to personal topics in general writing classes, a major change in the substance of the theme genre.

A related result was the breaking off from the theme of specialized
genres, such as the research paper, lab report, and literary analysis. The
change in the theme was again related to changes in the entire context
of genres in schools. The earliest themes (or rhetoricals) included what
would become the modes (to be discussed at greater length later) but also
narrower subtypes of discourse: Blair, in 1783, for example, grouped
prose compositions into historical, philosophical, epistolary, and ficti-
tious writing (Kitzhaber 51). By 1900 to 1920, teachers and textbooks
used the modes as the dominant subtypes of themes, but they also used
other subtypes. In Fred Newton Scott's program in 1903, teachers taught
the modes in the first two writing courses but new courses had been
added in literary interpretation, newspaper writing, and reviews (Kitzhaber 70). A 1924 text, *Writing by Types,* by Albert Baugh and others,
included the types critical essay, feature article, editorial, after-dinner
speech, and other "practical" writing tasks (Berlin 70–71). Increasingly
in the twentieth century, educators were using more specific types of
writing in more specialized courses that were attached to the purposes

of particular fields. The research paper appeared as a genre distinct from the theme from about 1920 on. According to Russell, the research paper responded to the new German "research ideal" of the American universities (*Writing* 71–74). According to Connors's similar view, teachers used the research paper to react against personal themes in an effort to develop knowledge from which students could write:

> The whole idea of a specific "research" paper would have been without meaning in 1880, of course, because prior to the reign of personal writing, teachers naturally assumed that students had no choice but to write something transmitted and synthesized from their reading. ("Personal" 178–79)

Creative writing, journalism, technical writing, business writing, all developed into identified separate school genres by the 1950s (Connors, "Rhetoric . . . 1850 to the Present" 62–63). As these genres and others (Russell discusses the essay examination and the lab report, for example) split into genres separate from the theme, the texts written in the writing class were left with a narrower range of possibilities. Connors argues that this factor and others in the educational culture led to composition's being left with nothing but expository writing ("Rhetoric . . . 1850 to the Present" 62–63).

The resulting freshman theme may deserve Kitzhaber's condemnation of a genre void of purpose or audience, for the separation of specialized fields left freshman writing with only generalized purposes and audiences. The scope of the freshman theme narrowed considerably as parts of it were subdivided into separate genres. The shift in culture and student knowledge left students with no knowledge base from which to write. While fulfilling the same function of allowing students to practice and display writing skills, the freshman theme was shifted as a genre from abstract discourses embedded in a liberal education to (dysfunctional?) personal or expository themes embedded in a specialized world. It is in the context of genres that the narrowness and vacuity of the theme genre appears most clearly, and it is the changes in the context of genres that largely led teachers to shape the theme into such a genre.

The contexts of genre, culture, and situation all interact in shaping the theme, as they did in shaping the business and presidential genres. Cultural changes create different situations, which create different actions, which create different genres and therefore different genre repertoires. The creation of different genre repertoires also enables different situations, which further spread emerging cultural changes. The reciprocal interaction of genres and their contexts appears clearly in these cases of genres changing. Such sweeping histories may illustrate contextual forces but may overlook finer distinctions in how a genre has changed and how contextual factors influence those changes. In fact, a closer look at our most detailed studies, of the genres of American presidential and business rhetoric, reveals significant nuances and suggests that generic change, like all change, is effected by individuals making decisions and acting within those changing contexts.

Contextual Distinctions and Individual Choices

Contextual changes do not necessarily sweep simultaneously through all situations. Some genres are created at a precise moment in time, as the constitutional presidential genres were, but even they bring to a head cultural and situational changes that had been building over time. In her examination of business communication, Yates demonstrates that people in local situations responded to the changes in different ways and at different rates. Examining the details of cases Yates considers, as well as the presidential genres, reveals the important influence not only of context but of particular individuals' actions. The cases discussed below also reveal another general principle: Genres change as individuals encourage or inhibit their change. The individuals may not intentionally be affecting the genres; they may not even be aware that their actions have any effect on the genres. In some cases, the individuals pursue a philosophy or a system that leads to generic change. In other cases, an individual may adapt a genre to suit his or her personality or personal philosophy. In still other cases, individuals may popularize social changes that lead to generic changes. In all of these cases, individuals have an identifiable effect on the origination of or historical changes in a genre.

Yates's study of business communication argues for the impact of individual influence, but it also demonstrates that individual influence works only when local situations combine with cultural context and individual initiative. The cases of business genres, in fact, develop at least a little bit differently in different companies. As Yates demonstrates, the general outline of changes in business communication must be elaborated with the details of specific companies and their communication systems. Yates examines three cases in detail: the Illinois Central Railroad, Scovill Manufacturing Company, and DuPont manufacturing. Rather than repeat Yates's history of each company here, I will use the details of each company to note how local and especially individual factors affected the history of the business communication genres.

The railroads were the first industry to develop a formal internal communication system, or genre set, and they did so in part because of contextual factors particular to the railroad industry (Yates 4–9). Those pressures were felt by individual railroads, including the one Yates studied in detail, the Illinois Central Railroad (Yates, chap. 4 and 5). Before 1887, however, the Illinois Central only very slowly developed systematic internal communication. Two events occurred in 1887 that pushed for substantial changes in Illinois Central's genre set, one event involving the cultural context and the other involving an individual. That year, the Interstate Commerce Act was passed, an act requiring extensive federal reporting of company information, and Stuyvesant Fish became president of the Illinois Central Railroad. Under Fish's leadership and under pressure from the Interstate Commerce Commission, the Illinois Central rapidly developed more precise internal reports and more reports, more forms, various manuals, and a generally complex internal communication system. One individual, Fish, clearly played an important role in making these management and genre changes, in consort with contextual forces. Similarly, the case of DuPont illustrates the impact of individuals on genre change (Yates, chap. 7 and 8). With a conservative head of the company, Eugene du Pont, the company's headquarters and main plant tended not to adopt innovations in technology and management methods. When du Pont died in 1902, however, the company was taken over by a team of three young du Ponts, who brought with them managers and ideas from more innovative companies. The new management team produced rapid and extensive change, adopting new technology and formal communication systems. Necessary genres developed quickly, including minutes and reports, manuals and circulars. By 1920, just eighteen years later, DuPont "was coordinated and controlled by a web of communication" (270). In the cases of both companies, the contextual factors encouraged change, but it appears to have taken the actions of powerful individuals to enact that change.

Yet not all individuals can have such effects on generic changes. One man at Illinois Central, a general manager, resisted the generic changes and managed only to lose his job. At another company, Scovill Manufacturing Company, slow change resulted even with a powerful supporter behind that change, as Yates recounts (Yates, chap. 6). The internal communication systems in manufacturing generally developed more slowly than those in railroads, but even so the changes at Scovill were slow and gradual. The company relied largely on oral communication from its beginnings in 1802 to 1900, in spite of the cultural factors of growth, new technologies, and systematic management philosophy and in spite of the individual factor of a manager who encouraged written communication from 1868 on. From 1900 to 1920, changes in the communication system finally accelerated, encouraged by rapid wartime growth, a manager, and eventually a statistician who actively pursued the goals of systematic management. Although generic change accelerated at Scovill in the first decades of the twentieth century and although contextual factors and individuals consistently encouraged change, Scovill's development of a complex, formal internal communication system came only gradually and slowly. Apparently but not surprisingly, generic change is not predictable, even when the "right" combination of context and individual combine. Inhibiting forces must exist alongside encouraging forces.

From all three cases, Yates draws some conclusions about the importance of different contextual and individual factors in effecting change in the internal communication systems (271–74). She concludes that such important contextual forces as growth, technology, and geographical dispersion encouraged but did not guarantee change. Finally, Yates concludes, "In all three cases, the single factor most immediately related to the emergence of communication as a managerial tool was the intervention of a strong manager championing the new theories" (273). Yates argues that the reason individuals were so essential is that the changes met opposition (because of costs and reduced importance of the individual), and it took strong individuals to overcome opposition. I would note, though, that some of those individuals championing the changes were not effective at first. And remember that some individuals resisting such changes were effective (such as Eugene du Pont) and some ineffective (Illinois Central's general manager). Power seems to be the most important requirement for an effective individual, but apparently even with power (in Scovill's case, for example), other contextual factors enter in. Perhaps generic change would always meet resistance, not just because of specific contextual factors such as dehumanizing systematization but because of human inertia and comfort with the status quo. Perhaps, then, it takes the "right" individual in the "right" local situation at a time of "right" contextual pressures for genres to change rapidly and thoroughly, while slow and gradual change, with resistance all the way, would be the more expected process of generic change.

Yet every genre tells a different story, and the presidential genres tell another tale of how individuals influence generic change. Rather than depending on the happily "right" combination of people and circumstances, the case of presidential genres suggests that some genres—perhaps those written by only a relatively few people and recurring relatively rarely—may change in ways more directly traceable to the actions of individuals.

The presidential genres may have originated in constitutional mandate and antecedent genres, but their development as recognizable genres with established conventions and expectations derive from another process: presidents being influenced by previous instances of a genre—that is, by how their predecessors acted within a similar situation. Washington was known to be conscious of how his every action set a precedent for future presidents, and that consciousness surely extended from deciding whether to shake hands to deciding how to instantiate a new type of discourse. Campbell and Jamieson assert that presidents tend to study past inaugural addresses before writing their own, for example (*Deeds* 33). The veto message was used only sporadically by early presidents, for another example, but James Madison's veto messages "initiated a pattern that persists into the present" and his lines of argument "were treated as precedents by his successors" (83). Especially for the early presidents as the presidential genres originated and evolved, previous presidents' rhetorical actions in similar rhetorical situations must have constituted a heavy precedent.

Perhaps as a result of that attention to what individuals before had done, one individual's choices to vary from precedent can also have persistent effect on a presidential genre. State of the union addresses were delivered orally at first, for example, but Thomas Jefferson, who was "a diffident speaker committed to reducing the pomp and ceremony of the presidency," changed all that by sending his in writing (52). Presidents after Jefferson sent their addresses in writing, until Woodrow Wilson, who delivered his address orally "in part because he believed that oral delivery created a climate conducive to cooperation" (66). Earlier presidents had desired cooperation with Congress; that contextual factor was not unique to Wilson. But his individual choice made a difference in the genre from then on. Later presidents varied, sometimes delivering the state of the union address orally, sometimes sending it written.

Two more recent examples from Campbell and Jamieson can illustrate the individual's power to change the genre in more significant ways. Ronald Reagan varied from the conventional substance of the state of the union address by emphasizing its ceremonial function and offering very little in specific legislative proposals. That shift in the address reflected the type of presidency and relationship with Congress that Reagan would establish (as well as responding to the contextual change of media-shortened attention spans) (70). To the extent that Reagan was effective (judged by popularity ratings, by legislative accomplishments, or by history), his concentration on the ceremonial function of the genre rather than on its additional function of legislative leadership may serve as a precedent to future presidents.

Ineffective choices may serve as a precedent in the opposite way, defining what one should not do in a genre. Gerald Ford has provided a model, in Campbell and Jamieson's opinion, of what not to do in a pardon. Ford's pardon of Nixon violated several of the necessary traits of the pardon genre, according to Campbell and Jamieson's analysis. The very "ineptitude of Ford's rhetorical act," in fact, proves the necessity of the generic traits they discovered (190). Because Ford used the pardon genre so ineffectively, his pardon will likely serve as a precedent not only to steer future pardoners away from his strategies but also to limit the use of the genre in general (190).

The presidents, perhaps because of their very rarity and the infrequency of their genres, can have significant individual impact on the genres they use. Although the power of the individual president to effect generic change may appear to be similar to the power of individual managers in Yates's study, as both are positions of leadership, I suspect that the president's generic power comes from a different source. There are many managers at any given time and many new managers learning the genres every day, but there is only one president every four years (barring deaths and resignations). There are few enough presidents for school children to learn them by heart. Each individual president, therefore, has considerably more impact on the genre (as well as on the institution) than the typical user of a genre who is one among many.

Finally, individuals may affect genres indirectly by having an impact on cultural context. Histories of ideas, for example, often trace individual influence on an idea that shapes a genre. The school theme and modes provide simple and quick examples. Scholars have frequently pointed to such individuals as Alexander Bain, Fred Newton Scott, and John Genung, among many others, as influencing the nature of first-year writing and its theme. And of course, individuals had a significant impact on the development of the mode genres, from their initial creation by Campbell and Bain to their promulgation by particular textbook authors ever since. Even a contemporary scholar, Robert Connors, could be described as an individual who had a significant impact on the development of the modes: his article "The Rise and Fall of the Modes of

Discourse" may have contributed to the slow decline (and near death?) of the mode genres.

In hindsight, it seems unsurprising that both contextual factors and individual influence appear to be necessary for many of the generic developments considered in this chapter. Yet some genre scholarship tends to emphasize social and cultural forces at work in change while others tend to emphasize the acts of significant individuals. It appears from these cases that neither may be sufficient in itself. Only detailed analysis after a generic change has occurred can tease out the various influences and pressures that might have led to a change, and other cases can be found where apparently similar factors contribute to different results. Contextual and individual forces clearly operate in conjunction with changes in genres, but their precise operation remains unclear. With genres as the nexus of so many interacting and reciprocal variables, I suspect that the history of genres will always be the history of individual genres. The multiple variations in contexts, local situations, and individuals may, even with more detailed study, lead always to the same conclusion: Every genre tells a different story, but a story with significant characters, events, and endings.

Flexibility and Stability

What makes genres functional in the midst of contextual changes and individual choices is their ability to balance both flexibility and stability. American business genres, along with new genres that developed, were flexible enough to adapt to major cultural changes. The case of presidential genres, in particular, exemplifies the importance of generic stability as well as the flexibility already so evident. The genres of theme and modes, on the other hand, have not achieved such a successful balance.

Campbell and Jamieson detail instance after instance of an individual president using a genre effectively or ineffectively, thereby demonstrating how flexible genres are. Presidential genres can clearly be changed by an individual's successes or failures. The genres themselves have never become so formulaic that there is not room for individual variation. The presidential genres adapt to particular historical circumstances and to individual political views. When Lyndon Johnson was sworn in as president after Kennedy's assassination, his inaugural address was incorporated within the genre of eulogy, a generic move chosen by other vice presidents ascending to the presidency (Campbell and Jamieson, *Deeds* chap. 3). The inaugural genre was flexible enough to accommodate the particular historical situation of each president. Each genre is also flexible enough to accommodate the philosophical differences of a James Madison and a

Jimmy Carter, of a Ronald Reagan and a William Clinton. As Campbell and Jamieson state, "The functions of each genre remain constant, but the rhetorical means through which these can be performed are variable" (216). The president decides "whether to issue discourse, when to issue discourse, and what strategies to employ in accomplishing an end" (217). The flexibility of the genres enables them to be shaped by the individual.

The flexibility of the presidential genres is balanced, though, by a generic stability. The genres must be flexible enough to bend to the individual president while maintaining the tradition of the institution of the presidency, for the presidential genres represent and constitute the institution of the presidency. As Campbell and Jamieson write, "The recurrence of recognizable forms of discourse in and of itself gives the presidency a sense of continuity and stability greater than that provided by the rhetoric of any single occupant" (214). Each genre "sustains the institution" (215) and creates "a coherent sense of the presidency" that "becomes part of the process through which presidents play their role as the symbolic, as well as real, head of state" (4–5). They further note, "The constitutive power of these genres creates a distinct identity for the presidency as an institution, while setting rhetorical boundaries for its occupants" (213). The genres must be recognizable and must maintain their identity to ensure that the institution of the presidency is maintained and that the individual's identity as president is secured. The result of this balancing act between generic stability and generic flexibility is a genre repertoire that enables individuality while fulfilling institutional needs. Campbell and Jamieson conclude:

> Functional, flexible genres serve to insulate the institution of the presidency from an Andrew Johnson, even as they sustain the initiatives of an Andrew Jackson or an Abraham Lincoln; they enable it to accommodate a Calvin Coolidge as well as a Franklin Roosevelt or a Woodrow Wilson. In sum, the institution of the presidency derives part of its coherence and its ability to survive from the constitutive power of its functional, flexible rhetorical genres. These forms of address enable individual presidents to adapt without undermining institutional stability, to speak both as individuals and as voices of an institution, and enable the less skillful to perform basic institutional functions while not impeding the great from eloquently transcending these formulas. (219)

Perhaps this balance between stability and flexibility is what all long-standing genres achieve. The relationship between the institution of the presidency and the few individuals who inhabit it may be unique, however. In such a strong institution with so few participants, the power of genres to maintain the tradition and the power of individuals to adapt and even change the genres may be exceptional. Although the case of business genres does not cover such a long historical period, the fact that so many of those genres persist today suggests that they, too, have remained flexible while supporting the institution of American business. Some balancing of stability and flexibility would seem to be necessary for genres to continue to function effectively.

Not all genres function effectively, though, and not all genres balance stability and flexibility effectively. The first-year theme may be a genre that was so flexible as to have no stable identity, while the modes may be a genre that became so stable as to have lost necessary flexibility.

The first-year theme is such an unstable genre that one might even question whether such a genre exists. Is there a type of text that is constructed by and helps construct a recurring rhetorical situation in the context of the first-year writing classroom? Is there a perceived type of discourse that sits at that nexus of the first-year writing class situation, the North American educational context, and the context of other, different school genres? Defined in terms of its recurrence in a common situational and cultural context, I believe the answer must be yes, but that genre has been flexible and has changed over time in dramatic ways as the culture has changed.[4]

Judged by the standard of whether a genre is recognized by its users, the theme meets the criteria of a genre. Teachers assign and students write the school theme, and many are eager to dissociate their favored kinds of writing (essays, literacy narratives) from it. But that rhetorical and social construct has also been called by different names in different contexts at different times. The term *theme* has been used at least since 1801, when John Walker in his *Teacher's Assistant* divided compositions into two types, themes and regular subjects. Themes, according to Walker, were argumentative texts and used a modified version of the classical *dispositio* (Connors, "Rhetoric . . . 1850 to the Present" 204). William Russell in 1823 extended the term *theme* to include explanatory as well as argumentative texts, and according to Connors, "[t]hus did the term become generalized, and all student papers have remained 'themes' up to the present" ("Rhetoric . . . 1850 to the Present" 205). According to Kitzhaber, the term was expanded in meaning one more time around 1900, when a theme became

> writing as an academic exercise to illustrate certain abstract
> principles or fulfill certain specifications imposed neither by
> the needs of the student nor by the requirements of the sub-
> ject or situation. It was writing in a social vacuum, with no
> motivation behind it except the necessity of handing in a
> theme. (223)

That may indeed be the meaning of "theme" to most teachers and students today.

The term was not without competition, however, even in the nineteenth century, and the inconstancy of reference may indicate an instability in the genre. When Harvard instituted its formal entrance requirement in English composition in 1874–75, it required each candidate "to
write a short English Composition" (qtd. in Kitzhaber 35), and the term
composition recurs repeatedly in descriptions of nineteenth-century
writing requirements.[5] Andrea Lunsford states that professors in Scottish universities debated whether to include "essay writing" in rhetoric
and composition classes, with essay writing defined as "a practice in
which a professor assigned general topics (such as 'solitude') and students amplified the topics as best they could" (435). Connors quotes an
1844 college-level textbook that called compositions "Essays" ("Rhetoric . . . 1850 to the Present" 206). Today, of course, the term *essay* is
loaded with multiple definitions. In a 1990 discussion of Kurt Spellmeyer's article on the essay in the academy, Susan Miller aligns the essay with freshman composition assignments, daily themes, and personal
essays, and she cites the essay as developing from collections of entries
from commonplace books, through Montaigne and published essays, to
the freshman essay. Spellmeyer, on the other hand, explicitly dissociates
the essay from common freshman composition assignments, and recent
scholarship on the essay as a genre increasingly limits the essay to something more particular than what students write in their writing classes.

Although the terms may vary, suggesting some lack of solidity, the
concept of a type of text that students write in writing class has persisted.
Defined in terms of its place in a context of genres, the theme is the
unmarked genre in writing classes, the one that is not a literacy narrative, letter to the editor, research paper, or other specialized genre, as
discussed previously. If we accept that the theme may be called by other
names, though, what gives the genre any constancy? How do we know
one when we see one? Its function in a setting might be one answer. It
gains some stability through its contexts, as a type of text written in

school in order to practice and demonstrate skill at composing.[6] Considering the theme from the perspective of its function in school, however, reveals even more flexibility and perhaps instability in the genre. It has persisted through a wide range of cultural views of education and writing pedagogy, but today's first-year theme ranges from the personal to the critical, from the narrative to the analytical, from the formulaic to the expressive. In terms of its function for a social group, the theme is often described as serving the needs of at least a part of the academic community, but the existence of an academic community itself has been called into question by a number of scholars. Russell, for example, argues that "today academia is a *discourse* community only in a context so broad as to have little meaning in terms of shared linguistic forms" (*Writing* 21). The specialized and field-divided group of academics may have long ago given up a common ideology, subject matter, and so on. If there is no academic community, if that social context itself lacks stability, it is no wonder that the first-year writing class, often seen as designed to teach genres that function for that community, is struggling to find an identity. If there is no common community, there are no common genres, and there is evidence that even the apparently similar genres such as the research paper or essay examination vary widely in the contexts of different academic disciplines. In such an amorphous nexus, with such vaguely constructed contexts, perhaps no genre could be effective. Perhaps as a result of the perpetual amorphousness of the first-year writing course, the theme has never quite achieved a balance of flexibility and stability. Either it has been so flexible as to disappear (perhaps the situation today) or so stable as to become petrified (as it may have done in the first half of the twentieth century).

In the users' struggle to balance flexibility and stability, the theme seems quite unlike the other genres considered in this chapter so far. Unlike the memorandum or the inaugural address, the freshman theme is called by different names, varies in subject matter and accepted styles, and can exist in different subtypes of discourse. The fluidity of this genre means that its history is less clearly defined. Compared with the other genres we have examined in this chapter, the theme has a less definite beginning (and end). Its historical relationship to other genres—especially the distinctions between it and other genres and its identity as a source for other genres—is also less well defined. Although not the focus of this chapter, the linguistic and textual traits of the freshman theme over time would also appear to be less easily identified than those of the other genres, even the highly individualized presidential genres. The primary thing that gives it credibility as a genre (apart from the fact that it has been labeled as such) is its identifiable recurrent contexts: composition done for a teacher audience in a North American college setting for the purpose of practicing and exhibiting composition skill in general ways not encompassed by more specialized genres.

Yet, in some ways, the theme may not be so unusual a genre. Although setting it apart from such flexible and stable professional and institutional genres as the memorandum or inaugural address, this instability may in fact make the theme more similar to other complex genres, perhaps even literary ones. Defining the novel, for example, tracing its origins, distinguishing it from the history of all other genres, and defining its linguistic and textual traits have all been tasks with which literary historians have struggled. Similarly for poetry. Perhaps the difficulty comes from the largeness of these genres; perhaps the generality of "novel," "poetry," or "theme" makes it necessarily a more fluid genre and one less easily pinned down, historically or otherwise. Or the difficulty may come from the long history of the genres, that they have taken so many forms in different cultural contexts over such a long time. Or from the widespread use of the genres, written and read by so many different people in different circumstances. Whatever the reason, it seems important to recognize that not all genres can be traced as neatly as the first two cases we examined. Although the contextual and individual influences are probably similar and the balancing act between flexibility and stability remains, the balance within the genre and among the genre, culture, and individual appears to be more complex in some large, long-standing genres than others. Some genres can be constantly developing and fluctuating as the cultural context fluctuates, with a resulting and potentially killing instability.

On the opposite end of the seesaw is a killing stability. The related school genres of the modes have proved to be so stable that they have become fixed and may not be adaptable to changing contexts. Since the modes were a genre constructed for scholarly and teacherly, rather than writerly, needs, the changes they must adapt to are changes in the critical and educational contexts. That is, the important influences are not ones that change the nature of "description" or "narration" but rather those that change the nature of the scholarly and educational endeavor that the modes serve. The flexibility and stability of the genre set over time must be sufficient to enable writing scholars to adapt their constructed set to the changing conditions of teaching and analyzing writing. What appears to have been true of the modes, however, is that they were not flexible enough to accommodate contextual models of writing. Kitzhaber condemns them not only for this rigidity but also and essentially for their createdness, for the fact that they were academic constructs rather than "naturally" occurring genres:

> The effect of the forms of discourse on rhetorical theory and practice has been bad. They represent an unrealistic view of the writing process, a view that assumes writing is done by formula and in a social vacuum. They turn the attention of both student and teacher toward an academic exercise instead of toward a meaningful act of communication in a social context. . . . [T]hey substitute mechanical for organic conceptions and therefore distort the nature of writing. Besides all this, they are an oversimplification, assuming that a composition consists of certain distinct ingredients that are, one might say, chemically pure, and that will be found to exist either in their pure state or in certain intentionally contrived combinations and proportions. (139)

As a constructed genre set, perhaps the modes were incapable of changing, of evolving to meet the changing needs of their community. As a constructed genre set, perhaps the modes were never sufficiently complex or fully realized textually to withstand change. Connors ("Rise") has given us an excellent exploration of the sources of the modes' demise, including contextual and individual factors that we have seen operating on other genres. The criticisms of Connors and Kitzhaber themselves have become influences on the demise of the modes, as the modes continue still in some conservative textbooks but are generally absent from scholars' classification systems. Whether because they were constructed or because they were poorly constructed, the modes have not been able to evolve into a functional genre set today.

At the end of his critique and indictment of the modes, Kitzhaber goes on to say, "Their [forms'/modes'] dominance, especially after 1900, had much to do with maintaining the stereotypical character of composition instruction for at least three decades" (139). The long and, in many eyes, destructive existence of the modes may have something to do with why scholars and teachers of writing today at times neglect genres. The modes were presented as a genre set, as a classification of discourse. That dominant genre set had been firmly attached to the current-traditional approach to writing. The only established, nonliterary genre set that many scholars of writing today have experienced is a schol-

arly, constructed one that "had much to do with maintaining the stereotypical character of composition instruction for at least three decades." It should be no great surprise that the modes have tainted the
whole enterprise of discourse classification for composition studies. Yet
the fact that the modes were a constructed genre set and were unrespon-
sive to context or to change should also suggest how new genre theory
differs from the modes. In the new genre theory, genres are dynamic
constructs evolving from use and context, helping to maintain the stability of a social group while flexibly enabling individuals to adapt to
its changing circumstances.

Genres Shaping History

The genres examined in this chapter give life and depth to that general
claim. Each demonstrates the complexity of how genres respond to antecedents, to contextual forces, and to individual choices. This examination of the histories of genres confirms the position of genre at the
nexus of the individual and the social, as the mediator between individual
action and cultural context. It also confirms the reciprocal nature of
genre and its contexts, for the genres studied not only were shaped by
their contexts but also shaped those contexts. Implicit in all these studies is the role that genre played in reinforcing and constructing the very
contexts out of which the genres develop.

The case of business genres seems fairly clear. As systematic management began to rule business, new genres developed and old genres
adapted to fulfill new functions. The development of these new genres
then shapes the context of genres, establishing a new genre repertoire and
influencing future instances of that genre.[7] At the same time, the creation
and use of these genres shapes the cultural contexts by reinforcing systematic management practices. The policy manual establishes those policies
by giving them a grounding that seems objective and necessary. Circular letters and committee meetings promulgate the new expectations, dis-
seminating the new beliefs to levels in the organizations that might otherwise have continued old ways. As individuals strove to encourage new
ways, the genres served as tools for that encouragement. As individuals
worked to resist these changes, they had to work against the genres they
were using. Explaining opposition is easier one-on-one than in a committee meeting; deciding practice on the basis of individual circumstances
is easier when no policy manual exists to dictate a different practice.
Without those genres, the new ideology would have difficulty infiltrat-

ing all layers of business; with those genres, the new ideology spreads more quickly and efficiently and gains instantiation, a textual reality less easy to resist. The new ideology shapes the business genres; the business genres reinforce, instantiate, and promulgate the new ideology.

The power of genres to maintain contexts as well as shape them is evident in the cases of themes and modes. Once created and accepted into the schools, the modes have had tremendous staying power, appearing yet today in more traditional textbooks. As the modes have stayed, so have the views of discourse that they represent. As long as modes remain, people will be taught that discourse is categorizable into a limited number of distinct types, each with distinct organizing principles. The flexibility of discourse to adapt to local situations will be neglected in favor of rigid categories. Similarly, the continued existence of the theme helps to continue the existence of a separate composition course. Since such a kind of writing as the theme exists, with identifiable qualities of good writing, it seems more reasonable to isolate writing into a course designed to teach theme writing. Were there no theme separable from genres written for more discipline-specific purposes, the difficulty of teaching writing apart from specific content would be more visible. The contexts create the genres, and the genres maintain the contexts.

The presidential genres likewise maintain their contexts, but their formative role is also more visible. The genres called for by the Constitution embodied and constituted some of the roles of the new president, establishing his relationship with the legislature, his authority in times of war, his position as agenda setter for the nation. The new presidential genres simultaneously develop from the new contexts and construct those new contexts. The history of presidential genres confirms what was discussed in detail in the first chapters, the nature of genres as both constructed and constructing, as reciprocally enmeshed in their situation, culture, and generic contexts. From this historical perspective, genres appear to act on history as well as being acted upon.

Quotidian Genre Change

The cases so far examined have the benefit of covering a wide array of social groups, time periods, and types of change. They suggest the complexity of genre's relationship to historical antecedents, changing contexts, and individuals' choices. Yet what they tend to emphasize—or at least what I have drawn from them—has been the global and rhetorical changes in genres and the actions of significant historical individuals. The reality of change in genres resides also in the quotidian details, the actions of everyday people who even unconsciously and without purpose enact change. Although deviating sharply from the approach taken so far in this chapter—and risking trying my reader's patience with grammatical details and quantitative results—I think it is important to examine genre change also at a different level of detail, in the linguistic choices made every day by ordinary people.

To examine genre change at this detailed level, I will use two of my studies of language change in progress (published as *Standardizing Written English: Diffusion in the Case of Scotland, 1520–1659* and "Genre as Textual Variable: Some Historical Evidence from Scots and American English"). In one case, I examined how Scots writers shifted their usage in texts of different genres between 1520 and 1659. To check those results, I studied a second case, how writers used a newly developing standard in colonial American English texts between 1640 and 1810. Both cases enable me to look at change in genres at a different level and from a different perspective, and the results will elaborate our understanding of genres in history.

The study of Scots writers in the sixteenth and seventeenth centuries found that genre is a significant variable in language change. During this period and beyond, the usage of England (Anglo-English) was coming to dominate the usage of Scotland (Scots-English), with Anglo-English becoming increasingly common in the writing of Scots as well as English writers. This shift in written usage in Scotland reflected the reunification of Scotland and England and the shifting of power even within Scotland toward England. During this time, 1520–1659, the previously independent nations of Scotland and England were merging politically and socially, with England dominant. With the seat of political power and social status shifted from Scotland to England, the seat of linguistic power shifted as well. Linguistic forms that previously had been considered standard in Scotland were being replaced by linguistic forms considered standard in England. Thus, Scots writers were shifting from writing some standard Scots-English forms to Anglo-English forms.

The specific linguistic forms I studied were the inflectional ending on the present participle verb (the *-ing* in *calling*, in current English); the spelling of the negative particle (*no* and *not*); the spelling of the indefinite article (*a* and *an*); the preterite or "past tense" inflection (the *-ed* in *called*); and the spelling of the *wh-* relative pronouns (e.g., *who*). The Anglo-English forms that were replacing the Scots-English forms are listed below:

Anglo-English form	replacing	Scots-English form
present participle inflection *-ing*		*-and*
negative particle *no/not*		*na/nocht*
indefinite article *a* before consonants and *an* before vowels		*ane* before all environments
preterite inflection *-ed*		*-it*
relative pronouns spelled with *wh-*		*quh-*

To study how the use of these forms changed over time, I counted the number of occurrences of these five features in randomly selected thousand-word passages from 121 texts spread over different time periods.[8] I also spread these sample texts across five different genres, common in Scotland at the time: religious treatises, official correspondence, private records (primarily diaries), private correspondence, and national public records (such as the records of the Scots Privy Council).

Not surprisingly, my results showed that anglicization (the adoption of Anglo-English standards) increased over time. Table 4.1 compiles the data for all texts. It shows that the use of each Anglo-English linguistic feature became more frequent over time. The negative particle, for example, was spelled in the Anglo-English rather than Scots-English form only 5 percent of the time in the Scots texts of 1520–39 but 95 percent of the time in 1640–59. The other features show similar movement, from Anglo-English forms being used less often in 1520 to more often in 1640–

Table 4.1

Anglicization of Scots Texts: Percentages of Anglo-English Forms over Time

	1520–39	1540–59	1560–79	1580–99	1600–19	1620–39	1640–59
-ing	62	52	76	83	95	97	99
no/not	5	23	53	57	75	97	95
a/an	16	18	28	41	51	72	74
-ed	5	6	22	23	46	68	87
wh-	0	15	14	17	47	62	83

Source: Devitt, "Genre as Textual Variable."

59. By 1640–59, in fact, Anglo-English forms clearly dominated across the board. Anglicization as a process was largely completed.

Also not surprising was that anglicization increased over time in all of the genres. What surprised me at the time, though, was that it did not increase at the same rate and time in each of the genres. Instead, the usage in some genres anglicized relatively quickly while in other genres the process occurred much more slowly. Tables 4.2–4.6 summarize the data from this study for each of the genres separately. Usage in each genre clearly anglicizes over time. For example, the -ed preterite inflection is used 17 percent of the time in religious treatises of 1520–39 but appears 100 percent of the time in religious treatises of 1640–59. Similar results appear for each genre, increasing from 4 percent to 88 percent in official correspondence, from 43 percent to 100 percent in private records, from 6 percent to 83 percent in private correspondence, and from 0 to 62 percent in public records. But the difference across the genres within one time period is vast. In 1600–19, for example, the use of the Anglo-English -ed form ranges from 6 percent to 100 percent. And that difference in genres does not occur only in that one form or time period: use of the a and an spellings of the indefinite article range from 6 percent to 48 percent in 1560–79; use of the no and not spellings range from 0 to 47 percent in 1540–59; and use of the wh- spellings of the relative pronoun range from 25 percent to 100 percent in 1620–39. Even though the general process of anglicization over time is evident in each case, anglicization occurred at quite different rates in different genres.

To confirm that these differences were not random, I conducted statistical tests on these results.[9] The differences that these tables suggest are in fact statistically significant. As an independent variable in an analysis of variance, genre was significant at the .0001 level. That is, there is less than a one in ten thousand chance that the differences across genres occurred randomly or by accident. In fact, genre proved as highly significant a variable as the variable of date, which was also significant at

Table 4.2

Anglicization in Religious Treatises (in percentages)

	1520–39*	1540–59*	1560–79	1580–99	1600–19	1620–39	1640–59
-ing	83	13	80	92	100	100	100
no/not	24	0	79	95	100	100	100
a/an	63	29	48	63	96	100	100
-ed	17	0	50	73	100	100	100
wh-	0	0	50	66	100	100	100

Source: Devitt, "Genre as Textual Variable."
*Fewer than four passages were examined for these dates.

Table 4.3

Anglicization in Official Correspondence (in percentages)

	1520–39	1540–59	1560–79	1580–99	1600–19	1620–39	1640–59
-ing	58	50	80	76	96	98	100
no/not	0	40	38	43	67	93	100
a/an	6	13	42	57	39	92	87
-ed	4	12	13	23	75	97	88
wh-	0	24	3	14	75	87	93

Source: Devitt, "Genre as Textual Variable."

Table 4.4

Anglicization in Private Records (in percentages)

	1520–39*	1540–59*	1560–79*	1580–99*	1600–19	1620–39	1640–59
-ing	—	—	80	83	99	93	100
no/not	—	—	100	83	66	100	100
a/an	—	—	32	35	63	68	89
-ed	—	—	43	5	33	50	100
wh-	—	—	21	0	41	25	100

Source: Devitt, "Genre as Textual Variable."
*Fewer than four passages were examined for these dates.

Table 4.5

Anglicization in Private Correspondence (in percentages)

	1520–39*	1540–59	1560–79	1580–99	1600–19	1620–39	1640–59
-ing	—	85	72	85	95	100	100
no/not	—	47	7	30	65	92	100
a/an	—	40	6	12	33	51	63
-ed	—	6	6	5	17	68	83
wh-	—	3	0	0	8	68	70

Source: Devitt, "Genre as Textual Variable."
*Fewer than four passages were examined for these dates.

Table 4.6

Anglicization in Public Records (in percentages)

	1520–39	1540–59	1560–79	1580–99	1600–19	1620–39	1640–59
-ing	55	48	67	78	85	95	94
no/not	0	0	50	48	75	100	75
a/an	0	0	13	37	22	49	32
-ed	0	2	3	4	6	22	62
wh-	0	0	0	1	11	31	54

Source: Devitt, "Genre as Textual Variables."

the .0001 level. In other words, two texts from different genres will differ as significantly as two texts from different dates. The difference between usage in a religious treatise and a public record in 1520–39, for example, is as significant as the difference between usage in a text from 1520–39 and a text from 1640–59. The variables of genre and date also interact over time, so usage changes at significantly different rates and patterns in different genres. In short, genre made a significant difference in how quickly and to what degree Scots writers shifted from Scots-English to Anglo-English forms.

Different genres anglicized at different rates and in different patterns. As these tables suggest, the religious treatises anglicize most rapidly and thoroughly, having shifted to Anglo-English usage almost totally by 1600. The national public records, in contrast, are the least anglicized of the genres, showing highly variable usage even as late as 1659. Table 4.7, which includes the data for 1640–1659 only, indicates the differences across genres. Between the two extremes of religious treatises and national public records, official correspondence and private records end up more highly anglicized than private correspondence.

In sum, with all the Scots texts combined, as in table 4.1, or the results for all texts in table 4.7, a historical change in language use appears, and it is clear that the variety of language called Scots-English is shifting toward the variety called Anglo-English. When those texts are separated into their different genres, though, very real differences appear in how that change is occurring. This study of Scots-English demonstrates that language change, and hence history, happened differently in different genres.

A second study confirms that these results are not unique to the case of Scots-English. To check the generalizability of this relationship between genre and language change, I examined writers' usage in colonial

Table 4.7

Percentages of Anglicization in All Genres, 1640–59

	-ing	no/not	a/an	-ed	wh-
Religious treatises	100	100	100	100	100
Official correspondence	100	100	87	88	93
Private records	100	100	89	100	100
Private correspondence	100	100	63	83	70
Public records	94	75	32	62	54
Average of all genres	99	95	74	87	83

Source: Devitt, "Genre as Textual Variables."

American texts. Though using fewer linguistic features and counting fewer texts, I similarly examined the change occurring in the use of two linguistic forms during the period from 1640 to 1810: the presence or absence of the genitive apostrophe (as in *dog's*); and the form of the third-person singular verb inflection (as in "he talks" spelled with the earlier *-th* or the newly written standard *-s*). Essentially the same five genres were included: official correspondence, private correspondence, religious treatises, private records (diaries and journals), and public records (though local rather than national, of course). The sixty texts examined yielded fewer instances of some features, so statistical tests would have been unreliable and these results must necessarily remain more tentative.[10] Still, the results of this study of American English confirm the discoveries of the Scots-English study.

Tables 4.8 and 4.9 show the data for the two linguistic features studied in American English. The use of the *-s* versus *-th* verb ending clearly changes over time, as the results for all texts reveal. Each genre does adopt the *-s* verb ending, but at different rates and to different degrees. By 1810, private records use the *-s* ending consistently, while public records still use *-th* at times. Before that date, three of the genres adopt the *-s* ending quickly, while religious treatises change more gradually and public records seem to adopt the new usage slowly. At any given date during this study, a sampling of texts might have shown variable usage, if the texts came from public records and religious treatises, while a sampling of texts that included only private records and correspondence might well have shown completely consistent usage. The language change was happening differently in different genres.

Table 4.8

Percentages of Third-Person Singular Present Verbs
Using the –s Rather Than –th Inflection, by Genre and Date

	1640–60	1690–1710	1740–60	1790–1810
Private records	100*	100	100*	100
Private correspondence	10	100	100	100
Official correspondence	39	97	100	100
Religious treatises	54	76	100	97
Public records	27	79	50*	88
Average of all texts	33	87	99	98

Source: Devitt, "Genre as Textual Variables."
*Fewer than five instances of the feature were recorded for these cells.

Table 4.9

Percentages of Singular Genitives Using the Apostrophe, by Genre and Date

	1640–60	1690–1710	1740–60	1790–1810
Religious treatises	0	10	100	100*
Official correspondence	25*	7	64	100*
Private correspondence	25*	31	87	91
Public records	0	77	84	60
Private records	40	32	14	29
Average of all texts	16	32	75	48
Without private records	6	32	83	86
Without private or public records	10	17	81.5	94

Source: Devitt, "Genre as Textual Variables."
*Fewer than five instances of the feature were recorded for these cells.

The data for the genitive apostrophe are somewhat more muddied, though they still confirm the importance of genre for language change. As table 4.9 shows, the use of the apostrophe in all texts combined appears highly variable. Separated by genre, however, a clear movement toward using the genitive apostrophe appears in religious treatises and the two correspondence genres. Public records, too, appear to be adopting a change, though how thoroughly or consistently remains questionable. Writers of private records appear not to be adopting the genitive apostrophe at all (a rejection of the genitive apostrophe that may be continuing today). Data that together might even question whether a change is occurring reveal a language change in progress when separated by genre, though with different degrees of acceptance among writers of different genres.

These two studies demonstrate that language change happens differently in different genres, but what does it say about genre? For one thing, these cases reveal that genres are not just conservative forces. Perhaps contrary to expectation, some genres seem to encourage more rapid change than do other genres. Genres, so often perceived as constraining constructs, apparently are not totally conservative but rather allow, perhaps even enable, change. Yet genres do not have such force in isolation. These cases again exemplify genre's role as tree rings, as an indicator of significant changes in the (cultural) climate and growing conditions. Although genre was a significant variable in a historical change, rather than pointing to genre as a moving force in history I would point to the contexts underlying genre. The fact that these language changes occurred differently in different genres points to the contexts that genres represent, the contexts that both construct genres and change over time. As argued in the previous chapters, genres mediate context and individual action. The contextual forces that influence individual decisions about what forms of the language to use appear to the writer through the genres he or she writes.

Each Scottish genre sat at the nexus of particular situational and cultural contexts, and the particular textual features it encompasses also reflect those contexts. Consider the slow anglicization of the Scottish national public records, for example. Although highly formal and public in situation, these records represent the remnants of the political power that Scotland until recently had retained within its own political bodies. The Privy Council may not have much legislative power anymore, but its records can still reflect that older Scots identity through using its older Scots language. These cultural forces resisting change, however, do not appear in explicit nationalistic movements arguing to keep the old forms. Nor do individuals encourage or inhibit these language changes as individuals encouraged or inhibited the changes in management systems, state of the union addresses, or freshman themes. Rather, the contextual forces operating to encourage or inhibit those language changes operated more or less forcefully in different genres according to the different contexts each genre represented. The genre embodied its cultural context and the social situation of its participants, an embodiment individual writers incorporated into their language choices. As a result of these underlying forces, when writing in national public records, writers used more traditional Scots-English forms and resisted change to the newer Anglo-English standard; when writers wrote official correspondence, they more readily adopted the Anglo-English forms, a resistance and readiness of which the writers seem unaware but which the genres construct.[11]

That writers seem unaware of these changes adds a critical detail to our understanding of the relationship of genre to historical change. I found no evidence of writers at the time discussing the need to preserve Scots-English in national records, no evidence of writers being conscious of what they were doing in that genre. The changes occurred so gradually, over 140 years, that individual writers were unlikely to be aware of the changes in progress in either case. Yet in each of the genres the change happened differently, in patterns clearly discernible only with hindsight. In fact, the different usages in the genres was not even noticed by scholars until this study discovered the pattern. The role of the individual here differs considerably from that of the other cases examined in this chapter. Rather than powerful individuals encouraging or inhibiting genre changes, individuals in these cases act as everyday people, with no special power over change, and they act unawares and without deliberate purpose. Individual actions are not less important in these cases; they are still necessary for the language to change. But the actions take on their importance over time and most of all collectively. What makes genres change as they do is many individuals, subject to the same contextual forces and working within the same genre set, acting in similar ways.

These smaller actions producing lower-level changes surely occur in every genre studied in this chapter, surely occur in every genre. What changes in such details as verb tense or voice might emerge in a closer study of how the memorandum changed to represent systematic management? What changes in such details as qualifiers or modals might be discovered in a closer study of war rhetoric from the presidents? In each genre that changes over time, what small details reveal the larger contextual changes, and what unconscious decisions do individuals make that shape and change the features of the genre? Some of these lower-level changes are probably unpredictable and explainable only after the fact. Most of these changes are probably imperceptible at the time and result from innumerable, nondeliberate individual acts.

Resistance to these changes, too, is the act of many individuals over time. These cases offer explicit evidence of resistance to change in genres. Usage changes slowly in some genres, even as usage by others is galloping along. Other cases in this chapter also showed evidence of resistance, as one railroad adopts new genres faster than another, for example. That resistance takes many forms, including evidently small bits of language that mark one genre as more conservative than another. But again these small bits of resistance are not remarked upon, noticed, or deliberate. The same individual might well have used anglicized usage in one genre and not in another; he might well have written a religious treatise using anglicizations and then written a private letter using Scots forms and never have been aware of the differences. For it is through the genre and not the individual writer that the collective pattern appears; it is through the genre that the contexts influence the individual writer's actions. These cases make evident that the individual and the contextual come together within genres.

What these cases add to our previously compiled understanding of genres in history, then, is attention to the small and the everyday, to the nameless individual and the collective nature of genre change, and to the apparent lack of deliberate purpose in many aspects of genre change.

Summary

The cases considered in this chapter include a variety of research methods and levels of analysis, and they range widely across contexts, from railroads and manufacturing plants to politics and academe. The different settings surely influence the different genres' histories and what we perceive in those histories. In the corporate settings of the business genres, for example, the functionality of communication may be more transparent than in other settings. The rhetorical situations that business genres construct tend to be immediate and local, and such contextual factors as the corporate structure and hierarchical relationships tend to be well defined. We also simply tend to think of business communication as serving specific purposes, fulfilling practical functions. When we consider the historical developments of genres in business communication, therefore, we may think first of how they change in response to corporate needs. Examining presidential genres, in contrast, individual contributions may come first to mind. Yet even examining the seemingly anonymous business genres reveals not only how corporate changes created new demands but also how individuals were needed to encourage particular ways of meeting those demands. Examining the seemingly individual presidential genres reveals not only how individuals crafted new genres but also how those genres emerged from antecedents and adapted to cultural change. The sweeping histories of the theme and modes, too, brush through contextual influences, antecedents, and individual actions, while the narrow studies of language changes within genres still revealed individual actions as well as contexts. So, while each genre's history appears to be a unique confluence of factors and decisions, some general claims about how genres change emerge.

Genre change is often but not always a gradual process of subtle adaptations. Changes of genres and genre repertoires can develop slowly or quickly, gradually or abruptly, though even the apparently rapid changes tend to have more gradual contextual changes behind them. The factors that encourage or inhibit the generic changes probably differ in every circumstance, but they appear to involve always both contextual and individual factors. Contextual factors range widely, from technological advances to philosophical ideas.[12] The influence of the individual on generic change is significant but difficult to generalize about. Individuals with power have proven capable of pushing substantial generic changes and of defeating, at least temporarily, such changes. Other individuals who wished to encourage or inhibit such changes, though, have proven ineffective. Most individuals who effect genre change may never even be aware that they are doing so. In all of the cases studied here, individual actions must compound to create collective change. The combination of contextual forces and individual forces is probably necessary for genre changes to have much currency or endurance. The role of the individual in genre change appears much stronger than previously acknowledged by rhetorical genre theory's emphasis on recurrence, but the role of context appears stronger than is often acknowledged by literary critics' emphasis on individual genius.

Not surprisingly, the development of new genres is influenced by antecedent genres, but Jamieson's work reminds us that those antecedents may sometimes be inappropriate and may limit the new genre's ability to fulfill its functions. Not only antecedent genres but also previous instances of a genre shape newly developing genres. It seems reasonable to suppose that all writers, not just presidents, confronted with situations new to them might look at texts others have written to fulfill similar functions.[13] The writing processes of presidents have been more often recorded, so that we know that presidents used previous instances of a genre to shape their own; it seems likely that the unrecorded processes of other writers might also include looking at previous instances. New tax accountants, in my study described in the previous chapter, also looked at previously written texts in the files to help construct their own instances of research memoranda and other genres. Even if such writers did not seek out previous texts, they would surely be influenced by such previous instances that they might have had occasion to read. In the development of a new genre, therefore, antecedent genres and previous texts responding to similar situations should prove important influences.

Those previous instances might also prove important to existing genres that adapt to change, as they did for presidential genres. Individual writers, faced with changing circumstances, decide to write something differently, as did individual presidents. Later writers, faced with continuing changes, adopt those differences for their own instances. Individual successes and failures may lead future writers to copy or avoid certain generic choices. Less visible choices, such as lower-level linguistic forms, may still be based on the precedents of other writers but less consciously so. Writers may follow others' choices without being deliberate, merely by following what seems expected in the genre. Deliberate or not, individual decisions not only encourage or inhibit generic change but actively create that change. The generic changes that result in turn reinforce the contextual changes that are occurring, placing even more pressure on individuals to act in ways that further change.

Since genres are so enmeshed in a fluid context and embedded in amorphous social groups, their histories reflect a constant balancing of tradition and change. As genres change, they need to maintain both stability and flexibility—stability to ensure that the genre continues to fulfill its necessary functions, flexibility to ensure that individuals can adapt the genre to their particular situations and their changing circumstances. Some genres achieve that balance successfully; some fail, dispersing into other genres and nothingness if too flexible, declining into arhetorical formulae if too stable. But the loss of a genre is not necessarily something to be mourned, not like the loss of an extinct species. The loss of a genre reflects the loss of a function, the result of changing needs and ideologies as society and individuals change. Contrary to common assumptions, it is in the nature of genres to change. Genres are changing all the time, in ways we often do not even recognize until much after the fact. And those changes create for a genre, like for the people who use it, a unique history. Genres are not the static conserver of traditional form that the old definition of genre might imply; instead, genres are as dynamic as history itself.

5

Creative Boundaries: An Argument for Genre as Standard, Genre as Muse

Nuns fret not at their convent's narrow room.
—William Wordsworth

Everything old is new again.

—All That Jazz

In the previous chapter, studies of particular genres illustrated that genre influences linguistic and social change, not just as a negative, constraining force but as a positive, encouraging force as well. Embedded as genres are in social, cultural, political, and rhetorical contexts, they necessarily reflect the dynamic nature of life. Yet, even accepting this dynamic perspective on genre, it can be difficult to overcome the romantic belief that genres somehow constrain life, that they restrict writers, inhibit self-expression, establish requirements that truly creative writers must resist and struggle to transcend. Even if genres have complicated social and rhetorical origins, even if genres change as their contexts change, aren't they still the givens that constrain creativity?

Rhetorical and literary scholars have complained that genre limits what writers can do. Rhetorician Thomas Conley, for example, accuses genre criticism of "forc[ing] experience to capitulate to rationality" (62). But Conley, like others who criticize genre as formulaic, formalistic, or deterministic, criticizes the actions of genre critics and of genre criticism done badly more than the concept of genre itself. The concept of genre does require a sameness among texts and writers, so genre theory has tended, as Dorothy Winsor notes, to emphasize "repetition and continuity (and thus underplays the role of agency and change)" ("Genre" 201). Or as Amanda McGinnis, a student in a seminar on genre observed,

"The individual does not cease to exist; he only ceases to be visible."
Of course genres do, in fact, constrain and limit the possibilities of what
individuals write, just as the rhetorical situations themselves constrain
and limit those possibilities. Writers adapt what they want to write to
suit the rhetorical situation and the genre that situation suggests. A writer
who wishes to present the results of an experiment in a science class will
"reach" the science teacher by writing a lab report, not by giving a first-
person narrative of the experience, including all the writer's hopes, fears,
and mistakes. Accepting that the rhetorical and social goals will best be
accomplished by writing a school lab report, the writer probably will
follow an expected organizational pattern, including sections of introduction, methods, results, and discussion, will use passive voice freely
to avoid first-person pronouns and to avoid calling attention to the researcher, will present results in numerical and tabular form, and much
more. The established genre of the school lab report will dictate much
of what the writer writes.

Yet consider also the limits of those constraints: How does an in-
animate genre "dictate" a person's writing? What if the writer has never
written or read a lab report before and does not know what is expected?
What if the writer does not want to reach the audience in the expected
way? What if the writer does not want to accomplish the assumed goals
but instead different goals, perhaps to startle a rigid teacher and to subvert the conformity required in science class? The existence of a genre
in an established rhetorical and social context, I would argue, does not
dictate any writing: it is a choice that can be made. Certainly, it is a choice
with powerful incentives and punishments attached, and the embeddedness of genres within ideologies and power structures will be considered further in this chapter. Yet the nature of genre as inhibitor of a
writer's freedom and creativity is not as simple as it might appear.

In this chapter, I argue that genre necessarily and simultaneously both
constrains and enables writers and that such a combination of constraint
and choice is essential to creativity. As I will explain, creativity theory
suggests that creativity derives from constraint as much as from freedom,
giving genres a significant role in making choices possible. This relationship between constraint and freedom parallels the relationship I will define between linguistic standardization and linguistic variation. Like language standards, genres conventionalize specific formal expectations; also
like language standards, genres make visible opportunities for variations.

The issue of genre's role in creativity resides amidst critical issues
for literary and rhetorical study and teaching. One view has always held

genre as an antonym to *creativity*, though its beliefs may rarely be stated so bluntly. By this view, writers of "genre literature" are hacks compared with writers of "real literature." Writers of "formulaic" genres like lab reports are just filling in the blanks, while "real" writers compose original essays (conveniently ignoring that essays, too, are genres with their own expectations and conventions). Yet this view in literary study has long been counterpoised by views that maintain the centrality of genre to all literary effort, hence all literary creativity: tragedy and comedy as the spine of all literature; multiple genres as Chaucer's playground; the rise of the novel as the enabler of both Fielding and Sterne. Similarly conflicting views of genre have appeared in composition and rhetoric as well. Recent debates over whether to emphasize individual "voice" in writing classes (Peter Elbow and others) or to emphasize expectations and conventions of academic writing (David Bartholomae and others) echo debates about whether an individual has an authentic self that transcends cultural (including generic) conventions or whether writers' personae are constructed through writing within those conventions. Most directly, the conflicting views appear in debates over whether to teach genres explicitly (quite apart from the debate about whether students can acquire a genre without being immersed in its community, to be considered in the last chapter). Does teaching students genres empower or entrap them, open their minds or brainwash them? Behind all of these debates lies the issue of whether genres merely constrain or also enable writers.

Other scholars in genre study have approached this debate but have not adequately recognized genre's positive creative power or delineated *how* genres act as constraints or enablers. Most notably, Frances Christie in "Genres as Choice" has argued that genre and choice are not inimical and that genre enables choice, but, as convincing as many of Christie's arguments are, that perspective still implies that constraint is bad and choice is good. My perspective is closer to that described by Conley, though he speaks of genre criticism rather than users and doubts that such a genre criticism is possible:

> Ideally, of course, the genre approach should be neither deductive nor inductive but "dialectical" in nature, playing off the general against the particular, the inexorably historical against the seemingly novel—which, to be sure, often turns out to be not so novel, after all. (65)

Instead of seeing a dichotomy between constraint and choice, then, my argument is dialectical, that both constraint and choice are necessary and therefore positive components of genre—both-and instead of either-or. Also in this chapter, I dig more deeply into the mechanisms by which genres constrain and enable choice. Applying research into language, creativity, and ideology to genre illuminates the nature of genre and its influence on individual actions.

Language Standards and Genres

Since genres encompass utterances, and utterances are made of language, genre bears some relationship to language. The exact nature of that relationship, however, is unclear, for larger linguistic, cognitive, and social theories are not yet adequate to pull all the elements of language use, including genre, together. Because language constitutes genre on some level, there are many rich commonalities between language and genre. To explore those commonalities and their implications for creativity, this section suggests some of the ways that language and genre—especially language standards and genre—would seem to be similar and then, on the basis of those similarities, argues that both language and genre entail choice as well as constraint.

One way that genres are inherently creative is in the same way that language is inherently creative: To use language is to say something never before said using words and structures that have often before been said. With the exception of a few routine utterances ("good morning," "how are you," "I love you," or "if you keep crossing your eyes they'll get stuck that way"), utterances are unique. When I write the sentence I am writing now, I am writing a sentence I have never written before. When I write this sentence that I am writing now, I am writing a sentence that no one else has ever written before. In fact, all of the sentences in this paragraph, all of our nonroutine utterances, are new and original in some basic way. If creativity involves novelty, then language is powerfully creative.

But that linguistic novelty can exist only because linguistic similarity also exists. Each element of a novel utterance has been uttered before. The individual sounds in an utterance are not new; the syntax in an utterance is not new; the words in an utterance are not new (or if they are they must be defined for an audience using words that are known). Without existing linguistic elements, nothing can be said, either novel or formulaic. The already existing patterns of a language must be present for the utterance to be understood, even as those patterns are used to express something never before said. This remarkable and necessary characteristic of language, this duality of patterning, has been described as generative, for new utterances are generated from preexisting patterns.

Since genres develop from utterances, genres, too, might be seen as generative. As existing patterns, they provide known ways of expressing something new. The writer or speaker of every individual text or piece of discourse uses existing genres to express something never before said. No two discourses are identical, yet many are perceived as using the same genre. To use a genre, then, like using language, is to say or write something never before said or written using generic patterns that have often before been used.

The similarities between genre and language are even more apparent in the nature of genre as a standard, a regularizing norm. Once established, genres operate as language standards, like "proper English." Both genres and language standards are sets of conventionalized expectations for using language. Language standards are the norms of language use, the rules of linguistic etiquette—rules of punctuation in writing and usage standards in speech and writing (subject-verb agreement, pronoun case, verb tenses, and so on, what some have called "grammar" but what Hartwell explains is more precisely called "usage"). Language standards represent established expectations of what "good" language users do in particular contexts; to subvert those expectations of language standards is to invite consequences, both good and bad. The nature of genres shares some similarities with language standards. Once genres have become established, they too conventionalize into expectations, even norms for appropriate behavior. Genres represent established expectations of what "good" writers write and "good" speakers speak in particular contexts; hence, to subvert those expectations entails consequences of various kinds, good and bad. (To conform to those expectations also entails consequences, good and bad, including acculturation and other ideological effects described more at the end of this chapter and in chapters 2 and 3.) Readers and writers, listeners and speakers, expect particular genres in particular situations, and they expect that discourse in those situations will conform to their expectations about those genres, will follow the generic conventions. Through the expectations of language users, then, genres do constrain discourse, and in that sense, genres are also like language standards.

People share similar attitudes toward genres and language standards as well. Just as some debate whether genres constrain self-expression or enable literary genius, some debate the social consequences of language standards. Some revile language standards as a constraint on individual freedom represented by individual idiolects, as restrictor of the home dialect and all it represents culturally, and as senseless formula contrived by members of the upper class to oppress members of the lower classes. Others revere language standards as the keeper of the gate against anarchy and unintelligibility or as the tool of empowerment for the disadvantaged, who can gain access to the circles of power if only they have access to the standard language. These two perspectives on language standards represent ends of a spectrum, a spectrum similar to the one concerning attitudes toward genre that I described earlier in this chapter. For example, the debate about whether to teach genre explicitly, as has been done in the Australian curriculum, revolves around whether the teaching of genre liberates the socially excluded or enforces artificial formulae.[1] The debates about teaching genres and teaching language standards echo one another, further suggesting that they involve common underlying issues.

To the extent that genres operate as do language standards, what is true of language standards may be true of genres. Examining the similarities between the two clarifies how genre operates, including how genre operates as a standard. As the more extensive research on language standards suggests, neither type of standard is solely constraining, and both entail variation and creativity as well as standardization and constraint. Since language standards, I will argue, inherently entail linguistic variation, genres similarly inherently entail creative choice.

The Nature of Generic Constraints

Both genres and language standards certainly, at least in part, regularize and standardize discourse. Both bring greater uniformity to language use, greater homogeneity; both act as centrifugal forces, holding language use together.[2] That both encompass centripetal as well as centrifugal forces is the crux of my later argument. These standardizing influences derive from socially constructed patterns of expectations for social purposes, so they are neither wholly arbitrary nor wholly predictable. Genres, embedded as they are in contexts, are not completely random; but, changing as they do over time and across groups, genres are not completely inevitable either. Similarly, language standards are neither wholly arbitrary nor predictable, and different language standards have existed for different groups at different times.

Standards, like genres, develop out of contexts and social structures. The history of Standardized Edited English (SEE), a standardized variety used in formal texts, is complex and multiple but clearly develops out of social as well as communicative purposes.[3] It may have first developed from scribal practices in Anglo-Saxon times; explicit commentary shaped it in the seventeenth and especially eighteenth centuries. Whatever history is traced, however, it is clear that SEE, like genres, developed partly out of social contexts for social purposes. The pragmatic need for a common dialect for widely intelligible printed texts may have encouraged the promotion of a single dialect, but the chosen dialect was not selected for purely pragmatic reasons. The chosen dialect for printed texts, which formed the basis of SEE, was not just that of William Caxton and other early printers but also that of the London-Cambridge-Oxford area, an area of prestige and power. The concurrent erosion of class distinctions may have leant to the emerging standard another social purpose, encouraging a more rigid prestige dialect that could more sharply mark social as well as linguistic distinctions. As historians trace these and other contextual factors in the development of SEE, it is clear that this language standard is neither wholly arbitrary nor inevitable. The regularities in both language standards and genres carry social as well as functional significance.

For both genres and language standards, these regularities of formal features can be specified. The genre of lab report includes an organizational pattern, stylistic features, and textual appearance described earlier. The language standard of SEE includes such formal features as the use of *whom* in objective case, use of a comma between independent clauses joined by a coordinating conjunction, use of *does* to agree with third-person singular subjects, and so on. In fact, for SEE we have a complex vocabulary for describing such formal features, called school grammar in Hartwell's terms and represented in such codifiers as dictionaries, usage glossaries, and handbooks.

Readers and listeners expect some of these features and may notice if there are variations or violations. That is, both genres and language standards have a linguistic "reality" for participants. The student who includes no "methods" section in her lab report will probably receive a lower grade; the student who writes "The chemical don't work" will probably be noticed negatively. As Joseph Williams points out in his important article "The Phenomenology of Error," however, not all variations are noticed equally, and neither is conformity to all rules. Some features of SEE are noticed only when they are violated (using *does* with third-person singular verbs, for example, or beginning a sentence with a capital letter) and others only when they are met (using the subjunctive, for example, and perhaps using *whom*). Some features are noticed neither in their violation nor in their conformity (the split infinitive may fit that category for many people; using a comma after an introductory phrase may as well). A case could be made for the same being true of genre features. Some are noticed only when they are violated: the afore-mentioned absence of a methods section in a lab report, perhaps, or including numerical results in prose rather than tabular form. Others are noticed when they are met: perhaps the poetic form of a sonnet written today. Still others are not noticed at all, in agreement or in violation: perhaps the use of passive or active voice in a lab report would not be noticed but only the use of *I*. Research could establish what genre fea-tures are noticed in what ways. Both genres and language standards are connected to specific formal features, and participants come to expect certain features and, at times, to notice how those expectations are met.

These formal features can and do change over time, however, indi-cating the inherent possibility of variation as well as standardization. In SEE, multiple negation was standard in Chaucer's time, and the once standard distinction between "less" and "fewer" is apparently becom-ing obsolete. In genres, the preceding chapter describes some formal changes over time; for another example, Charles Bazerman has traced in detail the changes in the form of the experimental article, including changes in the use of first person, of tables and graphs, and of organi-zation. Changes in the formal features, though, do not eliminate the genre or the language standard. As the historical cases demonstrate, genres persist even as their formal features change. The same might be said for a language standard: its specific features can change even as the standard, as a social construct, can remain in place. SEE still exists even though multiple negation is no longer acceptable and "less" more gen-erally is. Conceivably, a genre or a language standard could undergo so many changes in formal features so rapidly that participants would in-deed perceive and define it as a new genre or different language stan-dard. In terms of language standards, however, such redefinition tends to occur as a political rather than formal statement: for example, a gov-ernment declares for political reasons that a new standard will be im-posed, a standard that is a version of an existing standard. I suspect that the renaming of genres similarly tends to result sometimes from politi-cal rather than formal changes: "creative nonfiction" may differ formally from "essays," but the essay genre might have continued to encompass a wide range of forms were it not for the negative connotation of the freshman or school essay. Another factor in genre definition may be simple frequency: the popularity of the "nature essay" may lead it to genre rather than subgenre status. Political and popularity forces com-bined may lead to subdividing the academic essay into traditional or scholarly essays and "new" or personal academic essays. Changes in formal features alone, I suspect, are not enough to cause renaming of a genre or language standard without political forces encouraging such redefinition. The genre and the standard are much more than listings of their formal features.

So far, I have been writing as though SEE is the only language standard while drawing examples from multiple genres. In fact, both genres and language standards are multiple and vary in different contexts. Contrary to popular opinion, SEE is not the one and true standard for all occasions. Linguists have long noted the multiplicity of standards (e.g., Krapp), from a once national standard like Received Pronunciation in England to regional standards like upper-class southern American English. If the heart of a language standard is a regularized set of features expected by a group from its members in particular situations, then the multiplicity of language standards can be seen to extend across situations as well as regions, with the same speaker using a different standard in intimate conversation and in formal written academic essays.[4] Using SEE on the playground or in a letter to a friend would be considered "wrong," as using inappropriate language. Use of the subjective case of the pronoun in the subject complement position after a copulative verb may be "correct" in SEE, but "It is I" would be considered a joking response to the question "Who's there" after a knock on a dorm room door. The child who uses "whom" while playing marbles is likely to be laughed at or considered a "snoot," in David Foster Wallace's terms. Not only using an inappropriate standard but also avoiding the expected variety can be seen as speaking inappropriately: the African American living in a lower-class section of Detroit who speaks to friends without using African American English Vernacular, the young man at a bachelor party not using profanity, the college professor at a conference who does not use professional jargon. That is, a language standard exists on the playground and among less powerful groups in society as well, a standard in which the participants expect some features and not others. The standard of the less powerful or of the playground is no less a standard for not being institutionalized; its rules may be just as rigidly and even harshly enforced, and it may just as well mark insiders and outsiders. Language standards are also multiple across speakers, for different speakers apply different standards in different contexts. The aforementioned African American may use SEE in school or at work; a college professor may use Appalachian English when visiting home. There are some who never use SEE, just as there are some in England who do not use Received Pronunciation. To some, even upper-class southern American English seems "wrong" and nonstandard; to others that dialect seems affected and inappropriate for casual conversation. These multiple language standards with their different sets of features shift for everyone across context, situation, and individual.

People use multiple genres, too, in different situations, and like language standards they learn to shift genres for different settings. Just as people are bidialectal, people are bigeneric. Although group expectations are powerful forces for conformity, people participate in multiple groups and thus have a range of choices. Linguistically, individuals develop their own idiolects, unique varieties of the language that encompass all the varieties of language that they use in different settings. Individuals develop generic idiolects as well (idio-genres?), sets of genres in which they participate and from which they can choose, their individual genre repertoire. The theoretically complex multiplicity of genres was examined more thoroughly in chapter 1, including the variable judgments of what constitutes a genre, like judgments of what constitutes a language standard. Just as the definition of standards hinges on whose standards, the definition of genres depends on whose genres. Genres can be perceived, described, and classified in different ways, depending on who is doing the classifying. Like national versus regional language standards, a genre can be classified as narrative or fiction or novel or bildungsroman; another as persuasion or argument or essay or article or editorial. Different genres exist with different conventions for different people in different contexts as well as for different purposes in different situations. Both genres and language standards are multiple in multiple ways, with no single standard demanding conformity from all individuals at all times and in all settings.

Controlling multiple standards and multiple genres helps people perform well in their multiple tasks, for both language standards and genres are functional. The functional nature of genres is amply examined in the first chapters of this volume, but language standards, too, are functional. SEE originated in part from a functional need for communication across dialects. All language standards serve the needs of their communities both for increased intelligibility and as markers of membership. In reducing variation, they increase intelligibility across time and space; and, in restricting variation, they encourage conformity of group members and give them linguistic signals of who belongs and who does not. Both standards and genres serve important functions.

As the metaphor of linguistic etiquette suggests, another key concept for language standards is appropriateness. Appropriateness often seems to have overtaken functionality in language standards. Although originating from a communicative need, the standard of SEE entails certain features that have come to represent formality and education and so are most appropriate to use in formal, educated situations. The standard of upper-class southern American English entails certain features that have come to represent education, breeding, and regional loyalty. The standard of African American English Vernacular entails certain features that have come to represent ethnic identity and loyalty. The standard of the playground entails certain features that have come to represent intimacy, playfulness, and "coolness." Linguists now commonly view language standards in terms of appropriateness, but composition and rhetoric scholars more commonly view genre primarily in terms of function. Although their functions are well established, genres, like language standards, are also appropriate. Genres, too, are linguistic etiquette, exhibiting the "proper" (that is, appropriate) behavior at the proper occasion. Once genres have become well established, they are not just, as Bitzer described them, "fitting" responses to rhetorical situations and therefore functionally and rhetorically effective but also appropriate behavior in conventional social contexts and therefore socially effective. They meet expectations for proper behavior, for generic etiquette. The comparison of genre and language standard clarifies that both genres and language standards are both functional and appropriate.

Extending the etiquette metaphor from standards to genres can clarify the nature of genre as constraint. The functional nature of genres and language standards constrains the participant in part because genres represent effective means of fulfilling some purpose. Following the generic "rules" enables one to achieve a goal; not following them potentially leaves some important function unfulfilled. The appropriate nature of genres and language standards similarly constrains the participant because they are conventionalized proper behavior. Following generic etiquette "rules" enables one to "fit in," to be marked as belonging to the group; not following generic etiquette marks one as not belonging in some way. To get along well in society, one must learn or acquire the rules of generic etiquette. As is true of language standards, some people acquire even the most advanced rules early, as parents and friends and schools provide an environment in which the etiquette of many sophisticated genres is followed regularly; others must make an effort to learn the etiquette rules of some genres later and may never learn the rules sufficiently to fit in completely. Different groups may make that generic etiquette more or less accessible, depending on the strength of their desire to include and exclude people.

In addition to genres constraining people because they are functional and make rhetorical sense, then, generic etiquette constrains people if they want to belong to a group. Desire for membership in a group is a powerful constraint, more powerful perhaps than the trivialized notion of etiquette can capture. Depending on the society, the need to belong to a group—or the power of membership in a particular group—may be so strong that individuals choose to violate such etiquette only at great risk to their well-being. Or the social training to that etiquette may be so ingrained that individuals can "choose" to violate it only with great difficulty, so ingrained that many, in fact, may be unable to "choose" to do otherwise. Again, the comparison with language standards illuminates the difficulty, for sociolinguists have long recognized and amply demonstrated that individuals have strong and unconscious attachments to the dialects and standards they have been raised with, attachments that appear in the language they "choose" to use. Most noticeable to the nonlinguist perhaps is the virulence with which variations on an established language standard are attacked in letters to the editor and in editorials by linguistic prescriptivists and purists such as William Safire and James Kilpatrick. How dare we use *flaunt* when *flout* is intended! The constraint of linguistic, and so perhaps generic, etiquette is personally, socially, politically, and ideologically loaded. It is a powerful constraint, indeed.

Variation Within Genres

But even the most rigid and institutionalized language standard does not enforce 100 percent compliance. And even the most rigid and institutionalized language standard does not constrain all linguistic behavior, does not proscribe and prescribe every element of every word that is said or written. Neither does genre. Broadening the notion of language standard to encompass all "rules" for language use in different settings still does not provide a rule for every utterance. The sociolinguists who attempted to state rules for every usage and pronunciation called them "variable rules," ones that did not apply 100 percent of the time, and they allowed for what was once called "free" variation, unexplained differences in what individuals said. Within each language standard, in fact, remains great variation, what I might describe metaphorically as both free variation and variable rules. SEE specifies that *whom* be used in objective functions, for example, but it does not specify when *use* rather than *utilize* must appear. It specifies what will constitute subject-verb agreement, but it does not specify which verbs should be used. Added to such free variation are the many variable rules: use a comma after an introductory phrase, unless the phrase is short (how short? it varies); collective nouns are singular or plural, depending on context. A great deal of the language remains a matter of individual choice, necessary flexibility without which individuals could not mean different things. The same is true, I argue, for genres.

Genres, too, permit a great deal of individual choice, for not every aspect of every text is specified by any genre. Within any genre, there is a great deal of "free" variation. The lab report, for a continued example, may seem a relatively rigid genre, yet it does not dictate how the research question will be worded or which apparatus will be described first. Even the generic rules that we might consider specified are often really variable rules: the passive voice is common, but the researcher's activities can be and are described actively sometimes; the "results" section precedes the "discussion" section, except sometimes when a writer combines the results and discussion into a single section. Variation is permitted to the degree that it does not negate either function or appropriateness. (An interesting and important question for future research is how much and what types of variation still retain function and appropriateness.)

Not only is such variation available within genres and language standards; it is necessary for genres and language standards to exist. Without variation, it would not be possible to perceive standardization; without generic choice, it would not be possible to enact generic constraint. Conversely, language standards imply the existence of linguistic variation; generic constraints imply the existence of generic choices. If there were no variation in how people used the language, all people would speak exactly alike (a linguistic impossibility, in fact, but a hypothetical case that will serve for illumination). If all people spoke exactly alike, their similarities would probably go unnoticed, for there would be no contrast to call attention to any feature. If all speakers said "He doesn't," then no standard would have emerged to require it. Without the possibility of an alternative, no standards need develop.

That is in fact the case for linguistic and textual features that have no alternatives. In English, no language standard specifies that the definite article precedes rather than follows the noun; grammarians specify it, but it is a descriptive, not prescriptive rule. No native speaker will utter "dog the." The variation resides in what the standard does specify, the contrast between a noun phrase with a definite article ("the dog") and one without ("a dog" or "dog"). Similarly, the lab report genre does not prescribe that the text will break into paragraphs, that it will be written in sentences, or that it will be written and not sung. The meaning of the lab report genre resides where it does contrast with other texts, in the expectation of a methods section, in the avoidance of active agency, in the dependence on visual aids. It is in the "not-statements" (Freadman, "Anyone"), in the semantic and semiotic relationships (Halliday), in the variation within standardization, in the choice within constraint that generic meaning resides. Where there are no alternatives, there is no standard. Where there are both standards and variations, there is meaning.

Were there just variation and no standardization, meaning would also be impossible. Too much choice is as debilitating of meaning as is too little choice. In language, too much variation results eventually in lack of meaning: mutual unintelligibility. As the Latin-derived languages came to vary in more and more ways, they came to be so distinct as to be unintelligible, unmeaningful, to speakers of the other language—hence French and Italian. In genre, perhaps some genres permit more variation than others (the novel comes to mind), but variation cannot be infinite or the discourse becomes unintelligible. Even the varied *Ulysses* plays with narrative structure and stream of consciousness, traits of the novel genre. Even choice that is less than infinite can be paralyzing. Can each language user respond to each rhetorical situation anew? Can each utterance require a new organization? It is with some reason that many students panic when the assignment "allows" them to "write on any topic." As Christie argues, choice is enhanced by constraint, made possible by constraint. Further, I argue that meaning is enhanced by both choice and constraint. Meaning exists in the interaction of choice and constraint, in genre no less than in language.

Every utterance is constraint and choice, within the language itself, within the situation, within individual ability and characteristics, within the ideological and social context. Genre and language standards in fact accentuate the places of variation and choice by delimiting that variation and choice. Rather than genres and language standards inscribing only constraints, then, they encompass both constraint and choice. Sharing a basis in language, genre and language standards share the same fundamental trait of language, considered from two perspectives. Both constraint and choice, standardization and variation, are necessary for utterance, for meaning. Too much or too little of either is linguistically and rhetorically paralyzing. Language and utterances require both a centrifugal and a centripetal force to maintain the balance of meaning. Genre and language standards both exhibit that fundamental trait of language, a balance of standardization and variation, of commonality and difference.

Creativity Theory and Genre

Because genre encompasses both standards and variation, constraint and choice, genre encourages and even makes possible creativity. Although the term *creativity* may initially associate with things original and novel, scholars of creativity have largely rejected notions of creativity as unconstrained choice, novelty, and originality. Instead, they have added two perspectives: process views that examine how "new" things develop; and social views that emphasize the importance of which "new" things are valued. Both views contribute to understanding genre's role in creativity, but the first question of how new things develop addresses most directly the thorny question of originality within genres.

Several scholars in creativity theory have described the creativity from which new things develop as dual, two-sided. Albert Rothenberg identifies a specific thought process in creativity: Janusian thinking or "the capacity to conceive and utilize two or more opposite or contradictory ideas, concepts, or images *simultaneously*" (313). Arthur Koestler similarly describes creativity as "bisociation," "the perceiving of a situation or idea . . . in two self-consistent but habitually incompatible frames of reference" (35). By these definitions, genres could generate creativity: newly created hybrid genres could emerge from the joining of two existing genres; or a creative thinker could perceive an idea through the frames of reference of two different genres. I wish to use the duality of creativity to make a stronger claim here—not just that genres can be used as heuristics to creativity but that genres require creativity. Like variation, creativity inheres in genres.

Another creativity theorist who sees a duality to creativity is Charles Hampden-Turner. In his book *Maps of the Mind,* he describes the process of creative thinking as involving "divergent thinking"—"reformulating, elaborating and playing with the problem as presented"—followed by convergent thinking—"converging upon precisely the right answer" (104). "Divergence," he writes, "is the making in the mind of many from one. Convergence is the making of one from many. Mind is conceived as constantly branching out . . . before narrowing to a point of decision . . . , and so on in cyclical pattern. Creativity involves the entire cycle" (104). Creativity, to Hampden-Turner, requires the convergence as much as the divergence.

Hampden-Turner adds to this process Edward De Bono's distinction between lateral and vertical thinking, both required to work together. Vertical thinking begins with a given paradigm and works to fit new data (or ideas) into the paradigm. When a bit of data or an idea does not fit the paradigm, the thinker either rejects the datum or shifts to lateral thinking. With lateral thinking, the thinker generates several new paradigms and then tries them out on the data or ideas. Just as the creative thinker needs both convergence and divergence, she or he also needs both vertical and lateral thinking. As Hampden-Turner writes, vertical thinking is "grounded in a pattern which lateral thinking creates, qualifies and revises, allowing vertical thinking to re-orientate itself and once more plunge ahead" (110). Although "only lateral thinking can bring us back to the realization that we are self-organizing systems, pattern-making creatures, not just pattern recognizers and imprinted followers," "we must not fall into the trap of unlimited admiration for lateral thinking," he writes, for "lateral and vertical, right hemisphere and left, must work together" (111). For creativity to be generated, then, the creative mind must both discover patterns and follow patterns; both diverge from the already existing and converge into the now existing.

So too must the creative writer; hence genres, as patternings, become necessary to creativity. Of course, genres constitute the already existing from which the creative writer diverges, but they also constitute the divergence. They encompass the patterns followed in vertical thinking and the patterns discovered in lateral thinking. As such dynamic entities, they contain within themselves the seeds of divergence as well as convergence. (Remember the ability genres have to change over time, to diverge in response to changing needs of their users, even while often maintaining their status as genres.) Using lateral thinking, the writer or reader must perceive a genre by converging many unique texts into a single pattern, a genre. Using vertical thinking, the writer or reader creates a unique text within a genre by seeing how this text can diverge within the common pattern, the genre. To write and read requires both vertical and lateral thinking, both convergence and divergence, requires the unity from among the variation and the variation within the unity—that is, to write and read, with all the creativity both acts entail, requires genre.

Some examples will help bring those cognitive concepts back to experience. When a seasoned manager writes a memo announcing a meeting, the writer does not think about how to use a memo heading, how to get directly to the point, or how to name the time and place of the meeting—the conventions of the genre, the vertical thinking about how to fit into the pattern. Most of that thinking goes on without much conscious attention (perhaps it is routinized or operationalized, as activity theory might describe it). Instead, the manager thinks about what is unique to this particular memo: the specific agenda, the particular committee and its concerns, the potential conflicts with the assigned date, time and place. In other words, the manager thinks most about the divergence within the memo; the writer can concentrate on divergence precisely because the convergence is a given; the convergence takes care of itself.

Consider, for a second example, this chapter I composed that you are now reading. As I considered what to write and how, I explored possibilities, possible divergences. I knew that, given the rhetorical situation, I would write a chapter in a scholarly book and that scholarly chapters entail certain conventions. As a somewhat experienced writer of the genre, however, I did not concentrate my time on those common conventions or the common rhetorical situation. Instead, it is the unique aspects of the situation and of my ideas on which I concentrated. Yet I had room for such concentration, I knew what was unique and what merited my attention, only because I knew the genre. Because I know that scholarly chapters require interaction with the scholarly work of others, I knew to spend time educating myself about the particular works in creativity theory and linguistic standardization that this chapter would require. Because I know that scholarly chapters require well-articulated and well-reasoned arguments, I spent time determining precisely what I was willing to claim about the creativity of genres and precisely how I might support that claim. Because I know what the expectations of my genre are and have experience meeting those expectations, I am enabled to work efficiently and effectively on developing the unique aspects of this instance of the genre, on what is novel in this particular writing task and situation (including choosing the novelty of commenting on my own writing in this paragraph, necessitating the unconventional heavy use of the personal pronoun). Both my lateral and vertical thinking are defined by the genre within which I am working. The convergence of my situation with my specified genre enables me to write a scholarly chapter; the divergence of my situation from my genre enables me to write this particular scholarly chapter. Both depend upon my genre.

As these simple examples illustrate and as creativity theory supports, in practice genre enables writers to make choices as much as or more than it requires writers to conform. In theory, as I have argued earlier in this volume, the uniqueness of each utterance and each text means that genre patterns must be perceived from dissimilar texts, the divergent must be seen to converge. Genres, therefore, enable us to reduce the infinite possible divergence among texts to convergence. But genres in practice are usually the already existing, the given patterns. We don't need to discover them; they are already there. Writers and readers therefore typically use genres to construct their divergence rather than their convergence. Existing genres encourage lateral thinking about particular situations rather than vertical thinking about the given pattern. Genres encourage choice because their constraints are given. To produce an interpretable text, every writer must rely on the community's genres; to produce a unique text, every writer must exploit some of the possibilities for divergence within those genres. Since every text is unique, every writer must write creatively within a genre.

Valuing Both Constraint and Choice

This argument that all genres entail and even enable creativity returns us to the important role of social judgments in perceiving creativity. In Western society we value creativity highly and perceive it substantially in special uses of language—in literature and great oratory, in particular. Such ideology plays a role in our willingness or reluctance to call everyday writing within everyday genres creative. The issue of value in genres and creativity will be examined in greater depth in chapter 6, but it is worth noting here as we examine the extent to which all genres enable creativity. The novel is typically judged a genre that enables a writer's creativity, while the lab report is considered a constraining and noncreative genre. Although some think of the novelist as struggling for self-expression within the confining constraints of a (perhaps male-dominated language and) genre, the novelist also depends on the perception of similarities among novels that enables her to concentrate on the points where she must diverge. As noted before, even as James Joyce plays with point of view, narration, and language in *Ulysses,* he depends on some commonalities of character, structure, and literary allusion to keep his text interpretable. He can foreground innovation because of the background of the expected. Although some think of the scientist as writing her article by filling in the slots of methodology, results, and discussion, she too struggles to explain her modified instrumentation, to imply criticism of previous research, or to describe the heretofore undescribed double helix (especially within the constraints of scientific paradigms, as Thomas Kuhn has argued). Students of literature today might notice and value the creativity of the novelist over the scientist, but literary critics of old, such as Alexander Pope or William Wordsworth, recog-

nized the creativity required to work within the harness of highly specified genres, the ability of the tiny cell to be not a prison but a key to literary achievement. Scientists today, similarly, might value the creativity of
the scientist over that of the novelist, crediting much more highly the
scientist's achievement in contributing new knowledge within such well-
established methods and forms or even contributing to a paradigm shift.
Writers in all genres are creative, and all genres enable writers' creativity.

To accept such notions of everyday creativity is to question some
cherished notions about creativity and genius. It requires acknowledging the role of community values in calling an act creative and being more
appreciative of the creativity in all writing. To do so would challenge
the separation of the literary from the nonliterary, the "creative" writing from the "noncreative" writing, the James Joyce from the Jane Doe.
To do so would not require ignoring the qualities admired in a Joyce (and
again the question of aesthetic value awaits attention in the next chapter), but it would require seeing in those Joycean qualities both constraint
and choice, both uniqueness and conformity. It would also require admiring more qualities in the writing of a Jane Doe, admiring the divergence within the convergence, the ability to conform to expectations and
the ability to say something uniquely.

Although I will address the teaching of genre more broadly in the
last chapter, the particular issue of teaching genres as creative merits
attention here. To help students gain perspective on genres and creativity, we might take a lesson from how many have come to teach language
standards. With language standards, many teachers have come to an
uneasy compromise: they teach the diversity and social constructedness
of language standards, and they teach the possibility of resisting those
standards, while they also teach the one language standard, SEE, that
"educated" contexts require. What matters most is more an attitude
toward standards than a particular pedagogy or set of skills. A similar
approach to genre would seem to me appropriate. Teachers' attitudes
toward genres in the classroom could include several claims: that genres
are diverse, including the formal research paper and the friends' conversation; that their expectations are constructed in response to social and
rhetorical contexts; that it is possible to violate any generic expectation;
while at the same time some genres are most important to "educated"
contexts. Whether those genres ought to be taught explicitly I leave to
the last chapter.

As is true for the teaching of language standards, though, we scholars and teachers must confront directly the power of genres to constrain

and enable choice. We can confront it when we teach first-year writing and decide whether to teach "the essay" or how much to insist on the conventions of "academic writing." We can confront it when we begin our dissertations and consider the attitudes toward knowledge and personal experience that we must adopt if our dissertations are to be passed—or when we direct our student's dissertation and decide how much "dissertationese" we must require for our colleagues to accept it. We can confront it whenever we plan research on writing and select the genres within which our participants will work, a choice that may determine a community, an ideology, a voice, and much more. When in our past we failed to examine language standards, we taught them to our students unthinkingly and uncritically. When we saw language standards as evil constraints only, we failed to enable our students to use the prestige dialect to achieve their own goals. Only when we see language standards as both inhibiting and enabling can we give students the power to use them critically. Only when we understand genres as both constraint and choice, both regularity and chaos, both inhibiting and enabling will we be able to help students to use the power of genres critically and effectively. In such power is individual freedom.

Research on creativity helps us, too, with how to teach students to be both communicative and creative. Writers need both convergence and divergence; teachers can help students to develop whichever is lacking in particular writers and particular writing situations. For the students struggling with acceptable form, teachers might help them see the convergences among unique texts, help them use vertical thinking to discover patternings. For the students struggling with too much convergence, with formulaity, teachers might help them see the divergence of each text within its genre, the inevitability of divergence in their own texts, and encourage their lateral thinking to discover choices. Students need to learn how to make their texts fit within the patternings of converging situations and texts; they also need to learn how to diverge from those patternings in order to say what they want to say. Both kinds of learning are learning about genres. Both kinds of learning are necessary to encourage students' creativity. Both kinds of learning can also enable students to critique the social values, assumptions, and beliefs that have shaped those patternings, those genres. Helping students discover the rhetorical and social strategies behind the forms, their purposes and effects, what conformity they allow and what choices they require can develop students' critical as well as creative abilities.

Research into and teaching of professional genres can also benefit from an understanding of the creative powers of genre. In my research on the writing of tax accountants, for example, I found novice accountants having to concentrate on generic convergence but often inadequately recognizing the importance of divergence to the genre's success. For example, a junior accountant described how he copied relevant Codes of the Internal Revenue Service (that is, IRS Codes) into particular sections in a research memorandum, emphasizing convergence with existing genres; but a partner accountant described how the research memorandum applies relevant IRS Codes to a particular "fact pattern," a particular client's situation, emphasizing the uniting of divergence and convergence. As I interviewed accountants on the texts they had written, I found the divergence from the expected patterns to be as revealing about their genres as the convergence with those patterns. As I more recently worked on some projects with jury instructions, I found the genre constantly being defined by the confluence of convergence and divergence. Rewriting jury instructions to make them more intelligible but still technically accurate required me to distinguish acceptable from unacceptable divergence. As an outsider to the community that uses those instructions, I made unacceptable revisions several times. The insiders who knew the genre well quickly and easily noted those unacceptable divergences and could suggest divergences that would suit the genre and community better. The requirements of the genre guided those judgments of acceptable as well as unacceptable divergence. To say that the genre of jury instructions was constraining what I could write would be to misstate the role of genre in the divergence as well as the convergence: the genre of jury instructions enabled rewriting in particular ways, encouraged diverging in particular ways.

Research into these and other sets of genres may clarify this tension within genres, their ability to sustain both convergence and divergence, both vertical and lateral thinking, both standardization and variation, both constraint and choice.

Genre and Ideology

Emphasizing genre's positive role in enabling creativity is necessary to balance the usual negative connection of genre to constraint, but I do not want to ignore the genuine potential of genres to sustain and even enforce social meanings and belief systems, a topic I explored socially in chapter 2 but which I wish to revisit in the context of creativity. Because of its very nature, genre can empower and can impose power. Defining "ideology" generally as the socially constructed ways in which human beings understand the world,[5] the theory of genres presented in this volume must acknowledge genres' ideological power. Yet ideological power is not necessarily good or evil but rather, as J. M. Balkin describes it, ambivalent: it works for both good and bad, depending on how it is used. The potential for genres to enforce ideology is always present, just as the potential for genres to encourage creativity is always present. The difference lies within its use. Both constraint and creativity, though, are, as I have argued so far, necessarily inherent in the cultural construction that is genre.

In this section, I draw heavily on the theory of ideology argued by J. M. Balkin in his book *Cultural Software: A Theory of Ideology*, both because his explication of ideology is so thorough and well enmeshed in others' theories and because his theory acknowledges what humans gain as well as risk in their use of social constructions. Balkin calls socially constructed cultural information, what gets created and transmitted historically and through people, "cultural software." In spite of the machinelike metaphor, Balkin treats cultural information as tools for human cognition, ways of understanding the world, without which humans would be unable to make meaning. Like genres, though Balkin never mentions genres other than narrative structures, cultural information both enables understanding and potentially delimits what people can perceive. Such cultural software is created and transmitted by human beings; it does not exist as some suprastructure or system independent of the people who create and use it. Significantly, as I have been arguing for genres, cultural information in Balkin's theory both preserves similarity of constructions across individuals and permits innovation; thus cultural information can adapt to different circumstances and change across time (92). Applied to social scripts, Balkin describes these socially constituted ways of understanding experience as "platforms for innovation and improvisation" (195), a phrasing equally descriptive of the source of creativity within genres. Genres, as part of cultural information or "software," help humans understand their experience, are created and transmitted by other humans, and preserve stability while allowing change and creativity.

Because they are both inevitable and ubiquitous, cultural information, including genres, has often unrecognized ideological power. While that power is what enables human understanding, it is the same power that can have harmful effects. Balkin uses the example of narrative expectations to examine how extensively cultural information infiltrates our ways of being in the world; it can represent the potential effects of genres as well. Narrative, Balkin writes, "is simultaneously a method of memory storage, a method of framing and organizing experience, a method for indexing and retrieving information, a method of internalizing cultural expectations, and a method of explaining deviations from cultural expectations" (189–90). As such, it shapes much of our experience and has multiple possible ideological effects. Narrative expectations "give meaning to events" and "create the possibility of deviations from what is expected" (190–91), the dual role I have been arguing for genres and that Balkin even describes at one point as "Janus-faced" (191), comparable to the Janus-faced nature of creativity. This generative nature of genres Balkin describes for narratives as a heuristic: "[N]arrative thinking lets us organize the exceptional and the unusual into a comprehensive form. It allows us to learn by letting us match and reconfigure old expectations in light of new experiences" (191).

As this last point demonstrates, the very nature of narrative thinking—and other sets of expectations, including genres—more harmfully encourages a narrowing of possibilities, a reshaping of what is different into what fits expectations. Just as language standards require nonstandard usage to be justified or else judged negatively, the norms of genres require deviations from the expected to be justified rhetorically. Because cultural expectations define "what is canonical, expected, and ordinary," they bestow "legitimacy and authority on the expected," as Balkin writes (191). Thus, deviations from the expected are not only made more visible, thus enabling learning and innovation, but also made more questionable, thus challenging their validity and appropriateness. This role of genres to define the expected constitutes its most criticized feature. If genres help writers see what is expected, they may also disguise the legitimacy of what is not expected.

Genres can have other potential harmful effects that stem from their nature as ideological constructs. As one way of understanding experience, genres necessarily simplify that experience. Any categorization of experience, as I argued earlier in this volume, necessarily reduces unique situations to common, constructedly recurrent types of situations. The complexity and variation of each situation is thus reduced, and the view of that situation will necessarily be partial only. Further, if that partial and simplified view of experience comes to be endorsed by some institutional authority—a school curriculum, a handbook or style guide, a company manual—people are even less likely to see and value what is different, and they are less likely to critique the validity of what is expected. With institutional authority in place, the tendency of genres to

resist change also increases, as was demonstrated in the previous chapter by the slowness of Scottish national public records to adopt the newly
developing standards (though those new standards, of course, were also
promoting a new ideology). Cultural constructions, perhaps including
genres, also have the dangerous ability to "make themselves true," in
Balkin's words (211). As they are used, they become part of what is considered true about an experience. When multiple people use the same
perspective to describe an experience, others come to see that similarly
described perspective as social truth. As individuals use their existing
constructions to interpret new experience, too, they may force that experience into a different shape and may even encourage others to respond
to that experience in light of that interpretation. Balkin describes viv-
idly the cycle of such self-fulfilling interpretations:

> Depending on the narrative structures that we possess, the
> same behavior can be interpreted as a mere social slight, a
> misunderstanding, an aggressive action or a vital threat to
> national security. This interpretation can shape our response;
> the response, in turn, can induce behavior from others that
> confirms our worst fears. (213)

More particularly generic examples of "making themselves true" seem
apparent: if radio listeners and deejays perceive new music through their
generic filters of country music, rock music, or pop music, then an aspir-
ing musician or even a Shania Twain is likely to write music that fits country expectations in order to be playable on country stations; if tax accountants are trained to write research memoranda by copying heavily from
IRS regulations, then a new client's unique fact pattern will probably be
interpreted as an instance of a specific regulation; if students learn to support their academic arguments using logic and reason only, emotion and
ethos will come to be seen as inappropriate in academic arguments.

These potentially harmful effects of such cultural constructions as
genres are precisely what critics of genre most fear. Yet such potential
harm cannot be eliminated any more than the cultural constructions
themselves can be eliminated. People need cultural constructions, including genres, to make sense of their worlds, and making such cultural
constructions, including genres, appears to be part of human cognition.
Genres exist. And because genres exist, they will have ideological power.
Balkin contends that cultural constructions have power over individuals because they both enable and delimit understanding, because we come
to depend on them, and because using them requires us to open ourselves

to the influence of others, including to change and manipulation (273–75). Using genres at all requires us to let genres define our view of the world, brings us to depend on them as our default interpretations, and opens our minds to perceiving things as others do. The more significant a particular genre is in our interpretation of our experience, the more helpful and dangerous the genre is. As Balkin writes, "The more pervasive and powerful a form of cultural software in understanding the world, the more pervasive and powerful its potential ideological effects" (215).

What keeps such potential ideological power from overwhelming the benefits of genres, besides the resigned fact of its inevitability, is that genres are still created and transmitted by individuals, by human beings with all their imperfections, including the imperfect transmission of ideology. Balkin argues that ideology, his cultural software, must be created and transmitted by individuals and that the bits of cultural information are thus replicated in individual minds. But that cultural information is not replicated exactly the same in each individual. The inevitability of individual variation that Balkin sees in cultural information is a critical concept in language study also. No individual utters a word identically each time; variations of pronunciation always occur, even if only slight variations of pitch, the exact articulation of a vowel, or the precise movement from one sound to the next. Similarly, a genre is never experienced or transmitted identically from one person to the next. People learn each genre through their own experience with it, either through direct instruction, modeling, or more passive reception. That learning always necessarily differs from one person to the next, as individual experiences with genres differ. The construction of categories also differs from one mind to the next. Thus the conception of genre in each individual mind, though sufficiently similar to that of others in the society, inevitably varies. From such variation—and the transmission of such variation from one individual to another—comes the potential for change, for critique, and for creativity.

In addition to their learning and transmission of genre being necessarily imperfect and variable, human beings do not receive generic information passively. Rather they fit new knowledge in with existing knowledge, adapting and adjusting it as they go. As Balkin explains for cultural information, human minds adjust the cultural information they receive to fit within their own unique minds and experiences; and individuals combine and modify that information in their own ways (52). Just as I argue that the existence of genres enables creative divergence from those genres, Balkin notes that existing cultural information enables creativity by "providing thought with a necessary framework for problem solving and innovation" (52). What he sees as the essential creativity of human beings leads Balkin to conclude, "We are not simply the inheritors of a zealously guarded patrimony but entrepreneurial producers of a new cultural software, which will help constitute future generations of human beings" (52). Our story, he writes, is not one of slavery or of breaking free of slavery but one of creative freedom made possible by constraint.

That is not to say that genre entails ideology only positively but rather that genre entails both the positive and the negative, depending on how it is used. Genre exists in and is created only by individuals, actual human beings acting through language. Hence genre's power to manipulate comes through the actions of individuals manipulating other individuals, even as those manipulators themselves are reflecting the prior constructions and perhaps manipulations that they received from others. Balkin describes cultural software as both "a source of power over individuals and a source of individual autonomy" (279). Autonomy, which Balkin defines as "the ability to articulate one's values and act according to one's desires," is achieved through cultural software, "using the very means through which one is subjected to hermeneutic power. Hermeneutic power simultaneously facilitates autonomy and subjection" (280). Individual agency similarly derives from individuals' use of cultural software (293).

My argument, then, is that genre both empowers and subjects to power. Without genres, writers would lack significant ways of understanding their experiences and of making meaning through language. With genres, writers are subject to the manipulation of others and to the constraints of prior expectations, assumptions, values, and beliefs. Janus-like, genres inevitably look both ways at once, encompassing convergence and divergence, similarity and difference, standardization and variation, constraint and creativity. Rejecting these dichotomies and sustaining these tensions, genre can become, as language, infinitely and essentially creative.

6

A Comparison of Literary
and Rhetorical Genres

At this point in my theory, a little wishful thinking slips in.
—caption of cartoon by Sidney Harris,
Chronicle of Higher Education, 4 September 1998

Throughout this volume, my emphasis has been on rhetorical genres and their contexts, on the texts people use to communicate with one another and to perform linguistic actions. Even though in the chapter on creativity I addressed issues that are more typically raised about literary works—such as the nature of creativity, the sources of originality, and how writers vary from generic expectations—for the most part I have ignored literary genres in establishing a rhetorical genre theory and considering its implications. In this respect, this volume has conformed to the usual expectations of composition and rhetoric scholars within genre theory. Our genre theory is a reconceived, rhetorically based genre theory, not the categorization of literary kinds of old, when the term *genre* included only literary genres. Our main concern is with the everyday texts of everyday people, not the special texts of a cultural elite, the genres of which have already received considerable scholarly attention. So our genre theory—and mine in this volume—emphasizes rhetorical rather than literary genres, for good reasons and to good ends. Nonetheless, if our genre theory is to account for all genres—a goal that I hope we achieve—then it must account for literary as well as rhetorical genres. The extension of this rhetorical genre theory to literary genres is not, it turns out, a simple matter. Some basic postulates of rhetorical genre theory must be complicated to include literary genres, and those complications in turn lead to some new insights about rhetorical genres.

Whether there is a significant difference of kind between literary and nonliterary texts in the first place is a question long debated, a debate renewed recently by the work of those in cultural studies. The distinction between rhetorical and literary texts may thus be a false distinction, so that a rhetorical genre theory easily accommodates so-called literary texts. Even so, separate attention to literary genres is justified by the separation of literature and rhetoric in the long history of textual study. Although contemporary theorists might challenge the distinction, it has a long history that has led to distinctions between literary critics and rhetoricians and between literary theorists and composition theorists. The distinction has led to different fields of investigation with different questions and objects of study. Thus the focus of this chapter: Can a reconceived rhetorical theory of genre, drawing heavily from the questions, issues, and objects of study of rhetoric, contribute to an understanding of genres and texts traditionally labeled as literary as well as those labeled nonliterary? Can a rhetorical theory of genre respond to the questions raised by literary theorists and critics?

Of course, genre is not a new concept for literary study any more than it is for rhetoric, and questions about literary works have long been answered in terms of genre. Aristotle's *Poetics,* even more than his *Rhetoric,* uses the kind of text as a major organizing principle, beginning with his stated purpose in the first sentence of *Poetics:* "The art of poetic composition in general and its various species, the function and effect of each of them . . . these are the problems we shall discuss" (15). Generic questions have long been explored by literary scholars, becoming less popular only relatively recently. Past literary research bibliographies are full of works that explain texts by categorizing them into genres, that debate generic categorizations of particular texts, that describe characteristics of particular genres, and that argue over the nature of genres. Rene Wellek and Austin Warren, in their classic *Theory of Literature,* devote a chapter to literary genres as a necessary part of the "intrinsic" study of literature. Northrop Frye, in his 1957 *Anatomy of Criticism,* rejuvenated genre criticism with a new elaboration of genre to which literary critics since have responded. Even Frye's conception of genre, however, could not sustain genre criticism in the face first of romantic views of the author and then of poststructuralist and postmodern epistemologies. To the extent that genre had been defined in terms of common textual characteristics, genre criticism was out of place both in a world of individual inspiration and in a nonformalist theoretical world. The traditional literary views of genre, like the traditional rhetorical views of genre described in chapter 1, could not hold.

Today, however, literary studies, like rhetorical studies, is renewing its interest in genre by reconceiving the nature of genre. Literary scholars from comparative literature, cultural studies, historical studies, and other current schools of literary theory have been revisiting genre and restating its centrality to literary study. Adena Rosmarin published in 1985 *The Power of Genre*, in which she argues that genre can be reclaimed as a literary critic's tool. Ralph Cohen, in "History and Genre" in 1986, contributes to a treatment of literary genre as dynamic and changing. Marjorie Perloff in 1989 edited *Postmodern Genres*, providing a forum for major scholars to examine genres of all kinds, both literary and nonliterary, textual and nontextual, in light of postmodern epistemologies. In 1993, David Fishelov published his study *Metaphors of Genre: The Role of Analogies in Genre Theory* to survey past and recent genre theory in order to recover what could still be useful for the understanding of literary genres today. And the concept of ideology, which has become so central to much of literary theory, was connected to literary genre in 1994 in Thomas O. Beebee's book *The Ideology of Genre: A Comparative Study of Generic Instability*. Clearly, genre remains a significant concept for literary study, and literary theorists are recreating their views of genre to accommodate current approaches to literature.

Similar Questions, Similar Answers: Genre as Present, Varying, Dynamic

Those recreated views of literary genres are in some ways easily compatible with recreated views of rhetorical genres, and in some ways they raise difficult questions for all genre theories. Since literature, composition, and rhetoric, like other fields of knowledge, have all been affected by common philosophical shifts, it is not surprising that their reconceptions of genre share many qualities. All have moved away from formalism, and so all have moved away from defining genre as textual forms. Text, whether literary or rhetorical, is no longer seen as objective and static but rather as dynamic and created through the interaction of writer, reader, and context. Although literary theorists tend to emphasize the relationship of the reader and the text while compositionists tend to emphasize the relationship of the writer and the text, all acknowledge the interactive nature of textual meaning, the rhetorical triangulation of writer-reader-text, and the embeddedness of those relationships within context or culture. With such common new understandings of meaning come, not surprisingly, common new understandings of genre. Were genre to be defined as static categorization or textual features, genre

would hold little significance for today's theorists, whether from literature, composition, or rhetoric. Instead, genre has come to be redefined
in all these text-based fields as a dynamic concept created through the
interaction of writers, readers, past texts, and contexts.

For many literary scholars, genre has become part of the cultural
context with which writers and readers interact. Like culture and context, then, genre is inescapable. Thus, all literary texts participate in
genres. Many literary scholars no longer equate literary genres with classic categorizations of tragic, comic, and lyric (or epic); with older, rigid
forms, such as the sonnet; or with "genre writing," such as mysteries,
romances, science fiction, and westerns. Rather, every literary work is
seen as participating in genres. If literary scholars do not agree with E.
D. Hirsch's all-encompassing statement that "[a]ll understanding of
verbal meaning is necessarily genre-bound" (76), they might agree with
Jacques Derrida's more paradoxical statement, "every text participates
in one or several genres, there is no genreless text; there is always a genre
and genres, yet such participation never amounts to belonging" (65). The
nature of that participation without belonging is defined differently by
different theorists, but, in agreement with current rhetorical genre theory,
literary genre theorists (other than Croce and his followers) have largely
rejected the romantic notion that literary texts escape genre, that the
"best" literary works are those that cannot be categorized, those that
no genre can hold. (That the best literary works still "go beyond" our
expectations for genre is another argument that I will address later in
this chapter.) Fishelov describes the relationship of even the most innovative literary works to genre in a way that echoes rhetorical views of
creativity within genres:

> [E]ven in those areas of modern literature where it seems that
> generic rules are absent, the innovative areas of canonic lit-
> erature, generic rules are still a vital part of the literary com-
> municative situation. These generic conventions might be
> viewed as a challenge, or a horizon, against which the writer
> and his reader have to define themselves. The writer may
> stretch the generic rules, he may produce some unpredictable
> "match" between different existing conventions of existing
> literary genres (or even between literary conventions and
> conventions taken from other media), but in order to under-
> stand the overall significance of his text, we should be aware
> of the generic system against which he is working. A writer

does not create in a textual vacuum, and a rebellious child is still part of the family. (82–83)

As this comment suggests, contemporary literary genre theory also shifts somewhat from traditional literary genre theory by emphasizing the nature of genre as difference as well as similarity, of a *differance* that defines genre somewhat like Anne Freadman's "not-statements" define the negative nature of genre for rhetorical theorists. We know genres by what they are not as well as by what they are; a text participates in genres that it rejects as well as in those it accepts, in genres that it avoids as well as in those it embraces. Rosmarin describes genres as metaphors, a move that necessarily encompasses both likeness and unlikeness (as the metaphor "my love is a rose" derives meaning both from including the rose's perfume and from excluding the rose's thorns). Beebee goes so far as to argue that "a 'single' genre is only recognizable as difference, as a foregrounding against the background of its neighboring genres" (28). Cohen makes a similar argument in explaining why genres need not be defined by shared generic traits:

> A genre does not exist independently; it arises to compete or to contrast with other genres, to complement, augment, interrelate with other genres. Genres do not exist by themselves; they are named and placed within hierarchies or systems of genres, and each is defined by reference to the system and its members. A genre, therefore, is to be understood in relation to other genres, so that its aims and purposes at a particular time are defined by its interrelation with and differentiation from others. ("History" 207)

As Beebee points out, this complex interaction at the heart of current genre theory is also at the heart of our rejection of formalist genre theories, for "formalism is limited to describing what is 'there' in the texts, whereas any generic reading of a text is based equally on what is not there, on what the text does not say, and ultimately on what cannot be done with it" (263).

Since critics define the genres of literary texts by such similarity and difference, it is easy to see with literary genres how texts not only always participate in a genre but always participate in multiple genres simultaneously. As a result of genres' being defined by what they are not as well as what they are, Beebee argues, "every work involves more than one genre, even if only implicitly" (28). Perloff argues that more recently developing, postmodern genres appropriate multiple genres, "both high and popular," by "longing for a both/and situation rather than one of either/or" ("Introduction" 8), but Beebee argues that all genres, not just "postmodern" genres, involve such multiplicity: "Genre must be defined recursively: genres are made out of other genres" (264).

Current literary genre theorists, then, would seem to agree with rhetorical genre theorists that all texts participate in genres, that those genres are conceptual rather than formal, and that those genres encompass difference as well as similarity. Most literary and rhetorical genre theorists would also seem to agree that genres are dynamic and situated in specific historical circumstances. As I noted in chapter 4, Cohen offers the most elaborated dynamic and historical view of literary genres in his article "History and Genre." Cohen sees generic grouping as a process, as purpose-specific classifications that people construct at specific historical moments (205–10). This historical view of genres is more dynamic than the more often stated views of genres as institutions. Fredric Jameson, for example, states that "Genres are essentially literary *institutions,* or social contracts between a writer and a specific public, whose function is to specify the proper use of a particular cultural artifact"[1] (qtd. in Fishelov 87, Jameson's emphasis). The institutional view of genres is an old one, for Jameson's definition partly echoes an earlier statement of Wellek and Warren:

> The literary kind is an "institution"—as Church, University, or State is an institution. It exists, not as an animal exists or even as a building, chapel, library, or capital, but as an institution exists. One can work through, express oneself through, existing institutions, create new ones, or get on, so far as possible, without sharing in politics or rituals; one can also join, but then reshape, institutions. (226)

Today theorists might argue that one can never "get on" without participating in institutions or that institutions are not quite so separable from their participants. Theorists would also see institutions as more dynamic, reshaped by every action taken by its participants. All institutions, we see today, are culturally specific, historically determined; even the buildings, the chapels, libraries, and capitals, are culturally defined. So, too, are literary genres viewed today. Perloff states the matter baldly: "[G]enre, far from being a normative category, is always culture-specific and, to a high degree, historically determined" ("Introduction" 7). Although I argue in chapter 5 that genres are indeed normative categories

as well as culture-specific, Perloff's description of the historical speci-
ficity of literary genres agrees well with the local situatedness of rhetorical genres described in my previous chapters. Perloff's collection also
demonstrates this view; Lindenberger, for example, examines opera "to
show how a genre is rooted in particular institutional frameworks at
different historical moments" (31). Since genre is so historical, institutional, cultural, and situated, it is indelibly social and hence, as Beebee
argues at length, ideological, again a conception of literary genre that
agrees with conceptions of rhetorical genres.

Similar Questions, Different Answers:
Genre as Constructed and Constructing

From my interpretation of literary genre theory so far, it would seem that
rhetorical genre theory can comfortably apply to literary as well as rhetorical genres. Literary texts can be described as necessarily participating in at least one genre, and all literary genres can be treated as ideological concepts, historically and culturally situated, dynamically
interacting with multiple genres and defined by both their similarities
and differences with other genres. But underlying this apparent agreement may be a more essential disagreement about the nature of genres.
Rhetorical genre theory, as I have developed it throughout this volume,
is based in a functional, pragmatic theory of textual meaning. Genres
help language users achieve certain aims, fulfill certain functions, perform certain actions, do things with language. To the extent that genres
are perceived as being successful in achieving those functions, even as
situations and participants change, readers and writers operate within
them. Even apparently unsuccessful genres can operate on readers and
writers if the genres have become calcified or their proponents have
sufficient status and power in the group that uses them. Genres exist,
then, in the sense that they are patternings from repeated actions according to which (or in reaction against which) readers and writers use language. Can literary genres be understood as functional and pragmatic
in the same way? Do literary genres exist and operate on readers and
writers in the same ways? I would answer yes, but some literary theorists have answered the same questions differently.

Most quickly revealing of the possible conflict that I see is the genre
theory offered by Rosmarin. To Rosmarin, genres exist only in the critic's
mind and in the critic's use of them. The critic, not the writer, defines
the genre (29). From Rosmarin's perspective, genre is a critical tool rather
than a language-making tool, or even an operationalizing tool, as the

rhetorician David Russell would have it (see my discussion of Russell's view of genre within activity theory in chapter 2). To reduce genre to a tool at all is to deny its conceptual and ideological nature, making genre the consequence of culture and action rather than in an interactive and recursive relationship with culture and action. Defining genre as a critical tool in particular makes the critic all-powerful and rhetorical interaction negligible, as Rosmarin herself reveals:

> [O]nce genre is defined as pragmatic rather than natural, as defined rather than found, and as used rather than described, then there are precisely as many genres as we need, genres whose conceptual shape is precisely determined by that need. They are designed to serve the explanatory purpose of critical thought, not the other way around. (25)

Significant in this passage are Rosmarin's uses of the passive voice and collective "we." Who defines and uses genre? And whose need determines the conceptual shape of genres? To Rosmarin, the answer to both questions is the critic. Rhetorical genre theorists can agree with Rosmarin that genre is pragmatic, defined, and used, but some would disagree about whose actions are being described. In this move to the critic as definer of genre, Rosmarin privileges the reader's role—and a particular kind of reader role—above all others. In fact, she appears to omit the role of writers in genre construction altogether. She describes what she sees as a traditional "three-way conflict" in which "constitutive or explanatory power is in rapid and alternating succession located in genres, in the particulars of the historical text and context, in the theorist's 'envisioning' of those genres and particulars" (34). Translated to rhetorical terms, Rosmarin's three-way conflict alternates power in the text, the context, or the reader, but not in the writer. Beebee, in fact, describes a similar traditional conflict, but he includes the writer and adds it up to a four-way conflict:

> These four stages of generic criticism—genre as rules, genre as species, genre as patterns of textual features, and genre as reader conventions—correspond to the four positions in the great debate about the location of textual meaning: in authorial intention, in the work's historical or literary context, in the text itself, or in the reader. (3)

Certainly, some compositionists can sometimes be faulted for privileging the role of the writer over that of the reader, text, or context, producing the inverse of Rosmarin's preference. But capturing the pragmatic nature of genre requires capturing its complex functionality—in the writer's aims, in the culture and society's institutions and power maintenance, in the text's rhetorical strategies, and in the reader's or critic's responsive actions. As Beebee writes, in a different context, "genre is only secondarily an academic enterprise and a matter for literary scholarship. Primarily, genre is the precondition for the creation and the reading of texts" (250).

As a "precondition" for making meaning through language, genre also has power to shape texts, a power that Rosmarin's view of the critic as generic arbiter would preclude. The critic has power, in Rosmarin's view, to examine any text "as if" it participated in any genre. Only multiple examinations of a text through multiple generic screens will yield insight into the text, Rosmarin argues, and the choice of generic screen is limited only by the critic's ability to show that her use of a genre best justifies the "value" of a particular literary work (50–51). The necessity of seeing any text as participating in multiple genres is an insight that literary genre theory does seem to offer to rhetorical genre theory, as I will discuss further below. The critic and her aim to justify literary value are not the only powerful participants in genres, however, and the aims of the writers and needs of the cultural context must also be taken into account. The text, the writer, the context, and the critic, too, are shaped by genre. That is the fuller power of genre.

Not all literary genre theorists agree with Rosmarin's perspective, of course, and they offer counterbalancing views of the rhetorical nature of literary genres. Yet Rosmarin's position, though extreme, reflects a common privileging by literary theorists of the critic's role in creating genres. Cohen, in his seminal article "History and Genre," keeps genre rhetorically as well as historically contextualized in his major argument, which he summarizes as follows:

> Classifications are empirical, not logical. They are historical assumptions constructed by authors, audiences, and critics in order to serve communicative and aesthetic purposes. Such groupings are always in terms of distinctions and interrelations, and they form a system or community of genres. The purposes they serve are social and aesthetic. Groupings arise at particular historical moments, and as they include more and more members, they are subject to repeated redefinitions or abandonment. (210)

Yet his next sentence reveals his own essential privileging of the critic over all other participants: "Genres are open systems; they are grouping of texts *by critics* to fulfill certain ends" (210, emphasis added). In a similar move earlier in the article, Cohen emphasizes that genres are processes rather than determinate categories, which are changed by each member that is added to the genre. He continues, "The process by which genres are established always involves the human need for distinction and interrelation. Since the purposes of *critics who establish genres* vary, it is self-evident that the same texts can belong to different groupings or genres and serve different generic purposes" (204, emphasis added). To Cohen and Rosmarin, and to many other literary genre theorists, genre is a concept created and used by critics foremost or first of all. Even as literary theorists like Cohen acknowledge the roles of writers and other readers in genre formation, it is the critic whose conception of genre matters, who defines what is of interest to study, who makes genre matter. Of course, that privileging of the critic makes sense for scholars of literature who are most concerned to contribute to the literary critic's interpretive range. Again, let me remind that compositionists have tended to privilege the writer in similar ways, to use the writer's understanding of genre as defining what matters in genre study. Rhetorical genre theory, however, needs to account for what matters to critics, writers, and other readers, as well as to understand genre's embeddedness in text and context. If literary genre theory depends on genre being a construction of the critic alone, then rhetorical genre theory will necessarily contradict literary genre theory.

Fortunately, not all literary genre theorists agree with Rosmarin's complete preeminence of the critic as definer of genre and some may leave room for a rhetorically richer view of how genres are constructed. Cohen, as his earlier quoted statements show, gives writers and other readers a role in genre construction and function, even as he privileges the critic's role. Cohen's privileging of the critic seems more the result of his (and traditional literature's) interest in enabling literary criticism rather than the result of an exclusive definition of genre. Cohen sees the dynamic nature of genres for all participants, and his emphasis on the social and aesthetic functions of genre leaves room for functions other than the critic's. Among literary genre theorists, Beebee in particular seems to make genre a rhetorical concept encompassing writers, readers (including critics), texts, and contexts. Beebee echoes functional genre theorists rather directly in privileging "use-value" as the essence of genre: "[A] text's genre is its *use-value*. Genre gives us not understanding in the abstract and passive sense but use in the pragmatic and active sense" (14). The use-values that Beebee describes are comfortably familiar to new rhetorical conceptions of genre, involving the functions the genres serve for their users and the contexts in which they operate: "[G]eneric differences are grounded in the 'use-value' of a discourse rather than in its content, formal features, or its rules of production" (7). He further argues that, since use-values are necessarily social, genres (and genre theory) are necessarily ideological (14–15). In a detailed examination of how letter-writing manuals evolved into novels like Samuel Richardson's *Pamela* and others, Beebee argues that the manuals came to have functions, use-values, that the original *ars de dicta* could no longer fulfill, and so they developed differently in order to achieve the genre's functions:

> [T]he rhetorical manual must correspond to the social and political circumstances of its readers; it must represent the letter writer in order to produce a good letter. In other words, in order to fulfill the rather explicit function this genre has been assigned, it must do something else beyond the limits of its genre: it must become literature, create a (fictional) excess. In doing so, the *ars* becomes something other than itself. (110)

Although Beebee appears to be alone among literary theorists in defining genres according to their use-values, he is not alone in seeing generic change as originating in social and political change. His argument suggests that rhetorical genre theories based in pragmatic function can account for literary genres as well. In fact, most of Beebee's book demonstrates a literary generic criticism based in such a functional and rhetorical view of literary genres. Cultural studies approaches to literature in general would also seem to accommodate rhetorical genre theories, for cultural studies seems based in rhetorical understandings of how participants use "texts" in cultural contexts, and of how the texts and participants are shaped by the contexts. Such detailed genre studies as Janice Radway's study of the romance genre describe literature as fulfilling particular functions for its readers, and other studies of particular literary genres at least make reference to what genres do for their readers and for society. Such current literary studies also can emphasize the ideological nature of genres, as does Beebee, making it easy to see the ideological functions of particular literary genres. For genre theory to encompass both literary and rhetorical genres requires not that literary theorists abandon their attention to the critic's perspective on literature. Instead, our understanding of genre will advance from the separate emphases—on the critic or on the writer—if we can work within a common definition of genre to develop complementary concepts.

Different Questions, Similar Answers: Conformity, Variation, and Valuing

Another difference of emphasis that a common genre theory would have to accommodate is the emphasis on conformity to or variation from generic expectations. Where rhetorical genre theorists often seek texts that typify a genre, examine writers' conformity to generic conventions, and study readers' roles in promoting generic expectations, literary genre theorists are more likely to seek texts that break the rules of a genre, to value writers who challenge conventions, and to act as readers promoting unconventional generic readings.[2] Great authors have often been admired for their "breaking" of generic conventions, thereby expanding the literary universe. The words used to describe variation from generic convention themselves reveal the differing attitudes toward such variation and might be the basis of an interesting study. Some writers are said to "break," "violate," or "flout" conventions. Others "challenge," "push," "expand," or "play with" conventions. Current authors (like Laura Esquivel or Jorge Luis Borges) and some past authors (like Laurence Sterne in *Tristram Shandy*) are admired for their "resistance" to generic ideology, often through "appropriating" multiple genres, thereby giving us more "hybrid" genres. Can rhetorical genre theory deal with desirable variations within literary genres made by accomplished writers as well as the "errors" in rhetorical genres made by novices?

Describing the variation in individual texts should pose no problem for rhetorical genre theory. Methods of rhetorical criticism already exist to examine the rhetorical effectiveness of accomplished speakers (such as presidential inaugural addresses), methods that correspond and cooperate with literary critical methods. Even to account adequately for everyday texts, as I argued in chapter 5, rhetorical genre theory will need to embrace a definition of genre that encompasses difference as well as similarity, variation as well as standardization, and creativity as well as conformity. With a genre theory that sees genre as both-and rather than either-or, both the conformity and the resistance, the expected and the surprise, we can account for rhetorical and literary genres that themselves encompass both norms and variation, and we can describe rhetorical and literary texts that both reproduce and resist their genres. A genre theory that sees in every text and every genre both similarity and difference has much to contribute to the understanding of all texts, whether rhetorical or literary.

Yet all texts are not alike in the degree to which they conform to generic conventions, and not all genres are alike in the degree to which they encourage conformity or encourage variation. Some literary genres are seen as highly conventionalized, with specifically defined expectations, compared with less narrowly defined genres—haiku and sonnets compared with free verse, morality plays compared with theater of the absurd, mysteries compared with "literary" novels. While all of these literary genres can be seen, in light of current genre theory, as encompassing both standards and variations, the room for variation would appear to be larger in some genres than others. The same can be said for rhetorical genres—the expectations for lab reports are more narrowly specified than those for research papers, for resumes more narrowly than for application letters, for how-to articles more narrowly than for essays, for inaugural addresses more narrowly than for resignation speeches; the possible comparisons abound. However, more attention has been paid to these different levels of expectation in literary than in rhetorical genres. Rhetorical genre theory might benefit from examining these different levels in rhetorical as well as literary genres, from considering the effects of more or less specification on writers and readers. As long as these differences were seen as differences of degree and not of kind, rhetorical genre theory would seem to have no trouble including differences in the conventionality of different genres: All genres contain both specified expectations and allowable variations; some genres (not necessarily rhetorical) contain more specific expectations than do other genres (not necessarily literary). Relative freedom or constriction, therefore, cannot distinguish literary from nonliterary genres but only more conventionalized from less conventionalized genres.

Relative variation from those conventions might, however, distinguish literary from nonliterary works. Although all texts vary from conventions to some extent and in similar ways, the degree of variation might be higher among those texts considered to be most literary. Formulaic novels are labeled mysteries, for example, but mysteries that "go beyond" the formula are labeled novels (compare a Lillian Jackson Braun *The Cat Who . . .* mystery with an Umberto Eco *The Name of the Rose* novel). Other than popularity, what is the difference between the novels of a John Grisham and the novels of a John Irving? Both are called novels; the genre seems to be the same, as defined by its users. Yet one is commonly considered literary, the other not. The degree of variation from generic expectations may be part of the distinction.

Comparing literary to rhetorical texts, though, reveals a more complicated picture. Some rhetorical texts vary greatly from generic conventions. Unlike essays, a rhetorical genre that some have shifted to the category of literature, journal articles are surely a nonliterary genre yet they permit considerable range and variation. Some authors of journal articles are breaking generic expectations in many ways in recent years—Jane Tompkins includes a personal voice and experience, Victor Vitanza encourages his authors in *Pre/Text* to experiment—so much so in fact that the genre of the academic journal article seems to be developing in new ways with new expectations and conventions. Yet these articles are not considered literary. Variation from generic expectations is common in the genres that most encourage such variation—literary genres like literary novels, free verse, short stories; rhetorical genres like journal articles, editorials, research proposals—and less common in the genres that discourage so much variation—literary genres like westerns, romances, sonnets; rhetorical genres like resumes, obituaries, requests for proposals.

Not only do some genres encourage more variation than other genres, but also variation is more highly valued in some genres than others. Even if genre theory can thus encompass both the existence of variation and differing degrees of variation, it still needs to add a critical element for literary genres: the valuing of variation. Variation within literary texts is generally more highly valued than is similarity. At times, the value of a literary work seems definable wholly in terms of the work's variation from what others have done, its resistance to what is expected. Of course, literary value is much more complicated than simple surprise value, and the degree to which the unexpected is valued in literature has certainly varied over time as well. Nonetheless, the most highly valued literature is typically prized to some degree for its "originality," its "novelty." As I argued in chapter 5, current rhetorical genre theory can show how genre enables creativity, but the study of literary genres demonstrates that it will also need to explain how and why that creativity is valued.

The challenge for genre theory is not just to account for the fact of variation from generic expectations being valued, though that challenge alone is a substantial one. Variation is also valued differently at different times and in different contexts, and, even within one time and context, not all variation is valued alike. Some writers' variations are more highly valued in literary works than are other writers' variations, and some variations of one writer are more highly valued than other variations of the same writer, even within the same text. In addition to traditional aesthetic theories, recent social theories, critical pedagogy, and cultural studies all show promise in explaining this differential valuation, for each explains value as a cultural construct. New perspectives on ideology, appropriation, and resistance might be especially helpful if generic variation is viewed as generic resistance. As Beebee notes, "if genre is a form of ideology, then the struggle against or the deviations from genre are ideological struggles" (19). Laura L. Behling examines generic hybrids as ideological responses to multiculturalism and generic "passing" as connected to identity. Other studies of particular literary works in their cultural contexts should reveal the power relationships, prevailing ideologies, and generic expectations that lead to the valuing of particular variations, and comparative historical studies should reveal how those relationships, ideologies, and expectations change across different cultures and times so that different variations are differently valued. Current redefinitions of literary value, in other words, should also lead to fuller understanding of the value of generic variations.

The question of differential value also extends to the valuing of entire literary genres: some literary genres are more highly valued by readers than are other literary genres, and literary genres in general are more valued than nonliterary genres. The simple existence of variation fails to account for the different evaluation of different genres, for as we have seen, some rhetorical and less valued genres encompass considerable variation. Of course, the evaluation of genres changes over time. In some ways, recent questions within popular culture and cultural studies are all questions about the valuing of different genres. Does our culture still value the "high" arts more than the "popular" genres, or is that self-definition changing? Is poetry more highly valued than romances, seen as more artistic, beautiful, and refined? Or are romances more highly valued, since they are more widely read and make more money for their authors? What different kinds of value do different genres have? Literary scholars are investigating such questions with new vigor today, and they are extending to questions about nonliterary genres: Why do we commonly claim to value poetry above advertisements when we read more advertisements than poetry? What can we learn about ourselves by studying talk shows with the same detail that we used to give to studying dramas? The value of different genres—and genre knowledge as cultural capital—is at the heart of much redefinition of literary study and culture.

Such notions of value rarely, if ever, have arisen in rhetorical genre theory, though indifference to questions of value cannot persist in the face of recent turns to critical perspectives on genre.[3] Although some rhetorical genre theorists have been critical of the genres they studied, more common has been a descriptive or historical stance toward the genres studied, a stance that has contributed much to an understanding of how genres work but that now must be supplemented by a more critical stance. Perhaps such inattention to value may derive partly from the focus of many rhetorical genre theorists on the writing of novices, whether students or workers in entry-level positions. Dealing with texts often so little valued, and with generic variations most often viewed as "errors," such scholars have often resisted traditional notions of value in order to claim significance for their objects of study. The discoveries from such genre research have set the stage now for the kinds of complications that literary genres raise, including the complication of value. Genre theory already examines the roles of genres in the communities that use them; those roles can now be partly distinguished by how the users value those genres. Genre theorists are increasingly taking critical perspectives on genres, including examining how genres maintain or reinforce power relationships and how they shape world views, leading easily to interpretations of generic value in terms of the community's values. The developing notion of genre sets within genre theory elaborated in chapter 2 can fruitfully encompass differentiations among genres within those sets, with some genres more highly valued than others. In general, the quality of value can be added to the qualities of genres that genre theorists investigate, part of the cultural and rhetorical actions of genre.

Different Questions, Different Answers: Function, Community, Situation

So far, I have argued that questions typically raised in the study of literature can be addressed in rhetorical genre theory, though surely not to the satisfaction of every literary theorist and not always without considerable expansion of existing genre theory. The questions I have raised from literary theory about the nature of genre, its existence apart from the critic, the significance and appreciation of generic variation, and differences in how genres are valued at different times raise intriguing questions that enrich existing genre theory and can lead to significant new areas of research. When reversed, however, and literary answers to questions from rhetorical genre theory are considered, answers do not always come so easily. In particular, genre theory raises two questions that are answered about literature only with difficulty: What are the functions of literary genres? And what communities do literary genres serve?

A rhetorical genre theory based on functionality requires literary genres, too, to be describable in terms of their functions for their users. If the genres of tax accountants perform the work of tax accountants, what does literature accomplish, and for what group of users? The functions of literary genres have been long debated. Some, such as Bakhtin, argue for a general aesthetic function for literature as a whole. Sir Philip Sidney was not alone in specifying the functions of literature as "to teach and delight" (11). Somewhat more narrowly, Aristotle distinguishes tragedy and comedy not only on their differing subject matter and level of language but also on their differing effects on readers, serving different functions for readers. Many literary scholars have puzzled over the function of tragedy for readers who are saddened by reading it, some positing a purging of emotion or a reassurance that other people have worse circumstances. Others have explored the laughter function of comedy, perhaps a classical genre with the easiest association with a function. Poetry or the lyric, on the other hand, has been associated with a function for readers with greater difficulty, often resorting to expressiveness, that poetry expresses readers' deeper thoughts and emotions, that it helps readers reflect on their worlds. Once we move from classical genres to what some call subgenres—sonnets, dramatic monologues, novels—the functions of literary genres are described in more particular terms. Sonnets glorify love, monologues enable the poet to comment on the speaker's perceptions, novels give order to the human condition. More recent explanations of literary functions include Radway's description of romances enabling their readers to separate from their familial obligations and reasserting their belief in the heterosexual relationship. Though the nature of literary function is far from settled, literary theorists would seem to assume that literature must have a functionality, so requiring literary genres to be seen as having functions would not appear to be an obstacle to a common genre theory.

Radway's study of the romance as well as Aristotle's postulates about the effects of tragedy and comedy show how closely tied generic function can be to generic readership, for literary as well as rhetorical genres. As Radway notes, however, even her careful study examines only a small number of readers and only one kind of reader. The mothers reading romances at home while their children sleep or attend school are not the same readers as the secretaries reading romances at their desks during lunch or on the subway heading to work. Similarly, the New York philanthropist reading a poem in *The New Yorker* is not the same audience as the New York poet reading the same poem. Even more so, the playgoer on the floor of the Globe is not the same audience as the Shakespearean scholar studying the Hinman collated manuscript. With such multiple audiences for literary genres, can literary genres be described in terms of their communities of users, as posited by rhetorical genre theory? Perhaps the community of users of literary genres could be described always in multiple terms: literary poems are read by other poets, by editors, and by educated readers who aspire to cultural sophistication. Such a description would not be so far from a more complex understanding of the multiple users of rhetorical genres: business memoranda are read by the audience specified in the address line and potentially by those readers' staffs, by the writer's peers and bosses, and by anyone else to whom the memorandum is forwarded. Perhaps to account for both the business memorandum and the literary poem, we would do well to complicate our understanding of audience and function. Rather than connecting a genre to one group of language users and one function, a unitary and simple connection, the rhetorical situations of genres, whether literary or rhetorical, may need always to be described as multiple and complex.

Both questions—of the functions and communities of literary genres—cause difficulty in part because of a common quality of some literature: it is read by multiple audiences at different times and places, apart from its initial situation and community. What might in the past have been described as "transcendence" or "universality" permits some literary works to be enjoyed well beyond the initial rhetorical situations and cultural circumstances that first produced them, and, for some literary genres, such transcendence and universality seem to be part of their function.

I can leave to literary scholars and cultural critics the question of why some particular literary works appeal to later readers and other works never surpass their times. Surely much of the question of how and why literary works are read beyond their local situation can be answered by historical study and cultural critique. Different reading publics have developed at different historical periods, with different literary "tastes" and different commercial forces at work to encourage reading some works and even whole genres over others. The issues of value, raised earlier in this chapter, develop historically and culturally and influence what gets read and how. The fact, then, that some literary works are read centuries after they were written can be explained in historical and cultural terms, without reference to genre theories.

That simple fact, though, still poses difficulty for a genre theory that grounds genres in recurring types of situations. When literary works are read centuries after they were written, the situation within which they were produced has changed. Even if we can attach a function and community to a literary genre, as I argued above we can, can we claim that that function and community have remained unchanged centuries later? A Shakespearean tragedy was written within the drama genre of the time; it is read today within a drama genre that has surely changed, as all genres change over time in response to differing circumstances. We read an essay by Samuel Johnson today within a different set of expectations about essays than his contemporary readers would have had. Of course, we also acknowledge readily that our reading of a Shakespearean play is not the same experience as the viewing of the play by the groundlings in the seventeenth century, or that our reading of Johnson's essay does not coincide with how eighteenth-century publicans read it. Yet we do say that we are reading the same genre. We could read a nonliterary genre as if it were universal—say, letters to the editors from 1940s newspapers to understand the human condition or to be persuaded about comparable current issues—and we might well gain new understanding about ourselves. But if we read current letters to the editor for their universal meaning, we would be reading them as if they were participants in a different genre, not letters to the editor, just as reading scripture for its historical significance is reading it as a historical artifact, not as scripture. On the other hand, if we read current poems for their universal meaning, we would still be reading them as poems. If genre is tied firmly to rhetorical function and situation, then the genre itself must also be seen as different when experienced apart from its initial function and situation. Catherine Schryer establishes an important discovery for rhetorical genre theorists: that genres are never really stabilized, that they are always already changing in response to differing situations, that they are what she calls merely "stabilized for now" (and are, I will argue, not even that stabilized). From the evidence of literary texts being read in later times and under different circumstances, I would add that not only the genres but even the generic identity of particular texts are at best only stabilized for now.

Even with such historical and cultural clarification, the basic issue still challenges the very nature of genres as defined rhetorically: If genres fulfill certain functions or perform certain actions in particular, locally situated contexts, what is it about the nature of some literary genres that enables them to be read beyond their particular situations? In fact, some would distinguish literature from popular culture as art that may transcend local circumstances. If genres are defined as enmeshed in rhetorical situation, how do we explain that a function of at least some literary genres is to be used beyond their composer's space and time?

I certainly do not intend here to accomplish what literary theorists have struggled to do, to explain *how* literature can seem to transcend its original context. The inevitable historical situatedness of literature and its potential universality form a paradox that challenges students of all art. But I do believe that students of genre need to develop a theory that acknowledges the possibility of genres' going beyond their original functions and groups of users. As I argued earlier in this chapter and as I detailed in chapter 1, genres need to be seen as encompassing the interaction of writers, readers, texts, and contexts. Thus, if their readers or contexts change, the genres must change. One possibility is to describe genres read at different times and by different readers as being different genres. This explanation has some appeal, especially as applied to works that are read for different purposes. Scriptures, for a common example, can be read as holy texts, as historical artifacts, or as poetry, depending on the readers' purposes and situations. Texts of the scripture genre are read with differing expectations and world views, with attention given to differing qualities, as if one text were differing genres. A marriage poem, in this view, can be read as a celebration of a particular marriage in its original circumstances, participating in one genre, but be read as a celebration of all marriage in other circumstances, participating in a different genre. The function of a genre, then, might be said to change as its readers and contexts change, so that even the writer and text change in their interactions with the different readers and contexts. A text participates in multiple genres all the time, as we saw earlier in this chapter, so a text could shift genre participation over time and situation. Since genres adapt to changing historical circumstances, as I discussed in chapter 4, perhaps whole genres, too, can shift from one genre function and situation to another over time.

Perhaps when we read a literary work as if it transcends place and time, we are instead simply embedding the work in a different place and time. Reader response theory would suggest that readers recreate texts in their own contexts, and such an explanation fits easily within rhetorical genre theory and the idea that readers construct the genre's situation out of their differing material realities, as I discussed in chapter 1. One of the functions of many literary genres, however, seems to be directed toward future readers—that is, many literary genres strive to act not just in their contemporary situation but in future situations as well. Poetry written in celebration of particular events still strives to go beyond those events. Maya Angelou's poem written for the inauguration of President Bill Clinton speaks to larger circumstances, human issues, not just local ones, because that is what the genre of poetry is supposed to do. Certainly some literary genres are intensely locally situated (performance pieces seem an extreme example), though even they may be read differently in future generations (Did Shakespeare expect his historical plays to be meaningful two hundred years later?). When some literary works are read in different circumstances, we can say that they become participants in different genres. But what of the works, like poetry, that from the start would seem to encompass later audiences and contexts? Literary transcendence might indeed be an intriguing generic purpose to explore.

We could simply make universality one of the functions of those genres: just as letters to the editor are expected to address a current topic in a manner that might inform or persuade readers to change their actions (among other things), inaugural poems are expected to celebrate the incoming president in a manner that might inspire or arouse citizens of any time or place (among other things). When a literary work is particularized in a time or place, we can find ways of explaining its functions in rhetorical and cultural terms, thanks in large part to understandings of literature provided by cultural studies. But it seems to be a defining function of at least some literature to universalize. Is universalizing a function in the same way that persuading, celebrating, entertaining, or repressing can be seen as functions? Since genres have multiple functions, literary genres could have a function of universalizing in addition to locally situated functions. Perhaps it is just my inculcation into a traditional literary world view, but solving the problem by calling universality another kind of function seems to me to ignore the challenge these genres represent.

There is something significant for genre theory in how some genres can differ from other genres by more easily operating independent of their original time and place of composition. Those genres need not be literary genres. Poetry could develop as a genre so that currency and local situatedness are expected instead of speaking to universal human experience. Performance art, with its impermanence, is, in some ways, removing from art any contextually transcendent function. Satire has long sought universal statements through local situatedness. Literature could become valued for its currency, or rhetorical genres for their universality, and this discussion would be reversed. In fact, examining the universality of some literary genres helps us to notice that there are rhetorical genres as well that would seem to strive for transcendence of their local situation. Inaugural addresses accompany inaugural poems, and they, too, speak to human issues, strive to inspire actions beyond their local circumstances, and speak to future generations. Scholarly articles, for a quite different example, speak to future readers as well, attempting to contribute to a field that will continue past the writer's lifetime. Even a genre as mundane as the recipe is easily read in a variety of historical contexts and maintains its generic identity. Attention to future readers and uses, in other words, may not so much be a fact of all literature as a component of the context for some genres, both literary and rhetorical.

As long as some genres do have a quality of universality, genre theory must not tie generic function too closely to local situations or particularized functions without allowing generic function to include movement beyond those situations and particularities. We might extend our theory's acknowledgment that situation is always constructed and never actually repeats, to encompass the construction of situation and context in future times as well. Since situation never actually recurs and each individual's situation is unique and uniquely perceived, genres may be stabilized only at the moment of use. Some genres are used in a broader range of contexts or for a broader range of purposes. To recognize this flexibility that the genre users know and may exploit, then, our genre theory can encompass future situations and contexts at the nexus point where genre resides.

For the moment at least, a universalizing function would be an interesting generic study: Which genres encompass universality as a function, which do not? How does a universalizing function shape genres? How do readers recognize universality; how do writers attempt to achieve it (if writers do)? What does universality accomplish for the genre's users? What world views does it promote, what world views does it hide? What values are associated with a universalizing function, and how are they inculcated? How does the valuing of universality for a genre change over time? What makes particular works considered successfully universal and others not successful? How do those judgments change? Such questions, and the many others that could be explored, would help to elaborate the functions and audiences of literary genres in particular but also those of rhetorical genres commonly detached from the situation and context of their original composition. For both literary and rhetorical genres, then, the attachment of genres to function and context needs to be interpreted loosely and temporarily. While genres can be described in terms of their functions within groups at the nexus of contexts of culture, situation, and genres, the evidence of some genres should remind us to allow those functions and contexts to include not only the present but also the future.

New Questions, New Answers: Genre as Individual, Multiple, Destabilized

Even though the questions raised by literary genres are sometimes different from those raised by rhetorical genres, we can, I have argued, develop answers that enrich our understanding of literature and of genre theory. These answers for literary genres can also complicate and clarify our investigation of rhetorical genres. In particular, this investigation of literary genre theory raises several new possibilities for rhetorical genre theory: focusing on the variation within individual rhetorical texts; examining rhetorical texts as if they participated in multiple rather than single genres; considering whether rhetorical genres might have more complex, multiple functions and situations; and addressing questions of value within and among genres. In the end, reuniting literary and rhetorical genre theories can also reunite literary and rhetorical study and teaching, providing a common ground for students as well as critics and theorists.

Perhaps because literary works have long been studied for their particularities even more than for their commonalities, examining literary genres discourages us from depending too heavily on similarities and points us to differences—differences of one text from its generic expectations, and differences of one genre from other genres. Theoretically, rhetorical genre theory has addressed generic difference: Freadman's theory argues for defining genres in terms of what they are not, as well as what they are; Frances Christie explains how genres enable choice as well as constraint; my argument for genre as language standard and creativity enabler in chapter 5 encompasses variation as well as standardization. Practically, too, rhetorical critics have examined particular rhetorical works of special merit in order to discern how the rhetor responds to the situation in new ways, how the text diverges from the usual or expected, or what particular rhetorical strategies and styles are used. In general, however, rhetorical genre theorists have usually treated particular rhetorical works as examples of generic expectations rather than as individual texts with individual qualities. Typically, multiple samples of a genre are examined in order to understand the generic conventions, to trace generic change, or to discern ideological underpinnings of a genre. Individual works written by students or other novices are exam-

ined for their approximations to the generic expectations or their ineffective blends of learned and new genres. Thus, I gathered particular
works written by tax accountants in order to establish the participants'
generic categories and to learn what I could of how types of texts operated in that community. I examined particular works in order to learn
how particular textual conventions, like citation of sources, operated in
that genre. I did not examine any particular works in order to see how
effectively that particular writer used and varied from the expectations
of his genre. I did not study a particular work to understand the significance of the variations from generic expectations in that work. Such
emphasis on conformity, commonality, and expectations has served rhetorical genre theory well as it has developed a better understanding of
how genres operate for their participants, and it should continue to serve
genre theory well. Examining literary in addition to rhetorical genres,
however, should remind us that particular works are always more than
their representation of generic expectations. And no theoretical work
should continue for too long without returning to practice, in this case
to the rhetorical practice of close textual criticism.

As we reexamine rhetorical works for their variation as well as their
conformity, literary genre theory reminds us also of the multiplicity of
genres in which any text participates. In fact, literary perspectives such
as Beebee's remind rhetoricians and compositionists to beware of identifying any text too closely with a single genre. If genres are recognized
in terms of what they are not as well as what they are, then all texts are
participating in multiple genres and can best be understood in terms of
more than one genre. To some extent, rhetorical views of genre have
recognized the need for comparative genre work. The discussion of different kinds of genre sets in chapter 2 elaborates a basically intertextual
view of genres. To understand one genre, the analyst often needs to
understand other genres with which that genre interacts. As the example
of tax accounting genres in chapter 3 illustrates, to understand one genre
well requires understanding all the other genres surrounding it, both the
genres explicitly used and the genres implicitly referred to or shaping
what the genre is and is not. As Perloff noted, genres need to be understood in terms of both-and. Similarly, to understand a particular letter
to a client about a tax question, for example, one needs to examine not
only the genre of letters to clients but also the genres of client queries,
tax codes and regulations, IRS letters, and so on.

This interaction of multiple genres within a particular text is not a
perspective rhetorical genre theory has paid especial attention to, though

close rhetorical analyses often refer to multiple genres surrounding a particular text. Work such as that done recently by Anne Freadman ("Uptake") argues for the impact of related texts and genres on particular texts in other genres. But the multiple genre perspective argued for by some literary critics is of a different nature than that taken by rhetoricians. Literary critics often examine a particular literary work from the perspective of one genre, then another, or multiple genres together. Scholars in Perloff's collection on postmodern genres demonstrate traces of multiple genres in each "text," whether that text be Bob Dylan's songs or poetry by George Brecht. Such critique based on multiple genres would not be unusual in rhetorical criticism if the examined text were extraordinary in some way—an early example of a developing genre, a response to a new situation.[4] But to examine an "ordinary" text from the perspective of multiple genres would question the usual sureness of our generic identifications of texts. We know that a particular text is a letter to a friend and not a memo, or a research paper and not a personal narrative, or an essay and not a diary entry. If rhetoricians were to adopt literary scholars' questioning of genre and application of multiple perspectives, those ordinary texts might be seen in new lights. A research paper can be seen in terms of not only how it fulfills the aims of research papers, for example, but also how the particular paper draws on other genres of academic and nonacademic writing the student knows, how it reflects the assignment given by the teacher, and how it shares some of the language of the scholarly articles it cites. Some of this kind of work is being done with student writing, to see how students use familiar genres to learn unfamiliar genres. But imagine examining nonstudent writing, a memo written by an English department chair to his or her faculty, for example, to see how it might reflect not only other memoranda but also that chair's letters to friends, how its tone is derived from the curtly worded policy that it summarizes, even how it might reflect the community's appreciation for literary genres and accompanying literary language. Examining each rhetorical work from the perspective of multiple genres might develop new insights into the essentially interactive nature of all genres. It also might develop an understanding of what Beebee calls generic instability as being essential to the nature of genres and of particular works. Rhetorical genre theorists have come to speak of genres as stabilized-for-now, based on Catherine Schryer's phrase, but perhaps genres are not even ever really stabilized for now. If each text always participates in multiple genres, then even in that text a genre is moving, shifting, becoming destabilized for now and forever.

Even temporary stability may be an illusion of genre theory rather than a reality of genre-in-action.

The concept of constant generic instability might also lead to a significant reconception of generic function and situation. Schryer's amendment to describe genres as stabilized-for-now recognizes a large part of the instability of generic function and situation. Not only do generic function and situation change over time, as Cohen argues, but they may even be unstable at a given time. If the Bible can be read at the same time but in different settings as scripture, history, or poetry, perhaps its generic function is not as evident as we may have thought. If an inaugural poem inspires some listeners to renew their faith in their president and other listeners to critique the poem's quality, perhaps the genre's situation is not as static as we may have thought. Even such an apparently stable genre as the lab report has functions for its student writers that differ from those for its teacher readers and exists in different situations when it is being composed in notes in the lab, revised by the student at his computer late at night, and graded by the teacher in her office. If genres and texts truly participate simultaneously in multiple genres, multiple functions, and multiple situations, our understanding of genre theoretically becomes considerably more complicated.

A Common Purpose

With generic multiplicity and instability encompassed in genre theory, the challenge for writers and readers also appears considerably more complicated. Writers must work with multiple purposes, as has long been understood, but also with the multiple functions resonating in the chosen genres and their genre sets, some of which writers will not consciously select. The notion of using a genre as an operationalized tool, even when embedded within activity theory as Russell does so well, seems far too simple to encapsulate the complex interactions of multiple genres within a given activity system. How do writers enact so many genres? Do they concentrate on one genre, ignoring possible resonances and traces of other genres? The challenge for readers becomes similarly complex. Which genres are triggered for which readers? How do readers define themselves in such multiple situations, what roles do they choose?

Generic multiplicity and instability make our usual efforts at teaching students how to read and write genres seem far too simple indeed. To teach students the rhetorical and cultural significance of one genre will require teaching the significance of its genre set and the place of that genre within that set. Even then, any particular writing situation will bend that genre set into interaction with other, unanticipated genres from which writers, readers, texts, and contexts draw. On the other hand, the teaching of rhetorical genres will blend more easily with the teaching of literary genres. In teaching students to read literary works, teachers already show them how to use genre knowledge in conjunction with particular texts. We do not ignore the complexity of that interaction. In teaching students to read and write rhetorical works, teachers can show them how to use genre knowledge in conjunction with their particular situations, multiple though they may be, without ignoring the complexity of that interaction. If in turn we taught literary works as always participating in multiple genres, with functions and situations, we would be closer to teaching students a unified perspective on reading and writing. This perspective can come from teaching students a common genre awareness, a critical consciousness and rhetorical understanding of how genres work that I argue for in the next chapter.

A common teaching of reading and writing can motivate our search for a unified theory of genre. Our courses in literature and our courses in composition may emphasize different things, but they can depict reading and writing as a common activity. Literature courses may always emphasize the role of the reader, the writer's uniqueness, the text's significant variations from expectations, even literature's transcendence beyond local circumstances. Composition courses may always emphasize the role of the writer, the reader as common audience, the text's conformity to expectations, even the significance of the writer's processes. Both sets of emphases can be understood as only part of the picture of reading and writing. Both sets of emphases can be encircled within a genre theory that sees genres as involving readers, writers, text, and contexts; that sees all writers and readers as both unique and as necessarily casting themselves into common, social roles; that sees genres as requiring both conformity with and variation from expectations; that sees genres as always unstable, always multiple, always emerging. If genre theory can encompass the both-and, if genres can remain fluid and dynamic, then perhaps reading and writing can remain interactive and perhaps the discipline of English can remain fluid enough to encompass the multiplicity and instability of its participants.

I believe the previous paragraph in my more optimistic moments. In my more pessimistic moments, few though they may be, I realize that such an idealized, unified view of the compatibility of literature and composition works only if the scholars and teachers in literature and composition choose to be compatible. This chapter raises several significant differences in how scholars in the different areas view texts, contexts, readers, and writers, and it proposes ways that the differing views can be reconciled. If scholars working in rhetorical genre theory choose not to adapt their genre theory to literary genres, however, it may continue to emphasize function, community, similarity, and singularity in ways that exclude its application to many literary genres. If scholars working in literary theory choose not to adapt their critic-based definition of genre to a user-based definition, they may continue to define genres as classifications designed to serve critics' purposes and their classifications may exclude rhetorical genres. It seems to me that we in the fields of English and communication do indeed have a common object of study—discourse—and compatible though different perspectives on the object of study. But if people in these disciplines select the differences over the compatibilities, the work in one area will never contribute substantially to understanding the other area. Perhaps the question of our commonality comes down to a question of whether we will perceive our situations as recurring.

7

A Proposal for Teaching Genre
Awareness and Antecedent Genres

And gladly wolde he lerne, and gladly teche.
—Geoffrey Chaucer

To understand is to be given, at one and the same time, new
tools of potential understanding and new chains of potential
enslavement, and the two are not easily separated.
—J. M. Balkin, *Cultural Software*

Theory does not necessarily translate to practice, particularly to good
teaching practice, so the applications of genre theory to the teaching of
writing and literature need interrogation. This chapter begins such interrogation into teaching genres, but it awaits the work of future scholars
and teachers. If we are to use genre theory effectively in our teaching,
whether of literature or language, speaking or writing, it seems clear to
me from the argument of this volume that we must teach contextualized
genres, situated within their contexts of culture, situation, and other
genres. Generic forms must be embedded within their social and rhetorical purposes so that rhetorical understanding can counter the urge toward formula. Genres must be embedded within their social and cultural
ideologies so that critical awareness can counter potential ideological effects. Genres must be taught as both constraint and choice so that individual awareness can lead to individual creativity. The teaching of genres,
in sum, must develop thoughtfully, critically, and with recognition of the
complexity, benefits, and dangers of the concept of genre.

Particular curricula for and significant questions about the teaching of genre have already been raised by other scholars, so I can in this
section build from their discussions toward a refined proposal for teaching with genres. This proposal could apply to courses in literature and

rhetoric as well as writing courses and courses across the curriculum, though most of the discussion has involved the teaching of writing. While considering the most extensive arguments against the explicit teaching of genres and the curriculum that prompts such debates, I will argue *not* for teaching the textual features of particular genres, *not* for the goal of teaching students how to produce texts within particular genres, but rather for teaching genre awareness, a critical consciousness of both rhetorical purposes and ideological effects of generic forms. Such teaching, I propose, may enable writers to learn newly encountered genres when they are immersed in a context for which they need those genres but to learn the needed genres with greater rhetorical understanding and with more conscious acceptance of or resistance to the genres' ideologies. As a side effect of teaching genre awareness, students may also acquire new genres that can serve as antecedent genres for their future writing.

Arguments over Explicit Teaching

Although some volumes have argued for teaching specific genres and genre features (e.g., Cope and Kalantzis, *Powers;* Johns), resistance to the explicit teaching of genre comes from many sources, including teachers who fear rigid prescriptivism and theorists who fear ideological acculturation. Heather Kay and Tony Dudley-Evans describe the preconceptions and anxieties teachers had about teaching with genres even as they began a workshop on genre theory. While some of these fears can be addressed through pedagogical strategies—demonstrating how to teach genre in context and encouraging variation and creativity, as these same teachers suggest—some concerns about explicit teaching of genres cannot be so easily alleviated. Anyone proposing to teach genres now must consider the significant research-based and theoretically informed argument against the explicit teaching of genres offered by Aviva Freedman in her 1993 article in *Research in the Teaching of English,* "Show and Tell? The Role of Explicit Teaching in the Learning of New Genres." Freedman contributes an important caution against teaching the forms, rules, and principles of particular genres explicitly with the intention of helping students acquire those genres. Based in both composition theory and research on language acquisition, the argument contends that students learn new genres through situated immersion and textual input without any explicit instruction. The strong form of Freedman's hypothesis states "that explicit teaching is unnecessary; for the most part, not even possible; and where possible, not useful (except during editing, for a limited number of transparent and highly specific features)" (226). In fact, Freedman contends, such explicit teaching may even be harmful since students may misapply what they learn and misdirect their own intuitions and inclinations for effective writing.

While others have critiqued Freedman's claims for their own purposes (most immediately, the two responses by Jeanne Fahnestock and by Joseph Williams and Gregory Colomb in that same issue), I find Freedman's cautions reasonable and important ones but ones that do not necessarily preclude the kind of genre teaching I recommend. First of all, Freedman's argument is based on research in second-language acquisition. It is certainly possible that acquisition of rhetorical strategies within a first language develops differently from acquisition of formal features in a second language. Freedman's understanding of explicit teaching also leaves openings for other kinds of teaching. Freedman defines "explicit teaching of genre" as "explicit discussions, specifying the (formal) features of the genres and/or articulating underlying rules," which may also involve "explication of the social, cultural, and (or) political features of the context that elicits the textual regularities" (224). Freedman's emphasis on formal features first and contextual origins second are a reversal of what I would recommend. With such a definition, Freedman addresses most notably, though not exclusively, the kind of genre instruction advocated by scholars and teachers of the Australian curriculum. Developed out of Hallidayan linguistics, the curriculum involves explicit instruction in specific genres by moving students through stages.[1] The now familiar wheel model developed by J. R. Martin moves students from looking at models of a genre, through working collaboratively as a class to produce a text in that genre, to producing such a text in the genre individually (Cope and Kalantzis 10–11). Concerned about the potential formalism and prescriptivism of the wheel model, others have proposed different stages, including Cope and Kalantzis's own six-stage movement from asking a question through reading and analyzing sample texts to producing a text and evaluating the learning that may have resulted. All the processes of teaching described involve examining sample texts in order to generalize explicitly about generic features, followed by producing individual texts within that genre.[2] It is easy to see how such teaching could lead to rigidly prescriptive conceptions of a genre and to formulaic writing. If the goal of instruction is to enable students to learn particular genres, then the movement from models (or samples, which students are likely to treat as models) to production would seem to encourage producing texts that follow those models, would seem to encourage treating models as prescriptions and writing assignments as

imitations of those models. Julie E. Wollman-Bonilla's study of first graders, however, found that the children used some phrasings and structures
from the teachers' models but did not in fact copy them, claiming that
"[o]ver 90% of their texts were original" (59). What if the goal were
not to teach students particular genres but rather to teach students how
to analyze genres, to teach students a critical awareness of how genres
operate so that they could learn the new genres they encounter with
rhetorical and ideological understanding?

Freedman's argument is less relevant for (and less critical of) such
instructional goals. She argues that explicit explication of generic features is neither necessary nor possible, since writers learn genres on their
own and since no expert could ever fully articulate all the features in all
their contextualized complexity. (Of course, readers should turn to
Freedman's article itself for the full evidence and argument offered.) My
understanding of genre, as presented in this volume, would confirm that
no one could ever fully describe all the contextualized features of any
genre. Even experts in a genre, such as partners in tax accounting firms
or lawyers working on death penalty cases, cannot fully articulate either the necessary features of nor reasons behind a specific genre that
they use often and well (Devitt, "Intertextuality," "Where"). Fuller learning of a genre, Freedman argues, comes from immersion in the context
within which that genre is used. In such a context, writers learn the genre
without explicit instruction. In addition to the evidence Freedman offers, Stephanie Shine and Nancy L. Roser found that children learned
and responded to different genres differently without having been taught
them explicitly, and Wollman-Bonilla concludes that explicit teaching
may not have been essential for children learning science writing. Certainly my research into the writing of tax accountants confirms that
novices in a field learn the necessary genres, even though they may not
have been taught those genres, and Christine M. Tardy's study of grant
proposals found some researchers who learned the genre through "trial
and error." Experience commonly shows that people learn genres every
day without being taught them either in school or in the workplace.

But how are people able to learn these new genres without instruction, and what is it they are learning? Freedman reports her own studies of school children mastering narrative structure without having been
taught it and of students learning to write papers in an undergraduate
law course. In both cases, and others she cites, explicit teaching was not
necessary for students to be able to produce acceptable texts with appropriate features. Russell, too, describes how the newcomer "appro-

priates (learns to use) the ways with words of others" ("Rethinking" 516) by simply picking up the "tools-in-use" that others use. Yet, as Fahnestock mentions, students must have learned beforehand how to discern and then reproduce textual regularities (270). Learners must already know *how* to produce generic texts, and knowing how clearly seems to have helped them when they encounter new genres such as law essays. Further instruction in how to learn new genres might aid their learning. Of course, knowing how to learn new genres may also have been learned without explicit instruction, but what is the extent of that learning? The lack of explicitness of that knowledge is exactly what becomes most worrying: to what extent are these students aware of the rhetorical purposes and especially of the ideologies behind these genres they are learning implicitly?

Freedman herself describes the epistemic social motive behind writing the law essays:

> to enable students to become members of a new knowledge community. Through their writing, the students came to know and construe reality in specified ways, ways that were different from the ways in which they construed reality in other disciplines or in their everyday lives. ("Show" 228)

These students, through their implicit learning of a new genre, "were inducted into the ways of construing reality characteristic of those whose aim is to know and understand law" (229). Since they "were given no explicit instruction about the nature of this new genre" (229), I would argue that students were inculcated into the ideology of the law without the awareness needed to choose or resist that ideology. Even the schoolchildren who have learned narratives implicitly have learned to construe their experience in linear, episodic form, expecting complications and resolutions rather than a chaos of experiences. While Wollman-Bonilla describes how first graders adapted genres to their own contexts and audiences, and claims thus that even first graders can question generic conventions, I would not equate burgeoning rhetorical sensitivity to critical consciousness. Schoolchildren would surely be confused by instruction in the ideology of stories, but surely older students and working adults can be enlightened through considering explicitly the ideologies enmeshed in their school, workplace, and everyday genres.

Explicit teaching may not be necessary for people to produce acceptable texts with appropriate generic forms, then, but it may be necessary for people to perceive the purposes of those forms and their potential ideological effects. Williams and Colomb note the double-edged ideological sword of explicit teaching, both the worry over "academic colonialism" from teaching students any form of academic discourse and the hidden "ideological commitment and consequences of particular generic forms" from not teaching genres explicitly (262). Freedman herself acknowledges parenthetically that explicit teaching might enhance critical consciousness, which she defines as a separate issue from that of genre acquisition ("Show" 237). Her focus on acquisition is in fact critical to understanding her argument. Her skepticism about the benefit of explicit teaching is applied to the acquisition of new genres only, to acquiring the ability to produce new genres. On the basis of theory and research in second-language acquisition, she argues that acquisition lies below consciousness and so cannot be helped by conscious understanding of a genre, "however powerful such consciousness may be in allowing learners to reflect on, discriminate, and choose from among genres (hence from among ideologies and interpretations of reality)" (237). As this last quotation exemplifies, Freedman clearly believes in the importance of such consciousness. In fact, she and Peter Medway, in their introduction to their collection *Learning and Teaching Genre,* call for greater critical attention to genre. In her earlier article "Show and Tell?", though, Freedman argues that acquisition of a genre must precede critical awareness of that genre, for "such critical consciousness becomes possible only *through* the performance: Full genre knowledge (in all its subtlety and complexity) only becomes available *as a result of having written*" (236, emphasis in original). The great difficulty in such a claim (which Freedman admits is not yet demonstrated by research) is that it makes it impossible to learn a genre critically or knowingly. As I argued in previous chapters, by the time one has learned to perform a genre, one is already inducted into its ideology. If teachers are to help minimize the potential ideological effects of genres, they must help students perceive the ideology while they are encountering the genre. Once they are full participants in the genre, resistance becomes more difficult (some say futile) and choices become less visible (some say invisible).

Even if one rejects our ability to influence the ideological effects of genres, the explicit teaching of genres for awareness of rhetorical purposes may still be helpful. Since the research is not definitive, Freedman allows the possibility of a restricted form of her hypothesis: "under certain conditions and for some learners, explicit teaching *may* enhance learning" (226). Describing a model proposed by Ellis, Freedman hypothesizes that under specified conditions, particular kinds of explicit instruction may "raise the consciousness of some learners" so that they will better notice and internalize some linguistic features of a genre being acquired (243). Many of the conditions she sets for such learning can be met by the explicit teaching for awareness that I am proposing. I propose teaching genre awareness first so that students can learn new genres with a better understanding of their rhetorical purposes and contextual meanings. The actual acquisition of new genres, then, comes through input and immersion at the time that the writers actually need to use those genres. Under such teaching, writers are likely to meet Freedman's and Ellis's conditions that they be developmentally ready and that they encounter the new genres in authentic contexts. The biggest disagreement between my proposal and Freedman's (and Ellis's) model is that Freedman claims that students must be able to apply their new consciousness of linguistic features soon after learning them. Again, though, her time concerns apply to teaching explicitly the rules and principles of particular genres for the purpose of aiding acquisition of those genres. What is being taught in my proposal is the process of learning new genres rather than specific linguistic features of specific genres. Such meta-awareness of genres could be applied immediately as students learn new genres in other courses or, for workplace genre seminars, as workers practice the genres they need in their work. Such meta-awareness of genres, as learning strategies rather than static features, may also withstand greater distance in time between learning and application.

Another important critique Freedman raises is that it is not possible to articulate, much less explicate, all features of a genre or all the intricacies of a genre's context. If the goal were to teach someone how to perform a particular genre perfectly, this difficulty would leave our instruction at best partial and, as Freedman notes, potentially harmful. If, however, the goal is to teach someone how to approach a new genre and understand it as more than formulaic features, then the incompleteness of the teacher's knowledge of any one genre is irrelevant. The learner will acquire the genre through immersion in the authentic situation, either as an insider in the setting of a workplace genre or as a participant in the authentic setting of a school genre. Having learned how to perceive purpose behind form, the learner can discover the purposes behind the particular forms she or he notices. Having learned how to discern potential ideological effects, the learner can be alert to the ideologies underlying the genres she or he is acquiring.

Teaching Genre Awareness

Teaching for genre awareness may appear similar in some respects to teaching for genre acquisition, but the ends make all the difference. The goals of teaching genre awareness are for students to understand the intricate connections between contexts and forms, to perceive potential ideological effects of genres, and to discern both constraints and choices that genres make possible. Such genre awareness might also be applied to reading as well as writing. Sunny Hyon found in her study of second-language students that reading instruction based in particular genres helped build a general genre awareness; that genre awareness transferred to their reading of other genres and to their writing skills as well. Instruction in genre awareness thus enables a coherent curriculum across writing, speaking, language, and literature courses, indeed across an entire curriculum. Students learn strategies for learning that might apply in any context in which they encounter genres—in other words, in any context in which they encounter language.

A primary task for teaching genre awareness is to keep form and context intertwined. Using examples of already acquired genres and contrasting one familiar genre with another, teachers can lead students to discover the rhetorical purposes served by particular generic forms. Knowing the situations within which the familiar genres appear, students can come to see how the forms suit the context of situation; from there, students can be taught to discern how the context of culture influences the choices of forms. Eventually, the context of genres can be introduced as students see how one genre interacts with and responds to others. While I envision the teaching of genre awareness most explicitly and in most detail at the secondary and college level (and in workplace seminars), younger students could begin developing their awareness of how language differs in different situations and how those differences relate to different purposes. Many studies (e.g., Freedman, Langer, Shine and Roser) have demonstrated that children use different strategies in different genres; teachers can help them become consciously aware of those differences and their effects at levels appropriate for their cognitive development.

Although I propose teaching such awareness explicitly, I do not propose that a teacher lecture on these principles. Explicit teaching does not require presentational teaching. Environmental teaching, as described by George Hillocks in his meta-analysis of pedagogies, can most effectively lead students to explore and discover for themselves these principles, which the teacher then helps to articulate and pushes students to practice. For example, a teacher might have student groups collect and analyze samples of a familiar genre, perhaps guided by questions about repeated forms, audiences, purposes. Richard Coe in "Teaching Genre as Process" proposes one set of such questions about contexts for teachers to use for their own understanding of genres, though he then proposes that students may or may not need such conscious knowledge. Coe sometimes asks his students to reinvent a genre, giving them a situation and writing task with only ineffective samples of the genre. In his advanced writing courses, he asks students to analyze a genre and write a manual for others on how to write that genre. In my own courses, I ask students at first to examine such apparently simple genres as letters to friends, newspaper wedding announcements, or catalogue course descriptions. First, who uses these genres, both writers and readers, and for what purposes? What recurrent forms do students find, and how do those forms serve their participants and purposes? I have students work back and forth from the language to the context, from the context to the language.[3] One student examining apartment rental agreements, for example, understood from analyzing the genre's rhetorical situation that landlords and tenants were the participants and that the purpose was to regulate their relationship. By examining the language that appeared in the agreement, then, he was able to discover more—that the landlords were in control of this relationship and that the complex diction and passive syntax were shaping things in the landlord's favor. The language clarified the rhetorical situation of the genre, just as the genre gave him initial insight into the language he expected. Similarly, Bawarshi reports on a student who examined the patient medical history form, commonly completed by patients visiting a doctor for the first time. The student saw from her analysis how the form defined patients in terms of physical symptoms, allowing no room for the patient's emotions or own interpretation of the experience. Even without such perceptive discoveries, students gaining genre awareness can understand how the forms of a genre reflect the contexts within which the genre functions.

As students begin to understand the rhetorical nature of form, they can move to considering alternative ways of serving those purposes. Considering alternatives helps make visible both the choices possible within a genre and the ideology behind the expected forms. How else might one achieve that purpose, announce a wedding, for example? What other kinds of information might have been included? Why isn't it included? How could it be included? What other styles of language might have been chosen? Why weren't they? What would be the effects if that different language were used? Students might even be asked to write a new text that achieves different purposes or uses different means to the same purpose. Students in my first-year college writing courses, for example, have examined the course syllabus as a genre, using samples they received from various classes. Once they have described its purposes and participants and its appropriate forms, I ask them to write an alternative syllabus, one with a different purpose or one that establishes a different relationship between teacher and students. The resulting syllabi reveal much about expected language, tone, and content and show more clearly the ideology underlying the syllabus genre as well as the range of choices teachers can already make.

My point is not to argue for a particular pedagogical strategy as much as to argue for pedagogical strategies that keep generic form and generic contexts united. Unlike Coe, I believe students need to make their understanding of genres explicit, for I want them to gain conscious critical awareness of how genres work. I also want them to practice moving within genres. They need to discover that genres allow a range of choices, as well as set constraints. Creating alternative genres is one way of seeing the play within genres. More directly, students can be asked to revise existing samples of a genre to achieve a different relationship or alter somewhat their purpose or ideology: make the tone of this syllabus friendlier; put less emphasis on grades in this syllabus. Students can see how far they can stretch a genre. What if you didn't want the impersonal tone of a lab report? How much personal experience or vivid language could you incorporate? Suppose your experiment goes awry; how could the genre of lab report encompass that experience? What if your wedding included your children, a stepfather, or a barn dance instead of a reception? How could the genre of wedding announcement include that reality? What if you wanted the world to know about your love instead of the participants, locations, or decorations of your wedding? How could you change the genre to emphasize what you value? Would a newspaper publish it? If not, how could you distribute it? On a more analytical level, students can be shown how much creativity and variation is possible within existing genres by showing them as wide a range of samples as possible, ones reflecting different uses of language and form even while achieving similar purposes in similar settings.

If time and student level permit a more advanced pursuit of genre awareness, students can conduct mini-ethnographies to understand how genres work in particular contexts. Mary Jo Reiff has described how she uses ethnographies to teach genres, both at the undergraduate and graduate level. In advanced composition courses, I have asked students to contact experts in using the genres they wish to study, people who have been using the genres for some period of time. From the experts and other sources, they gather samples of the genres to analyze. They interview the experts, including discourse-based interviews based on their analyses of the samples. They may draw on published descriptions of their genres as well, though they often discover that those are too context-free to be of much help. As a result of their research, they write an analysis of their genres, including the genre's features, how those features suit the contexts, and what potential ideological effects the genre has. Their experts are asked to review that analysis, to make suggestions or correct misconceptions. Finally, students write a text within that genre, not to demonstrate that they have acquired the genre but to deepen their understanding of the expectations of the genre. Their text might try to conform to some prototypical sense of the genre, might try to push the boundaries of the genre, or might create an alternative to the genre. They also add to their now-portfolio on the genre a description of what they have learned further about the genre by writing that text. Students report that they feel more confident about tackling new writing tasks in the future after having conducted such an extensive and thorough analysis of one genre. I hope they have learned strategies for learning any genre they might need.

If their genre awareness continues beyond their college years, they might also be able to acquire better the genres they will need in their workplaces. In my study of the writing done by tax accountants, many new associates reported that they did not know how to write the research memorandum genre when they started their jobs. They tried to learn the genre through looking at memoranda written by those before them, by talking to senior associates, and by learning from the Partners' responses to their drafts (the last a strategy recognized but often disdained by the Partners themselves). Writers tackling a new genre often look to samples of that genre in order to learn how to write it. Explicit instruction of genre awareness can teach them how to examine such samples, what to look for and how to interpret what they find, especially discerning the required from the optional elements and the rhetorical purposes behind those elements. Genre awareness can teach students to seek the rhetorical nature of the genre, to understand its context and functions for its users, in order to avoid formulaic copying of a model rather than rhetorically embedded analysis of samples.

Whether such explicit instruction in genre awareness does result in deeper understanding of the genres they acquire later is an issue requiring research. I believe conscious awareness of anything makes mindful living more possible than it would be otherwise. Yet it is possible that such explicit instruction of genre awareness as I propose would not apply later when writers come to learn new genres. They may not be able to apply their understanding to new situations. Or the ideological effects of genre may be so powerful as to preclude awareness. Or Freedman might be right that no genuine critical consciousness is possible until after learning to perform the genre, in which case the ideological effects are likely to make genre awareness difficult. I hope, instead, that even after writers learn to perform within a genre, they can use the genre awareness they have learned to understand what they are doing more deeply, more purposefully, and more rhetorically, that their learned genre awareness will keep them from following formula blindly because they will always be wondering about the contexts behind the forms.

Aiding Genre Acquisition Through Choosing Antecedent Genres

A pedagogy of genre awareness offers a new rationale for the teaching of writing courses in general and first-year composition courses in particular. Some scholars and teachers have called for abolishing writing courses apart from disciplinary contexts. First-year writing courses in particular have been attacked as not useful, in part because of a potential lack of transferability of the general writing skills learned in composition courses to the particular writing tasks students will later confront. The teaching of genre awareness rather than particular skills gives a new potential justification for first-year writing courses and a way of helping students transfer general rhetorical understanding to particular rhetorical tasks. In that respect alone, a pedagogy of genre awareness can rescue first-year writing courses.

Yet a side effect of teaching genre awareness also provides support for the first-year writing course and suggests a new angle on the issue of transference. In learning genre awareness, students inevitably also learn new genres. Those new genres can serve as antecedent genres for students as they move on to other contexts. The notion of genre antecedents provides a powerful new perspective on the issue of transferability and the value of composition courses. Each genre with which students become familiar as they increase their genre awareness, and especially each genre students acquire in the process, serves as a potential antecedent for their learning future genres. As I will argue in this section, the genres teachers choose as illustrations or as writing assignments may become part of students' genre repertoires, become available to them as antecedents for learning new genres, and inculcate in them particular perceptions of situations. These consequences provide a new argument for the value of teaching first-year composition, and they clarify the criteria for choosing the genres we use.

Teachers in writing classes must always use some particular genres, for writing always involves writing in a genre. In school settings, Judith Langer reports research indicating that children's use of discourse is always genre-specific and that their strategies vary from one genre to another. Thus, our teaching always involves genre-specific activities. Christie, arguing for the Australian school's approach to teaching genre, observes,

> Whether the point is acknowledged or not, successful writing at any time always involves mastery of a particular kind of genre. If its presence is not acknowledged by the teacher and hence explicitly built into the patterns of working in which teacher and students engage, it simply becomes part of the hidden curriculum of schooling. ("Language" 38)

While not leading necessarily to teaching genre features explicitly, Christie's point should be recognized. Even if genre awareness and not genre acquisition is our primary goal, teachers cannot avoid expecting students to be able to write in particular genres. To keep genres from being part of the hidden curriculum, we need to choose deliberately the genres we have students write and we need to help students succeed at performing within those genres.

The criteria for choosing genres should include which genres best supplement students' existing genre repertoires and may serve as especially rich antecedent genres. Not only can we not avoid using specific genres, but some of those genres will also become part of students' genre repertoires and may serve as antecedents for their future writing tasks. When people write, they draw on the genres they know, their own context of genres, to help construct their rhetorical action. If they encounter a situation new to them, it is the genres they have acquired in the past that they can use to shape their new action. Every genre they acquire, then, expands their genre repertoire and simultaneously shapes how they might view new situations. The genres they learn in school, whether consciously or not, will form part of that repertoire and will be available to them when they write in different contexts. Historical evidence supports the influence of existing genres on new ones, as discussed in chapter 4. Historically, new genres often emerge from old, as policy manuals emerged from rules books and circular letters. Jamieson examines this point most fully in her study of the papal encyclicals and state of the union addresses, and she concludes that existing genres serve as powerful antecedents in shaping newly emerging genres. The historical evidence suggests that people use familiar genres to act within new situations. Since genres emerge only through individual actions, individuals must themselves be drawing on these existing genres to use what they know to construct discourse in a changing situation. Although more cognitive research on how people acquire new first-language genres is needed, the process may be similar for developing and acquiring new genres. Kevin Brooks, for example, posits that knowledge of familiar genres helps his students address the less familiar genre of hypertext. Individuals can only draw from genres they know, however. The more genres they know, the more potential antecedents they have for addressing new situations. If the genres they know influence how they learn the new genres they encounter, then knowing more genres would give individuals more different genres on which to draw. The more genres they know, seemingly the more likely they would be to have access to a genre that would serve as a sound basis for learning any new one.

The notion that known genres serve as antecedents for writers argues for the importance of first-year composition courses as a bridge between genres acquired before and those acquired during and after college. Rather than being artificial genres serving only composition courses, the genres students acquire in our writing classes serve as antecedent genres when students move into other contexts—into discipline-specific courses, into workplaces, and into civic lives. If we ask students to write analytic essays in first-year composition, that genre will be available for them to draw from when they need to write a causal analysis in their history class, a report at work, or a letter to the editor. If students write research papers, they can draw on that experience when they need to write case studies in their psychology class, proposals at work, or letters to their congressional representatives. That composition genres are relevant to later writing tasks has been argued before to defend the value of first-year writing courses. But I am describing a specific mechanism by which first-year instruction affects later writing, as people draw on whatever genres they have acquired from whatever sources when they encounter unfamiliar writing tasks. Faced with academic writing tasks in their majors, students can draw from the five-paragraph theme, personal narrative, analytic essay, or ethnography, if those genres are in their repertoires. But they cannot draw from analytic essays or ethnographies if they have never acquired those genres and will instead have to draw from genres that may have less relevance to the specific situation.

As the last examples suggest, many different genres can serve as antecedents later in a student's life. Which genres a teacher chooses to include in a genre awareness pedagogy depends on the course's goals and its institution's objectives. Writing courses can choose from an array of genre examples and assignments to supplement the genres students probably already know. To deepen students' education beyond home and media genres, Charles Cooper points out that "genres must be assigned and genre knowledge assessed" (27), but the choice of how students' education should be deepened and hence which genres should be included is largely a matter of institutional curricula and individual goals. School requires acquisition of a variety of genres, from law essays to literary interpretations, from history essay exams to lab reports, from composition themes to class notes. Even if explicit teaching did help students acquire those genres, even if teachers could know and articulate every nuanced detail of every genre, no writing class could possibly teach students all the genres they will need to succeed even in school, much less in the workplace or in their civic lives. Hence the value of teaching genre awareness rather than acquisition of particular genres. The choice of genres to use as exemplars and assignments then must derive from the place of the course in its institution and the teacher's goals within that institution. For courses designed to prepare students to write in other courses, the exemplar and assigned genres are likely to be more analytic and source-based, like analytic essays and researched position papers. For courses emphasizing the use of writing to enrich personal experience, such genres as journals, literacy narratives, and reflections are more likely choices. Courses with goals of increasing students' critical consciousness and awareness of diversity might use such genres as literacy narratives and ethnographies. The wealth of options for writing courses today—or the confusion over their rightful purposes, depending on your perspective—means that the genres used can be designed to serve as antecedents for a wealth of future roles and activities for students. Selecting genres with the most potential as antecedent genres for a particular student population while teaching how to learn genres, as I proposed above, may be the most responsible reaction to these facts.

Genres that students learn in writing courses thus can be chosen to provide antecedents for tackling future writing tasks, but they should also be chosen with an eye to the limiting effects of those antecedents.

Jamieson demonstrates how Washington's knowledge of the monarch's speech from the throne colored his first state of the union address and even subsequently affected how Congress replied. Antecedent genres are also antecedent ways of structuring the world. Given genre's role in constructing as well as reflecting situations and contexts, as I discussed in the first chapter of this volume, the genres students acquire—or do not acquire—in writing courses will also shape how they view new situations and contexts. Acquiring the analytic essay promotes Western logic and dispassionate approaches to subjects. To the extent that logic and distance are appropriate strategies for other academic tasks, acquiring that genre should help students succeed in later courses. To the extent that logic and distance minimize emotion and involvement, acquiring that genre could hinder artists or those in fields requiring empathy and compassion. The pitfalls of academic writing and the value of different types of writing assignments have been discussed by many in other scholarship, but the full significance of the teacher's choice of genre and the role that genre plays have not perhaps been adequately considered. Teaching nontraditional academic genres, like literacy narratives or ethnographies, for example, creates antecedents for students that will also change how they potentially approach new writing tasks, for both good and ill. Whatever genres are taught will also entail not teaching others, thereby failing to provide other antecedents. If first-year writing genres do in fact serve as potential antecedents for future writing, we must choose our genres carefully in order to serve our students best. What we assign today may appear in new guise tomorrow.

I suspect that the mechanism for writers selecting antecedent genres is not quite this straightforward. Writers may choose their antecedents for many reasons not necessarily related to the similarity of situation, including such reasons as their comfort level with a particular genre or their resistance to a teacher or the genre the teacher promoted. We certainly need considerable research into how people make use of known genres when acquiring new genres. Whatever genres they have acquired in the past may serve as antecedent genres, but writers may or may not make use of them. Not all genres serve as equally appropriate or helpful antecedents either, and people do not always draw effectively from their genre repertoire, so part of our work as teachers must be to help students learn how to choose and use the genres to which they have access. Jamieson's work again points out that antecedent genres can be poorly chosen, as they may have been for state of the union addresses, or that antecedent genres can encourage poor rhetorical choices and disguise differences in the rhetorical situations, as they may have done for papal encyclicals. Simply having access to more genres does not ensure choosing antecedents wisely (or for strictly rhetorical reasons).

Of course, even a well-chosen antecedent will lead individuals to some rhetorical approaches that are ineffective for the different situation and contexts. When learning a new genre, individuals must change and adapt their knowledge of existing genres, but that learning process takes time and practice. As most teachers' experience probably confirms, students often continue to use inappropriate strategies from familiar genres as they acquire new genres. The five-paragraph theme persists when the teacher assigns an analytic essay, or plot summaries overwhelm literary critical papers, or encyclopedia paraphrases substitute for research papers. Yet each of those antecedent genres also gives students the basis for meeting the new challenges. The five-paragraph theme provides a sense of organization and thesis that can adapt to organic structures and controlling ideas. The plot summary enables students to understand literary texts as a precursor to analyzing them. And encyclopedia paraphrases enable students to summarize information in ways that can apply to summarizing more advanced scholarship. Given that students will draw on known genres to tackle unfamiliar situations, it is better that they have access to some genres with situations and contexts that significantly overlap those of the new genres they need to acquire.

Second-language research also suggests how antecedent genres can interfere as well as help with learning new genres. Second-language research demonstrates that students' first languages influence what they find easy or difficult to learn about the second language. Similarly, perhaps, the genres students have acquired make it easier or more difficult to acquire elements of the new genres. First-year composition courses can help students acquire genres that would serve as bridges to the new genres later learned by immersion. A writer who has acquired only the five-paragraph theme for academic contexts will struggle with acquiring the case study research report, for example, in ways different from the writer who also has acquired the analytic essay and the ethnography or the writer who also has acquired the literacy narrative and the research paper. The writer who relies on personal narratives to write a lab report will be challenged in different ways from the writer who has practiced writing literary criticism or the writer who has practiced journal writing. I am not saying that we can necessarily predict which writer will have the easiest time learning which genres. We know too little yet about how writers move from one genre to another, and the rhetorical

strategies of each genre are too complex and tacit for analysts to identify all possible relevancies. I am saying that the genres we teach in writing courses potentially influence students' learning of genres later in their
lives and that we must choose those genres deliberately and carefully,
taking advantage of all we do know about how genres shape people's
rhetorical practices and perceptions.

Our task as teachers, then, is to help students understand the differences in rhetorical situations and contexts while using the familiar to
acquire the unfamiliar, to establish what Prince calls "mediating links
between familiar and unfamiliar generic contexts" (730). Establishing
such links does not require teaching formal features explicitly, but it does
require our being conscious of those antecedent genres, their limitations,
and their differences from the genres we are asking students to acquire.
Teachers can and responsibly must also aid their students' acquisition
of the genres they require students to produce. Arguing that the genres
used in writing courses may serve as antecedent genres for later writing
tasks still does not necessitate that those genres be taught explicitly. We
must help students succeed at understanding and writing the genres we
assign, but that need still does not entail explicating genre features so
that students can follow those models. What teachers can still provide
to aid acquisition is textual input in the form of samples of genres and
"pushes," in Freedman's terms, in the form of sequenced writing tasks.
Teachers can help by providing multiple samples of each assigned genre,
samples demonstrating a variety of approaches within the genre and
showing as wide a range of creative choices as possible. Such textual
input will help students move beyond a simple formulaic treatment of
them as models, though some students are still likely to treat samples
as models. Cooper uses such samples as exemplars and asks students to
discover the criteria for good writing within each assigned genre. He then
uses those criteria as students work through staged writing processes to
produce each genre. Such explicit teaching of criteria may aid some students who are ready for it, as Freedman notes, and may aid all students
in their monitoring processes, especially in their revision work. I would
caution, though, that the criteria be described in terms of their purposes
and settings in order to discourage students' focusing on form to the
exclusion of rhetoric. I would also caution that assignments and sequenced processes be designed to encourage purposeful creativity within
those criteria. Students could be led to discover not only criteria for effective texts but also the range of variation as well as regularities within
the exemplars. Since variation is as much a part of genres as standard-

ization, study of sample texts can fruitfully reveal choices and creativity as well as criteria.

It may be enough to aid students' genre acquisition to provide multiple samples within a genre and to assign the writing task. If indeed students use more tacit knowledge when writing genres, then providing the input and push may enable students to access appropriate antecedent genres and to access whatever tacit knowledge they have gained through the course's immersion in the context. A writing course grounded in genre awareness will, according to acquisition theory, need to provide samples of the genres to be written, including the particular genres of genre analysis and ethnography that such a pedagogy often requires of students. Courtney Cazden asserts, "All concept learning . . . benefits from clearly presented prototypical exemplars" (10). Providing such input may be more than many teachers of discipline-specific courses currently provide, but it seems clear from all research that writers need to be familiar with a genre to write it well. This connection may in part explain the truism that reading improves writing. Even for writing courses, teachers may at times provide insufficient input for students to acquire an assigned genre and may need more deliberately to provide samples of the genres they expect students to perform.

There is danger, though, in providing samples of genres. Students easily turn samples into models, and models easily turn writing into formula. People commonly select one instance of a category as a prototype of that category, as more representative of that category than other examples (Rosch; Lakoff). Even given a range of samples of a genre, writers might well narrow their view to a single text, which they then treat as a prototype or exemplar of that genre. Prototypes easily become evaluative norms, as Balkin points out (255). How reasonable, then, appear the fears of the teachers in Kay and Dudley-Evans's workshop, who feared that teaching genres would lead to teaching prescriptive formulae for producing texts always inadequate in comparison with the generic model.

The alternative to offering samples that might become evaluative models, however, is to offer no models at all, and that way lies unreasonable amounts of anxiety for novice writers. As Freedman notes, "exposure to written discourse is a *necessary but not a sufficient condition*" (238). One affective variable is the level of anxiety: "The less the anxiety, the greater the learning" (238). To ask students to write new genres with no samples of those genres is to reduce their learning by increasing their anxiety. Scott Turow, in his account of his first year at Harvard

Law School, *One L,* describes the effects on him of being asked to write with no generic samples:

> Henley asked us to try our hand at briefing the case—that is, preparing a short digest of the facts, issues, and reasoning essential to the court in making its decision. Briefing, I'm told, is important. All first-year students do it so they can organize the information in a case, and the various student guide books make it sound easy. But I have no idea of what a good brief looks like or even where to start. What in the hell are "the facts" for instance? The case goes on for a solid page giving all the details about how this woman, Olga Monge, was fired primarily because she would not go out on a date with her foreman. Obviously, I'm not supposed to include all of that, but I'm not sure what to pick, how abstract I'm supposed to be, and whether I should include items like her hourly wage. Is a brief supposed to sound casual or formal? Does it make any difference how a brief sounds? Should I include the reasoning of the judge who dissented, as well? Is this why students hate the case-study method?
>
> Twenty minutes ago, I threw up my hands and quit. (30)

Turow's reaction to being asked to write something unfamiliar comes even with textbooks that describe to him why he should write a brief and what some of its parts are. But without samples, he does not know "what a good brief looks like or even where to start," and his book amply describes the tremendous anxiety he felt. To provide samples may be to allow some to create formulas, but to provide no samples is to create unnecessary anxiety for all.

Return to Genre Awareness and Ideological Effects

Although it increased his anxiety, the lack of samples in Turow's case did not prevent him from learning the genre nor from acquiring the kind of legal argument expected in the legal world in which he was immersed. Turow's account also describes how he and his classmates built their understanding of what is expected through the input of their teachers' questioning and evaluation in class sessions:

> We were learning more than a process or analysis or a set of rules. In our discussions with the professors, as they questioned us and picked at what we said, we were also being

tacitly instructed in the strategies of legal argument, in putting what had been analyzed back together in a way that would make our contentions persuasive to a court. We all quickly saw that that kind of argument was supposed to be reasoned, consistent, progressive in its logic. Nothing was taken for granted; nothing was proven just because it was strongly felt. All of our teachers tried to impress upon us that you do not sway a judge with emotional declarations of faith. (84)

As Turow comes to understand the ways of thinking expected of him in his speaking and writing as a lawyer, he also becomes aware of its ideological effects. After his wife complains that he "lawyers" her when they quarrel, applying his new strategies in inappropriate contexts (overgeneralizing, in our terms), Turow worries that learning legal argument will "calcify" his way of approaching subjects (86). With great critical awareness, Turow comes to recognize the ideology behind legal thinking, including that lawyers must be "suspicious and distrustful," take nothing at face value and yet accept "ridiculous fictions" in order to preserve legal tradition and logical consistency (86). Finally, Turow realized the harmful ideological effects for him:

> What all of that showed me was that the law as a way of looking at the world and my own more personal way of seeing things could not be thoroughly meshed; that at some point, somehow, I would have to *learn* those habits of mind without making them my own in the deepest sense. I had no idea quite how I'd go about that, but I knew that it was necessary. . . .
>
> "It's a problem," I said, and I realized it was one that nobody yet had shown us how to solve. (86–87)

Had Turow been taught genre awareness, he would still have felt the ideological effects of legal genres and legal argument, and he would still have felt the clash between his previous way of seeing and acting in the world and that of Harvard Law School; but perhaps he might have become aware of those purposes, values, beliefs, assumptions, and ways of seeing the world earlier in his first year, with less struggle and confusion. Perhaps, though nobody could really show him, he might even have once before considered "how to solve" the "problem" of conflicting ideologies.

It is this potential for giving students more control over language that most drives me to argue for teaching genre awareness. Of course, genre awareness cannot solve the problem of harmful ideological effects. And genre awareness itself has potentially harmful ideological effects. As concerned teachers often recognize, making students more aware of the power of genres could lead to oversimplification as well as overgeneralization. Some students could reduce the complexity of contextualized forms to decontextualized forms: some could believe that if they can make their text sound like a genre they don't need to understand the genre. The danger of models as formulae I have already addressed, but the use of models and exemplars rather than varied samples could produce students who expect always to write imperfect approximations of ideal texts and who expect to be told the formula for any writing task. The Australian system, it appears to me, may too easily encourage just such an approach to learning genre. Prescriptivism and rigidity may return too easily to the teaching of writing if genre awareness reduces to teaching school or academic genres. The theory of genre elaborated in this volume would require treating genres as enabling as well as inhibiting creativity, as roomy enough to adapt to individual situations, and as rhetorically responsive and dynamic. I do not want students ever to lose sight of the inherent variation within all genres, the creativity essential to keeping genres alive and functioning well for their users. It is all a matter of how genre is taught and how it is learned.

I argue still for teaching genre awareness explicitly in hopes of arming students against rigid prescriptivism as well as against hidden ideologies. If they understand the fluidity and variation of genres, they might resist those who try to dictate a genre too rigidly. If they understand the rhetorical purpose of generic forms, they might better understand why and when standardized forms of the language are appropriate and why and when they are not. In fact, genre awareness can lead to more conscious language choices. The influences of genre on language are subtle and silent. Recall the study I reported in chapter 4 of the language used in Scots-English texts. This study showed that the linguistic differences among genres lay deep, influencing such small linguistic units as inflectional endings and spellings. The correlation of language forms with genre goes much deeper than matters of style, which a writer might notice and try to control; it goes to the smallest level of linguistic detail. I doubt that the writers of the sixteenth and seventeenth centuries were consciously or deliberately altering their language for rhetorical effect. The sixteenth century was, after all, long before the eighteenth-century period of heightened linguistic insecurity that produced so much of our self-consciousness about correctness and language standards. Standards and expectations existed, of course, but variation in form was much less noticed and individual differences more unremarked. Yet writers were varying their usage in different genres, apparently responding to different rhetorical purposes and contexts without being aware of how the genres were influencing their use of language. In short, whether or not we teach writers to adjust their language for different genres, this study suggests that writers *will* use different language in different genres, perhaps in ways of which the writers themselves are unaware.

I doubt that most writers can resist such subtle pulls of language once they are immersed in the genre. It is precisely when they are studying a genre and its language explicitly that they stand a chance of recognizing what the genre and its language are promoting, before they are active participants for whom the genre and its language may seem self-evident. Writers stand a much better chance of making their language choices deliberate if they have studied the extent to which genre inculcates form, if they have examined explicitly those forms that are evident in particular genres, and if they have practiced controlling which forms they use. The kind of direct instruction in genre awareness that I advocate here may worry some about the danger of teaching it badly, forcing assimilation and conformity, promoting formulaic use of language, and encouraging acceptance of the existing power structures that genres reflect. Recognizing from my Scots-English study how subtle and silent the encouragement of particular language forms within a genre can be, however, I prefer to risk the benefits of teaching genre awareness well. Teaching language and genre explicitly risks enforced conformity to formula, but such teaching has the potential reward of helping students integrate their understanding of rhetoric (purpose, audience, their own position) with the linguistic and generic forms that they produce. Having seen the extent to which genre shapes language, I am reluctant to leave my students ignorant of those effects. Language, genre, and writing interact, sometimes in quite small and subtle ways. To ignore that fact is to mystify writing, to allow genre and situation to encourage linguistic conformity on writers unaware, and to deny students access to a better understanding of why as well as what they write. It may be dangerous to teach expected forms, but it may be even more dangerous not to teach them. The question for me is how genre and its language can be taught so as to critique as well as to understand generic and linguistic expectations. I believe that is a challenge that thoughtful teachers can meet.

8
A Conclusion

Mind in its purest play is like some bat
That beats about in caverns all alone,
Contriving by a kind of senseless wit
Not to conclude against a wall of stone.
—Richard Wilbur, "Mind"

The previous chapters have argued for a dynamic and paradoxical theory of genre, one encompassing multiplicity and variation as well as regularity and standardization, one diachronic as well as synchronic, one individual as well as social. By definition, genres are both form and context, and they both shape and are shaped by contexts of situation, culture, and other genres. Socially, genres reflect and reinforce the group but are enacted individually. Historically, genres require both cultural support and individual action in order to change, and they require both stability and flexibility in order to endure. Genres serve as regularizing standards and as enablers of variation and creativity. For students and teachers, genres offer both rhetorical understanding and ideological training. The theory of genres presented in this volume resists dichotomies and accepts paradoxes. For genres to work as they do, they must maintain the tension between these apparent dichotomies, just as the phrase of my title, "writing genres," maintains the tension between *writing* as verb and *writing* as modifier.

Confronting these dichotomies requires further work not just in theory but also in research. A great deal of research remains to test the genre theory proposed in this volume, to examine whether its propositions continue to fit the experiences of people participating in genres. This volume is not, I hope, the last word on genre. Nor is it intended to delimit what other scholars might argue or pursue. As a theory of genre and not discourse, it does not encompass every element important to symbolic action and so does not claim that genre alone influences rhetorical choices. It agrees with scholars like William Benoit who contend that other relationships also explain discourse. It offers one perspective on genre that I hope covers enough range and depth to highlight areas that other scholars of genre might wish to examine more closely. As one theory, it emphasizes some aspects of genre and minimizes others. Where this theory treats some important aspects of genre too cursorily, I hope others will offer closer examinations. Where this theory omits important elements, I hope others will include them. Where this theory is misguided, I hope others will argue for correction. I hope that my work provides some avenues for future research and that others test some of the proposals here, for I believe that scholarship in composition, rhetoric, linguistics, and literary study can all benefit from incorporating a contemporary understanding of genre.

I have elsewhere discussed the implications of genre for the linguistic study of textual variables ("Genre as Textual") and for growing distinctions between text linguistics and composition ("Developing"). Chapter 6 in this volume largely considers the significance of genre for studying literary texts and literary genres. Both linguistics and literary study have been developing more rhetorically sound conceptions of genre and have begun reexamining the generic nature of texts. For rhetoric and composition scholars, the new conception of genre presented in this volume might fill some significant gaps in existing theories of writing. I have already suggested throughout this work how genre can help to reintegrate several dichotomies in our view of writing. Most particular to genre theory might be the better reintegration of form with content and of text with context, the former a long-standing marriage we still struggle to explain to others, the latter a more recent split whose divorce we are just beginning to contest. Can we speak of context apart from text? Contexts are always textualized. Through genre we can speak of both, as do many scholars who study particular genres in particular communities (such as Bazerman and Myers, in their studies of the experimental article in science and articles in biology, respectively). Studies of particular genres and of particular genre sets (as, for example, the research-process genres in Swales or the genre sets of tax accountants in my "Intertextuality" article) can reveal a great deal about the communities that construct and use those genres, and studies of particular texts within those genres can reveal a great deal about the choices writers make.

The theory of genre I present in this volume draws relatively little from cognitive research, compared with its reliance on social and rhetorical studies, but its arguments can also help raise new questions and posit new answers to some cognitive concerns. The reintegration of product and process that this new genre theory enables can clarify the value of studying products or texts, but it also can contribute to our understanding of process and text making. Some of the long-standing (and often unspoken) questions about writing processes can be addressed through considering genre's role, as I described in an earlier article ("Genre, Genres") and as I wish to return to here. Two such questions will illustrate: Where do writers' goals come from? How do writers know what to change when they are revising?

One of the classic articles on writing processes, Linda Flower and John Hayes's 1981 article "A Cognitive Process Theory of Writing," might have had a different emphasis had a better understanding of genre been well shared when it was written. Flower and Hayes concentrated in part on how writers generate and regenerate goals. In one paragraph, they acknowledge a small role for genre:

> [B]ut we should not forget that many writing goals are well-learned, standard ones stored in memory. For example, we would expect many writers to draw automatically on those goals associated with writing in general, such as, "interest the reader," or "start with an introduction," or on goals associated with a given genre, such as making a jingle rhyme. These goals will often be so basic that they won't even be consciously considered or expressed. And the more experienced the writer the greater this repertory of semi-automatic plans and goals will be. (381)

The new genre theory would support the notion that "well-learned, standard" goals are "so basic that they won't even be consciously considered or expressed," and that more experienced writers will be well stocked with "semi-automatic plans and goals." However, rather than being uninteresting because unconscious and rather than being trivial ("such as making a jingle rhyme"), these "basic" and "well-learned" generic goals may be the stuff of which all writing goals (at least partly) are made. To understand the contextual and social constructs behind genres may be to understand more deeply the goals that writers have and the forces at work in their generation and regeneration. Following up on this idea, Bawarshi has elaborated a genre-based theory of writers' motives and intentions, leading him to critique such social but genre-less theories of invention as that developed by Karen Burke LeFevre. Understanding writing processes, then, must include understanding generic goals: what they are—the historical, community, and rhetorical forces that shape them—how writers learn them, and how writers use them.

Similarly, a better understanding of genre may help us understand better how writers know when and what to revise. Scholars have described the perception of dissonance, between intention and text or between intention and execution, as an important part of revision (e.g., Sommers; Flower et al.). But James Reither asserts, "Composition studies does not seriously attend . . . to the knowing without which cognitive dissonance is impossible" (142). A large part of that "knowing" must be knowing genres. How, Flower and coauthors ask,

> can we say that a writer detects a dissonance or a failed comparison between text and intention when the second side of the equation, an "ideal" or "correct" or intended text doesn't exist—when there is no template to "match" the current text against? (27)

Genre might provide at least part of that template, for it might provide at least part of the writer's notion of the ideal text. If a writer has chosen to write a particular genre, then the writer has chosen in some respects a template, a standard, in the terms of chapter 5, an interaction of contexts and an appropriate reflection of those contexts in sets of expectation. As chapter 5 also argued, that genre standard also entails a range of possible variations, room within that standard to meet the demands of the individual situation and the individual's creative choices. In revising, a writer may check the contexts and forms of the evolving text against those of the chosen genre, its expectations and possible variations: where there is a mismatch, either between the evolving text and the chosen genre or between the chosen genre and the writer's goals, there is dissonance. Genre by no means solves the problem of determining why writers revise what they do; but, without incorporating genre, a complete solution to the problem is impossible.

As these brief discussions of goals and dissonance illustrate, studies of writing processes and cognitive perspectives on writing can benefit from taking genre into account. In fact, researchers most interested in the cognition of individual writers can make essential contributions to genre theory by studying how writers learn and use a variety of genres. Where and how do newcomers learn a genre? Does the process differ in different contexts or are there typical processes of learning? My argument that school genres may serve as antecedent genres for more complex genres learned later is subject to verification or refutation through research. If I am right about the role of antecedent genres in individuals' learning to write new genres, then perhaps all writing is rewriting.

Those most interested in social and rhetorical perspectives on writing can contribute especially by studying further the creation, transmission, and modification of genres. Further research is needed, for example, on the range of variation possible in a genre and the distinction between acceptable variation and unacceptable violation of a genre. How does a group sanction or reject variations? The range of variation possible might be a function of the nature of the group as well as the nature of the genre. The study of how genres function for groups is in its relative infancy. Collaborative research between sociologists and genre theorists might bring insight into the nature of different groups and the roles genres play within them. Different genres function differently for different groups—what factors make a difference and why? The range of possibilities within a single genre remains relatively unexplored, at least for everyday genres. Some genres admit more creative choice than others. Which ones, and why? What marks the difference between effective and ineffective variation? Some texts are ineffective instances of a genre. What can studying bad examples tell us about how genres operate and how writers work—and sometimes fail—within those genres? More close historical studies might trace how perceived needs within a group lead to new genres with new functions. Who starts a new genre and how? The emergence of new genres out of old deserves further detailed study, including the development of so-called hybrid genres but also the nature of all genres as hybrids of previously existing antecedent genres.

As someone who has been working on understanding genre for many years, I see the potential benefits of genre in virtually every article or book I read on the study and teaching of writing, language, and literature. Studies of the relationship between reading and writing need to acknowledge that genre connects readers and writers, both their products and their processes. Studies of both literary and everyday genres need to investigate how interpretations of genre vary (or do not) among different writers and readers and among different groups that use similarly named genres. Research on assessment and on school assignments needs to consider the power of differing generic demands to influence results. Judith A. Langer, in her research on elementary students, for example, found that "genre distinctions were stronger than grade distinctions in their effects on student writing" (167). Researchers of basic writing need to continue working beyond the forms of academic genres to see their contextual constructs, with ideologies and roles that may pose conflicts for some basic writers. A study of the Athabaskans, a group of Alaskan Indians, discussed by Michael B. Prince, found that learning to write a new genre "implied cultural and personal values that conflicted with pre-existing patterns of thought and behavior" (741). Scott Turow and other Harvard law students are not the only ones who feel the pinch of new ideologies acquired along with new genres. The social implications of a new understanding of genre are extensive and deserve attention by scholars, teachers, and policy makers.

Genres pervade lives. People use them, consciously and unconsciously, creatively and formulaically, for social functions and individual purposes, with critical awareness and blind immersion, in the past and yet today. They shape our experiences, and our experiences shape them. As we study and teach these ways of acting symbolically with others, we may be approaching an understanding not just of genres but of the messy, complex ways that human beings get along in their worlds.

Notes

References

Index

Notes

1. A Theory of Genre

1. That is not to say that previous work in literary theory dealing with genres has not made valuable contributions to the understanding of particular works and particular genres and to our understanding of literature. Some critics, like Northrop Frye, for example, have developed sophisticated analyses of literature that include genre. Useful though some of these systems are for the study of literary works, however, as long as they are most concerned with a classification system, they are minimizing the true power of genre, a point I will expand considerably in chapter 6, on literary genres.

2. It is possible that architects' notebooks are physical objects rather than genres—that is, the architects' notebooks are like blue books, sketch pads, or locking diaries, physical holders into which certain genres are typically placed (essay examinations, drawings, personal journals) but which form part of the context rather than the essence of their genres. One could use a sketchbook for a personal journal, a blue book for grocery lists. The physical containers are associated with a genre. In this respect, they relate to genres as do formal features: they may be associated with a genre but are not necessary for a genre to exist— neither necessary nor sufficient. The difference, though, between blue books and architects' notebooks, as I understand Medway's reports, is that the students see their architects' notebooks as a kind of text; that is the label they give to what they write in it as well as to the physical object. If so, the architect's notebook would seem to be a genre with little formal similarity from one text to the other.

3. Of course, people can and do use genres without explicitly understanding the rhetorical nature of their formal conventions, and people can still respond inappropriately even while using an appropriate genre. That is, people can use genres ineffectively. This theory of genre can help explain how and why some uses of genre fail because it pinpoints the nature of and possible sources for those failures.

4. David Bleich, in his article in *Pedagogy,* argues that genres must be seen as material because they are made material through language. While his reminder that genres are in the end grounded in material language is well taken, to say that genres materialize through specific instances is not to say that the conception of a genre, the defining of a material experience as a recurrent situation and therefore calling for particular uses of material language, is also material.

5. I am grateful to David Blakesley for pointing out this similarity in Burke's approach to contexts.

2. An Analysis of Genres in Social Settings

1. I am grateful to Lisa Ede for helping me clarify this distinction.

2. See Hyon for this outline of three schools.

3. I recognize that those goals, values, and identities are also created by the group and reproduced by the genres. I am not asserting here some prior existence of the group identity over the genre for any individual member nor the existence of such identities separate from the people in the group.

4. I have no doubt that sociologists could offer other categorizations of social groups that would prove more valid sociologically. My goal here, though, is not to describe groups accurately but to provide starting points for thinking about how different group features might affect genres. I would hope that future research (and reanalysis of existing research) would demonstrate the group qualities that most significantly influence how genres operate socially.

5. Some academic classes might develop enough frequency and enough sense of shared endeavor to become a community, especially if the students and teacher have worked together before, as in a graduate program or such specialist programs as creative writing. I doubt that most classes can achieve community status by meeting for a few hours each week for only a few months, with students and teachers who meet each other for the first time in the class, and with students having a range of purposes for the class.

6. A genre can exist in more than one group. A syllabus, for example, is a genre within both an academic class collective and within an academic department community; the research paper exists in a class, a department, a university, and a discipline. The genre's significance for the collective differs from that of the community. Within a class, for example, the syllabus sets the rules for the collective's interactions and defines the nature of their common endeavor, as well as defining the teacher's and students' roles. Within a department, the syllabus reflects the rules of the department and university and particularizes the department's course description and curriculum, as well as defining the professor's role as a teacher among colleagues. Even more complex, the research paper acquaints students with methods and sources and demonstrates their understanding in a class, it may add particular skills at a particular level for students in a department, it may ensure research experience within a university, and it may represent a discipline's basic knowledge and methodologies. The same genre has different meaning, and it functions for different groups in different ways.

7. I do not use duality of structure in chapter 1 to describe what are reciprocal relationships in part because Giddens's theory treats human actions as "reproducing" rather than "constructing" the social structures.

8. Is it coincidence that Berkenkotter and Huckin refer to social agents with the relative pronoun "that" rather than "who"? Although their theory emphasizes cognition as well as culture and power and they cite Giddens's emphasis on human agency (17–18), people often seem to have relatively little agency in their work or in the work of other genre scholars, including much of my work.

9. I thank Yates's scholarship for the insight that genres, as rhetorical acts, must remain flexible.

3. A Study of Genres in Context, a Theoretical Intermezzo

1. See Devitt, "Intertextuality," for a fuller account of the study and its results.

2. See Devitt, "Intertextuality," for the details of how tax accountants refer to the Tax Code and Regulations.

3. I realize that using the academic community here raises issues of defining community as well as defining genre. Is the academic community a single community or multiple communities? Is the research paper a single genre or a grouping of several genres? As for the genre question, I would return to my argument that genres should be defined by the community who uses them and that the community's label should be respected. Academics speak of a research paper as a single genre (it is what many expect students to have learned in their English classes). As for the community question, the debate about the coherence of the academic community still rages and is being subjected to research. It is a question deserving more complex discussion than space in this chapter allows. Since academics have been known to define themselves as a group, however, there must be some sense in which the notion of an academic community makes sense to its participants.

4. See Williams on the range of acceptability of different usage items.

4. A History of Genres and Genres in History

1. In "Epic in the Novel," Bakhtin asserts that all genres other than the novel are fixed and that the "primordial process of their formation lies outside historically documented observation" (3). However, Bakhtin also treats genres on that same page as "pre-existing forms", as containers into which meaning is poured. That view of genre is inconsistent with his treatment of genre later in the same essay "not in its formalistic sense, but as a zone and a field of valorized perception, as a mode for representing the world" (28) and is certainly inconsistent with his treatment of genre in his essay on speech genres.

2. Campbell and Jamieson explain that they do not consider all of the genres presidents use. They are interested particularly in those genres dictated by the Constitution and used to assert the institution of the presidency. What I consider in this section, therefore, is but part of a larger genre repertoire.

3. I thank James Hartman for giving me this metaphor of genre as tree ring.

4. I am not considering saying that the theme is not a genre because I use recognition by users as a determining criterion. To say that the theme is not a genre is to deny the reality of many teachers in writing classes today. If I were writing a history of composition courses, I might want for those purposes to identify different genres and exclude the theme as a helpful category. If I were arguing for what students *should* write, I might deny the validity of the theme as a genuine rhetorical construct. But for my purposes, the historical persistence of the label "theme"—as well as my perception of it as a type of discourse at a specific nexus—justifies my treating it as a genre.

5. Harvard sophomores and juniors also wrote themes in 1858–59 and 1874–75 (Kitzhaber 33–34), however, and Harvard apparently adopted

Kitzhaber's definition of theme when the Report of the Committee on Composition and Rhetoric in 1892 "urged that theme-writing be classed once and for all as a part of elementary education and not a concern of the university or college" (qtd. in Kitzhaber 45).

6. The theme surely has more purposes than just to practice and demonstrate skill in composing, but that purpose is the primary, defining purpose that distinguishes it from other school genres. As other purposes become primary, new genres such as the research paper, the lab report, and the essay exam develop.

7. See Yates and Orlikowski on how the memorandum, once developed, shapes future memoranda.

8. For a detailed report of the methodology of this study, including the statistical tests conducted, see the relevant sections of Devitt, *Standardizing.*

9. The statistical tests used include analyses of variance, coefficient differences, and *t*-statistics, taking into account standard error and 95% confidence intervals. See Devitt, *Standardizing,* for details.

10. For details on this study, see Devitt, "Genre as Textual Variable."

11. For further discussion of why change occurred as it did in each of the particular genres, see the discussion in Devitt, *Standardizing.*

12. The few cases examined here do not begin to cover the kinds of contextual factors that influence genre origin and change, of course. Elizabeth Hoger's review of the history of music criticism, for just one example, notes the importance to the beginnings of journalistic music criticism of changes in music audiences as well as the development of new periodicals as forums. The contextual factors in each genre's development are surely unique.

13. Not all genres are learned by reading examples of others, presumably, especially ones for which samples are difficult to come by. Randall Popken examines the intriguing case of the resume, which, Popken argues, was learned not by reading others' confidential resumes but by being taught a model of the resume in business discourse courses. He notes the premature stability of the emerging genre that results, among other things, in its becoming rigidly formulaic as well as exclusionary.

5. Creative Boundaries: An Argument for Genre as Standard, Genre as Muse

1. See, for example, the relevant chapters in Reid and in Cope and Kalantzis, the discussion around Aviva Freedman's article "Show and Tell?" in *Research in the Teaching of English,* and the final chapter in this volume.

2. For perspectives on language standards, see, for example, Devitt, *Standardizing,* especially the first chapter; Heath and other articles in Shopen and Williams; Haas; Crowley; and Joseph.

3. See Heath, Fisher, and Crowley for three accounts of the history of SEE.

4. For more on this view of standards, see chapter 1 in Devitt, *Standardizing.*

5. I recognize that the definition of ideology is a point of much debate among major philosophers and scholars, and I do not pretend to enter that debate here. For my purposes, in this definition I am following what J. M. Balkin

describes as the issues common to various theorists' definitions of ideology (2). Balkin's own definition of ideology is much more complex and precise, as detailed more fully in his book *Cultural Software: A Theory of Ideology.*

6. A Comparison of Literary and Rhetorical Genres

1. In addition to the static nature of Jameson's definition, it includes a circularity that pertains to the functions literary genres serve. The function of a literary genre, according to Jameson here, is to specify how readers should use it. Its function is to specify its function. On the other hand, Jameson's statement also reinforces the centrality of function to literary as well as rhetorical genres, for Jameson sees function as the reason for genres' existence.

2. This oversimplification of the different emphases of rhetorical and literary theorists is not meant to ignore either literary theorists who examine generic expectations or rhetorical critics who examine the generic deviations of particular texts. There is, of course, a long history of close rhetorical criticism that examines particular rhetorical texts using interpretive methods similar to those used by literary critics. Presidential inaugural addresses, for just one example, are closely analyzed for the particular aims, rhetorical strategies, and uses and variations from generic expectations they encompass. I am characterizing the approach taken most often by many new rhetorical genre theorists rather than that taken by rhetorical critics.

3. See, for example, Freedman and Medway's argument for a critical turn in "Locating."

4. For a good example, see Jamieson's study of papal encyclicals and presidential state of the union addresses.

7. A Proposal for Teaching Genre Awareness and Antecedent Genres

1. For the fullest description and historical background of the Australian curriculum, see Cope and Kalantzis, *Powers.*

2. See Callaghan, Knapp, and Noble 194–95 for another example.

3. For a more detailed demonstration of how I have used genre as a basis for advanced literacy, see my first-year composition textbook coauthored with Anis Bawarshi and Mary Jo Reiff, *Scenes of Writing* (2004).

References

Aristotle. *Poetics*. Trans. and ed. Gerald F. Else. Ann Arbor: U of Michigan P, 1967.

———. *On Rhetoric: A Theory of Civic Discourse*. Trans. and ed. George A. Kennedy. New York: Oxford UP, 1991.

Bakhtin, M. M. *The Dialogic Imagination: Four Essays by M. M. Bakhtin*. Ed. Michael Holquist. Trans. Caryl Emerson and Michael Holquist. Austin: U of Texas P, 1981.

———. "Discourse in the Novel." Bakhtin, *Dialogic* 259–422.

———. "Epic and Novel." Bakhtin, *Dialogic* 3–40.

———. "The Problem of Speech Genres." *Speech Genres and Other Late Essays*. Ed. Caryl Emerson and Michael Holquist. Trans. Vern W. McGee. Austin: U of Texas P, 1986. 60–102.

Balkin, J. M. *Cultural Software: A Theory of Ideology*. New Haven: Yale UP, 1998.

Bartholomae, David. "Writing with Teachers: A Conversation with Peter Elbow." *College Composition and Communication* 46 (1995): 62–71.

———. "Response." *College Composition and Communication* 46 (1995): 84–87.

Barton, Ellen. "Constructing the Personal and the Professional: The Volunteer Narrative." Conf. on Coll. Composition and Communication Convention. Chicago. Mar. 2002.

Bawarshi, Anis. "The Genre Function." *College English* 62 (2000): 355–60.

Bazerman, Charles. *Shaping Written Knowledge: The Genre and Activity of the Experimental Article in Science*. Madison: U of Wisconsin P, 1988.

———. "Systems of Genres and the Enactment of Social Institutions." *Genre and the New Rhetoric*. Ed. Aviva Freedman and Peter Medway. London: Taylor, 1994. 79–101.

Beebee, Thomas O. *The Ideology of Genre: A Comparative Study of Generic Instability*. University Park: Pennsylvania State UP, 1994.

Behling, Laura L. "'Generic' Multiculturalism: Hybrid Texts, Cultural Contexts." *College English* 65 (2003): 411–26.

Benoit, William L. "Beyond Genre Theory: The Genesis of Rhetorical Action." *Communication Monographs* 67 (2000): 178–92.

Berkenkotter, Carol, and Thomas N. Huckin. *Genre Knowledge in Disciplinary Communication: Cognition/Culture/Power*. Hillsdale, NJ: Erlbaum, 1995.

Berlin, James A. *Rhetoric and Reality: Writing Instruction in American Colleges, 1900–1985.* Carbondale: Southern Illinois UP, 1987.

Bhatia, Vijay K. "Introduction: Genre Analysis and World Englishes." *World Englishes* 16.3 (1997): 313–19.

Bitzer, Lloyd F. "The Rhetorical Situation." *Philosophy and Rhetoric* 1 (winter 1968): 1–14.

Bizzell, Patricia. "Cognition, Convention, and Certainty: What We Need to Know about Writing." *Pre/Text* 3 (1982): 213–43.

Bleich, David. "The Materiality of Language and the Pedagogy of Exchange." *Pedagogy* 1 (2001): 117–41.

Bourdieu, Pierre. *Language and Symbolic Power.* Cambridge: Harvard UP, 1991.

Brooks, Kevin. "Reading, Writing, and Teaching Creative Hypertext: A Genre-Based Pedagogy." *Pedagogy* 2 (2002): 337–56.

Burke, Kenneth. "The Philosophy of Literary Form." *The Philosophy of Literary Form: Studies in Symbolic Action.* 3rd ed. Berkeley: U of California P, 1974. 1–137.

Callaghan, Mike, Peter Knapp, and Greg Noble. "Genre in Practice." Cope and Kalantzis 179–202.

Campbell, Karlyn Kohrs, and Kathleen Hall Jamieson. *Deeds Done in Words: Presidential Rhetoric and the Genres of Governance.* Chicago: U of Chicago P, 1990.

———, eds. *Form and Genre: Shaping Rhetorical Action.* Falls Church, VA: Speech Communication Association, 1978.

Cazden, Courtney B. "A Report on Reports: Two Dilemmas of Genre Teaching." May 1993. ERIC ED 363593.

Chapman, Marilyn L. "Situated, Social, Active: Rewriting Genre in the Elementary Classroom." *Written Communication* 16 (1999): 469–90.

Christie, Frances. "Genres as Choice." Reid 22–34.

———. "Language and Schooling." *Language, Schooling and Society.* Ed. Stephen Tchudi. Upper Montclair, NJ: Boynton, 1985. 21–40.

Coe, Richard M. "An Apology for Form; or, Who Took the Form Out of the Process?" *College English* 49 (Jan. 1987): 13–28.

———. "Teaching Genre as Process." Freedman and Medway, *Learning* 157–69.

Coe, Richard, Lorelei Lingard, and Tatiana Teslenko. *The Rhetoric and Ideology of Genre: Strategies for Stability and Change.* Cresskill, NJ: Hampton, 2002.

Cohen, Ralph. "Do Postmodern Genres Exist?" *Genre* 20 (1987): 241–58.

———. "Do Postmodern Genres Exist?" Perloff, *Postmodern* 11–27.

———. "History and Genre." *New Literary History* 17 (1986): 203–18.

Conley, Thomas. "The Linnaean Blues: Thoughts on the Genre Approach." *Form, Genre, and the Study of Political Discourse.* Ed. Herbert W. Simons and Aram A. Aghazarian. Columbia: U of South Carolina P, 1986. 59–78.

Connors, Robert J. *Composition-Rhetoric: Backgrounds, Theory, and Pedagogy.* Pittsburgh: U of Pittsburgh P, 1997.

———. "The Rhetoric of Explanation: Explanatory Rhetoric from Aristotle to 1850." *Written Communication* 1 (1984): 189–210.

————. "The Rhetoric of Explanation: Explanatory Rhetoric from 1850 to the Present." *Written Communication* 2 (1985): 49–72.

————. "The Rise and Fall of the Modes of Discourse." *College Composition and Communication* 32 (1981): 444–55.

————. "Personal Writing Assignments." *College Composition and Communication* 38 (1981): 166–83.

Consigny, Scott. "Rhetoric and Its Situations." *Philosophy and Rhetoric* 7 (summer 1974): 175–86.

Cooper, Charles R. "What We Know about Genres, and How It Can Help Us Assign and Evaluate Writing." *Evaluating Writing: The Role of Teachers' Knowledge about Text, Learning, and Culture.* Ed. Charles R. Cooper and Lee Odell. Urbana, IL: NCTE, 1999. 23–52.

Cope, Bill, and Mary Kalantzis, eds. *The Powers of Literacy: A Genre Approach to Teaching Writing.* Pittsburgh: U of Pittsburgh P, 1993.

————. "The Power of Literacy and the Literacy of Power." Cope and Kalantzis 63–89.

Crowley, Tony. *Standard English and the Politics of Language.* Urbana: U of Illinois P, 1989.

d'Angelo, Frank. "Nineteenth-Century Forms/Modes of Discourse: A Critical Inquiry." *College Composition and Communication* 35 (1984): 31–42.

Derrida, Jacques. "The Law of Genre." Trans. Avital Ronell. *Critical Inquiry* 7 (autumn 1980): 55–82.

Devitt, Amy J. "Intertextuality in Tax Accounting: Generic, Referential, and Functional." *Textual Dynamics of the Professions: Historical and Contemporary Studies of Writing in Professional Communities.* Ed. Charles Bazerman and James Paradis. Madison: U of Wisconsin P, 1991. 336–57.

————. "Generalizing about Genre: New Conceptions of an Old Concept." *College Composition and Communication* 44 (1993): 573–86.

————. "Genre as Language Standard." *Genre and Writing: Issues, Arguments, Alternatives.* Ed. Wendy Bishop and Hans Ostrom. Portsmouth, NH: Boynton, 1997. 45–55.

————. "Genre as Textual Variable: Some Historical Evidence from Scots and American English." *American Speech* 64 (1989): 291–303.

————. "Genre, Genres, and the Teaching of Genre." *College Composition and Communication* 47 (1996): 605–15.

————. "The Developing Discipline of Composition: From Text Linguistics to Genre Theory." *History, Reflection, and Narrative: The Professionalization of Composition, 1963–1983.* Ed. Mary Rosner, Beth Boehm, and Debra Journet. Stamford, CT: Ablex, 1999. 177–86.

————. *Standardizing Written English: Diffusion in the Case of Scotland, 1520–1659.* Cambridge: Cambridge UP, 1989.

————. "Where Communities Collide: Exploring a Legal Genre." *College English* 65 (2003): 543–49, 557–58.

Dubrow, Heather. *Genre.* London: Methuen, 1982.

Elbow, Peter. "Being a Writer vs. Being an Academic: A Conflict in Goals." *College Composition and Communication* 46 (1995): 72–83.

————. "Response." *College Composition and Communication* 46 (1995): 87–92.

Fahnestock, Jeanne. "Genre and Rhetorical Craft." *Research in the Teaching of English* 27 (1993): 265–71.

Fishelov, David. *Metaphors of Genre: The Role of Analogies in Genre Theory.* University Park: Pennsylvania State UP, 1993.

Fisher, John H. *The Emergence of Standard English.* Lexington: UP of Kentucky, 1996.

Flower, Linda, and John R. Hayes. "A Cognitive Process Theory of Writing." *College Composition and Communication* 32 (Dec. 1981): 365–87.

Flower, Linda, et al. "Detection, Diagnosis, and the Strategies of Revision." *College Composition and Communication* 37 (Feb. 1986): 16–55.

Freadman, Anne. "Anyone for Tennis?" Reid 91–124.

————. "Uptake." Coe, Lingard, and Teslenko 39–53.

Freedman, Aviva. "Show and Tell? The Role of Explicit Teaching in the Learning of New Genres." *Research in the Teaching of English* 27 (1993): 222–51.

————. "Situating Genre: A Rejoinder." *Research in the Teaching of English* 27 (1993): 272–81.

Freedman, Aviva, and Peter Medway, eds. *Genre and the New Rhetoric.* London: Taylor, 1994.

————. "Introduction: New Views of Genre and Their Implications for Education." Freedman and Medway, *Learning* 1–22.

————, eds. *Learning and Teaching Genre.* Portsmouth, NH: Boynton, 1994.

————. "Locating Genre Studies: Antecedents and Prospects." Freedman and Medway, *Genre* 1–20.

Frye, Northrop. *Anatomy of Criticism: Four Essays.* Princeton, NJ: Princeton UP, 1957.

————. "Rhetorical Criticism: Theory of Genres." *Anatomy of Criticism.* Princeton, NJ: Princeton UP, 1971. 243–337.

Geertz, Clifford. "Blurred Genres: The Refiguration of Social Thought." *Local Knowledge: Further Essays in Interpretive Anthropology.* New York: Basic, 1983. 19–35.

Giddens, Anthony. *The Constitution of Society: Outline of the Theory of Structuration.* Berkeley: U of California P, 1984.

Giltrow, Janet. "Meta Genre." Coe, Lingard, and Teslenko 187–205.

Haas, William, ed. *Standard Languages: Spoken and Written.* Mont Follick Ser. 5. Totowa, NJ: Barnes, 1982.

Halliday, M. A. K. *Language as Social Semiotic: The Social Interpretation of Language and Meaning.* London: Arnold, 1978.

Halliday, M. A. K., and Ruqaiya Hasan. *Language, Context, and Text: Aspects of Language in a Social-Semiotic Perspective.* 2nd ed. Oxford: Oxford UP, 1989.

Hampden-Turner, Charles. *Maps of the Mind.* New York: Collier, 1981.

Harris, Joseph. "The Idea of Community in the Study of Writing." *College Composition and Communication* 40 (1989): 11–22.

————. *A Teaching Subject: Composition since 1966.* Upper Saddle River, NJ: Prentice, 1997.

Hartwell, Patrick. "Grammar, Grammars, and the Teaching of Grammar." *College English* 47 (1985): 105–27.

Heath, Shirley B. "Standard English: Biography of a Symbol." Shopen and Williams 3–32.

Hillocks, George, Jr. *Research on Written Composition: New Directions for Teaching.* New York: National Conference on Research in English; Urbana, IL: ERIC Clearinghouse on Reading and Communication Skills, National Institute of Education, 1986.

Hirsch, E. D. *Validity in Interpretation.* New Haven: Yale UP, 1965.

Hoger, Elizabeth Anne. *Writing in the Discipline of Music: Rhetorical Parameters in Writings about Music Criticism.* Diss. Purdue Univ, Dec. 1992.

Hyon, Sunny. "Genre and ESL Reading: A Classroom Study." Johns 121–41.

———. "Genre in Three Traditions: Implications of ESL." *TESOL Quarterly* 30 (1996): 693–722.

Jameson, Fredric. *The Political Unconscious: Narrative as a Socially Symbolic Act.* Ithaca, NY: Cornell UP, 1981.

Jamieson, Kathleen M. "Antecedent Genre as Rhetorical Constraint." *Quarterly Journal of Speech* 61 (Dec. 1975): 406–15.

Johns, Ann M., ed. *Genre in the Classroom: Multiple Perspectives.* Mahwah, NJ: Erlbaum, 2002.

Joseph, John Earl. *Eloquence and Power: The Rise of Language Standards and Standard Languages.* London: Pinter, 1987.

Kansas City Star 13 Dec. 1998: I4.

Kay, Heather, and Tony Dudley-Evans. "Genre: What Teachers Think." *ELT Journal* 52 (1998): 308–14.

Killingsworth, M. Jimmie, and Michael K. Gilbertson. *Signs, Genres, and Communities in Technical Communication.* Amityville, NY: Baywood, 1992.

Kitzhaber, Albert R. *Rhetoric in American Colleges, 1850–1900.* Dallas: Southern Methodist UP, 1990.

Koestler, Arthur. *The Act of Creation.* New York: Dell, 1964.

Krapp, G. P. "Standards of Speech and Their Values." *Modern Philology* 11 (1913): 57–70.

Kress, Gunther. "Genre in a Social Theory of Language: A Reply to John Dixon." Reid 35–45.

Kuhn, Thomas S. *The Structure of Scientific Revolutions.* Chicago: U of Chicago P, 1962.

Labov, William. "The Social Motivation of a Sound Change." *Word* 19 (1963): 273–309.

Lakoff, George. *Women, Fire, and Dangerous Things: What Categories Reveal about the Mind.* Chicago: U of Chicago P, 1987.

Langer, Judith A. "Children's Sense of Genre: A Study of Performance on Parallel Reading and Writing Tasks." *Written Communication* 2 (Apr. 1985): 157–87.

LeFevre, Karen Burke. *Invention as a Social Act.* Carbondale: Southern Illinois UP, 1987.

Lindenberger, Herbert. "From Opera to Postmodernity: On Genre, Style, Institutions." Perloff, *Postmodern* 28–53.

Lunsford, Andrea A. "Essay Writing and Teachers' Responses in Nineteenth-Century Scottish Universities." *College Composition and Communication* 32 (1981): 434–43.

Malinowski, B. "The Problem of Meaning in Primitive Languages" (suppl. I). *The Meaning of Meaning: A Study of the Influence of Language upon Thought and of the Science of Symbolism.* By C. K. Ogden and I. A. Richards. 10th ed. New York: Harcourt; London: Routledge, 1952. 296–336.

Martin, J. R., Frances Christie, and Joan Rothery. "Social Processes in Education: A Reply to Sawyer and Watson (and others)." Reid 58–82.

Medway, Peter. "Fuzzy Genres and Community Identities: The Case of Architecture Students' Sketchbooks." Coe, Lingard, and Teslenko 123–53.

Miller, Carolyn R. "Genre as Social Action." *Quarterly Journal of Speech* 70 (May 1984): 151–67.

———. "Rhetorical Community: The Cultural Basis of Genre." Freedman and Medway, *Genre* 67–78.

Miller, Susan. *Textual Carnivals: The Politics of Composition.* Carbondale: Southern Illinois UP, 1991.

———. "Two Comments on 'A Common Ground: The Essay in Academe.'" *College English* 52 (1990): 330–34.

Milroy, James, and Lesley Milroy. "Linguistic Change, Social Network and Speaker Innovation." *Journal of Linguistics* 21 (1985): 339–84.

Milroy, Lesley. *Language and Social Networks.* Oxford: Basil Blackwell, 1980.

Myers, Greg. *Writing Biology: Texts in the Social Construction of Scientific Knowledge.* Madison: U of Wisconsin P, 1990.

Odell, Lee, Dixie Goswami, and Anne Herrington. "The Discourse-Based Interview: A Procedure for Exploring the Tacit Knowledge of Writers in Nonacademic Settings." *Research on Writing: Principles and Methods.* Ed. Peter Mosenthal, Lynne Tamor, and Sean A. Walmsley. New York: Longman, 1983. 220–36.

Olsen, Leslie A. "Research on Discourse Communities: An Overview." *Writing in the Workplace: New Research Perspectives.* Ed. Rachel Spilka. Carbondale: Southern Illinois UP, 1993. 181–94.

Ongstad, Sigmund. "The Definition of Genre and the Didactics of Genre." Rethinking Genre Colloquium. Ottawa, Ont. 3–5 Apr. 1992.

Orlikowski, Wanda J., and JoAnne Yates. "Genre Repertoire: The Structuring of Communicative Practices in Organizations." *Administrative Science Quarterly* 39 (1994): 541–74.

Pattison, Robert. *On Literacy: The Politics of the Word from Homer to the Age of Rock.* New York: Oxford UP, 1982.

Perloff, Marjorie. "Introduction." Perloff, *Postmodern* 3–10.

———, ed. *Postmodern Genres.* Norman: U of Oklahoma P, 1989.

Popken, Randall. "The Pedagogical Dissemination of a Genre: The Resume in American Business Discourse Textbooks, 1914–1939." *JAC: A Journal of Composition Theory* 19 (1999): 91–116.

Porter, James E. *Audience and Rhetoric: An Archaeological Composition of the Discourse Community.* Englewood Cliffs, NJ: Prentice, 1992.

Prince, Michael B. "Literacy and Genre: Toward a Pedagogy of Mediation." *College English* 51 (Nov. 1989): 730–49.

Radway, Janice A. *Reading the Romance: Women, Patriarchy, and Popular Literature.* Chapel Hill: U of North Carolina P, 1984. Introd., 1991.

Reid, Ian, ed. *The Place of Genre in Learning: Current Debates.* Melbourne, Australia: Deakin University Centre for Studies in Literary Education, 1987.

Reiff, Mary Jo. "Accessing Communities Through the Genre of Ethnography: Exploring a Pedagogical Genre." *College English* 65 (2003): 553–58.

Reither, James A. "Writing and Knowing: Toward Redefining the Writing Process." *College English* 47 (Oct. 1985): 620–28. Rpt. in *The Writing Teachers' Sourcebook.* Ed. Gary Tate and Edward P. J. Corbett. 2nd ed. New York: Oxford UP, 1988. 140–48.

Rosch, Eleanor. "Cognitive Reference Points." *Cognitive Psychology* 7 (1957): 532–47.

Rosmarin, Adena. *The Power of Genre.* Minneapolis: U of Minnesota P, 1985.

Rothenberg, Albert. "The Process of Janusian Thinking in Creativity." *The Creativity Question.* Ed. Albert Rothenberg and Carl R. Hausman. Durham, NC: Duke UP, 1976. 311–27.

Russell, David R. "Rethinking Genre in School and Society: An Activity Theory Analysis." *Written Communication* 14 (1997): 504–54.

———. *Writing in the Academic Disciplines, 1870–1990: A Curricular History.* Carbondale: Southern Illinois UP, 1991.

Ryan, Marie-Laure. "Introduction: On the Why, What, and How of Generic Taxonomy." *Poetics* 10 (1981): 109–26.

Schryer, Catherine F. "Records as Genre." *Written Communication* 10 (1993): 200–34.

———. "Genre Time/Space: Chronotopic Strategies in the Experimental Article." *JAC: A Journal of Composition Theory* 19 (1999): 81–89.

Shine, Stephanie, and Nancy L. Roser. "The Role of Genre in Preschoolers' Response to Picture Books." *Research in the Teaching of English* 34 (1999): 197–254.

Shopen, Timothy, and Joseph M. Williams, eds. *Standards and Dialects in English.* Cambridge, MA: Winthrop, 1980.

Sidney, Sir Philip. *Sir Philip Sidney's Defense of Poesy.* Ed. Lewis Soens. Lincoln: U of Nebraska P, 1970.

Smart, Graham. "Genre as Community Invention: A Central Bank's Response to Its Executives' Expectations as Readers." *Writing in the Workplace: New Research Perspectives.* Ed. Rachel Spilka. Carbondale: Southern Illinois UP, 1993. 124–40.

Sommers, Nancy. "Revision Strategies of Student Writers and Experienced Adult Writers." *College Composition and Communication* 31 (Dec. 1980): 378–88.

Spellmeyer, Kurt. "A Common Ground: The Essay in the Academy." *College English* 51 (1989): 262–76.

Swales, John M. *Genre Analysis: English in Academic and Research Settings.* Cambridge: Cambridge UP, 1990.

———. *Other Floors, Other Voices: A Textography of a Small University Building*. Mahwah, NJ: Erlbaum, 1968.

Tardy, Christine M. "A Genre System View of the Funding of Academic Research." *Written Communication* 20 (2003): 7–36.

Thompson, John B. "Editor's Introduction." *Language and Symbolic Power*. Pierre Bourdieu. Cambridge: Harvard UP, 1991. 1–31.

Titunik, I. R. "The Formal Method and the Sociological Method (M. M. Baxtin, P. N. Medvedev, V. N. Volosinov) in Russian Theory and Study of Literature." Volosinov 175–200.

Todorov, Tzvetan. *Genres in Discourse*. Trans. Catherine Porter. Cambridge: Cambridge UP, 1990.

Turow, Scott. *One L*. New York: Penguin, 1977.

Vatz, Richard. "The Myth of the Rhetorical Situation." *Philosophy and Rhetoric* 6 (summer 1973): 154–61.

Volosinov, V. N. *Marxism and the Philosophy of Language*. Trans. Ladislav Matejka and I. R. Titunik. Cambridge: Harvard UP, 1986.

Wallace, David Foster. "Tense Present: Democracy, English, and the Wars over Usage." *Harper's* Apr. 2001: 39–58.

Wellek, Rene, and Austin Warren. *Theory of Literature*. 3rd ed. New York: Harcourt, 1956.

Williams, Joseph. "The Phenomenology of Error." *College Composition and Communication* 32 (1981): 152–68.

Williams, Joseph, and Gregory G. Colomb. "The Case for Explicit Teaching: Why What You Don't Know Won't Help You." *Research in the Teaching of English* 27 (1993): 252–64.

Winsor, Dorothy A. "Genre and Activity Systems: The Role of Documentation in Maintaining and Changing Engineering Activity Systems." *Written Communication* 16 (1999): 200–24.

———. "Ordering Work: Blue-Collar Literacy and the Political Nature of Genre." *Written Communication* 17 (2000): 155–84.

Wollman-Bonilla, Julie E. "Teaching Science Writing to First Graders: Genre Learning and Recontextualization." *Research in the Teaching of English* 35 (2000): 35–65.

Yates, JoAnne. *Control Through Communication: The Rise of System in American Management*. Baltimore: Johns Hopkins UP, 1989.

Yates, JoAnne, and Wanda Orlikowski. "Genres of Organizational Communication: A Structural Approach to Studying Communication and Media." *Academy of Management Review* 17 (1992): 299–326.

———. "Genre Systems: Structuring Interaction Through Communicative Norms." *Journal of Business Communication* 39 (2002): 13–35.

Index

Amy J. Devitt is a professor of English at the University of Kansas and, until 2004, Conger-Gabel Teaching Professor. She teaches courses in writing, composition and rhetoric, and the English language. She has published a historical linguistic study of changing language standards, *Standardizing Written English: Diffusion in the Case of Scotland, 1520–1659*, a textbook for writing courses; *Scenes of Writing: Strategies for Composing with Genres*; and articles on genre in *College Composition and Communication, College English*, and elsewhere.